Missouri Advanced Real Estate Practice

1st Edition

PERFORMANCE
PROGRAMS
COMPANY

Ryan Mettling
Stephen Mettling

Material in this book is not intended to represent legal advice and should not be so construed. Readers should consult legal counsel for advice regarding points of law

6810 190th Street East, Bradenton, FL 34211
info@performanceprogramscompany.com
www.performanceprogramscompany.com

ISBN: 978-1965482506

Missouri Advanced Real Estate Practice (MAREP)

Table of Contents

Missouri Advanced Real Estate Practice

Course Overview

The Missouri Advanced Real Estate Practice (MAREP) program has been developed to satisfy Missouri's 24-hour real estate practice education requirement following completion of the 48-hour prelicense course. The course fulfills the Missouri Real Estate Commission's objective of giving new Missouri licensees a carefully developed reinforcement of key real estate brokerage principles, concepts, and practices necessary to initiate a productive, professional career in real estate.

Beyond an initial review of key principles, the MAREP program takes on a further examination of essential skills and practices necessary to meet client and customer transactional requirements within Missouri's legal framework. Skills examined include compliance with Missouri agency and disclosure laws; how to properly represent both sellers and buyers in real estate transactions; and an in-depth look at Missouri transaction contracts, including listings, the sales contract, offer and acceptance, earnest money, and closing costs. In addition to its agency and contracts topics, the MAREP program further examines the other key subjects required by the Commission: ethics and the NAR Code of Ethics; cooperating with other licensees; compensation in the post-NAR settlement environment; risk management and avoiding misrepresentation; types of financing; and an introduction to construction terminology essential for working with Missouri buyers and sellers in the field.

Taken as a whole, the Missouri Advanced Real Estate Practice program is designed to deepen the new licensee's understanding of how brokerage works in actual practice, and how it is supposed to be undertaken in view of today's standards of professionalism, ethics, and legal compliance in Missouri.

ABOUT THE AUTHORS

Ryan Mettling Mr. Mettling is an accomplished online curriculum designer, author, and course developer. He is responsible for the company's strategic planning, general management, printing and production, e-pub and retail platforms, and multi-channel marketing. Mr. Mettling is a member of the Real Estate Educators Association (REEA), and graduated Valedictorian from the University of Central Florida's College of Business Administration.

Stephen Mettling. For nearly fifty years, Stephen Mettling has been actively engaged in real estate education. Beginning with Dearborn in 1972, then called Real Estate Education Company, Mr. Mettling managed the company's textbook division and author acquisitions. Subsequently he built up the company's real estate school division which eventually became the country's largest real estate, insurance and securities school network in the country. In 1978, Mr. Mettling founded Performance Programs Company, a custom training program publishing and development company specializing in commercial, industrial, and corporate real estate. Over time, Performance Programs Company narrowed its focus to real estate textbook and exam prep publishing. Currently the Company's texts and prelicense resources are used in hundreds of schools in over 48 states. Mr. Mettling has authored over 100 textbooks, real estate programs and exam prep manuals.

Module 1: MISSOURI AGENCY RELATIONSHIPS & AGENCY DISCLOSURE

I. Acting as an Agent, Dual Agent or Transaction Broker
II. Obligations of Agents to Clients and Customers
III. Missouri Broker Disclosure Form
IV. Termination of Brokerage Relationships

Acting as an Agent, Dual Agent or Transaction Broker

1) Explain the duties, limitations, and disclosure requirements associated with conventional agency relationships, dual agency and transaction brokerage.
2) Explain the requirements for lawfully practicing dual agency in Missouri.

Obligations of Agents to Clients and Customers

1) Identify the specific duties Missouri licensees owe to seller, buyer, and transaction brokerage clients and explain how those duties differ depending on the type of agency relationship in place.
2) Describe the disclosure requirements for each brokerage relationship type in Missouri.
3) Explain the permitted activities and confidentiality obligations of a Missouri transaction broker.

Missouri Broker Disclosure Form

1) Identify the required elements of Missouri brokerage service agreements.
2) Describe the purpose and proper use of the Missouri Broker Disclosure Form.
3) Explain the disclosure requirements Missouri licensees must follow regarding licensed status, ownership interest, and controlled business arrangements in order to protect consumers and comply with state license law and federal regulations.

Termination of Brokerage Relationships

1) Identify the ways an agency relationship can be legally terminated in Missouri.
2) Explain the rights and responsibilities of both the client and the broker when ending an agency relationship.
3) Describe which fiduciary duties survive the termination of agency in Missouri and recognize which changes in circumstances do not constitute termination of the agency relationship.

I. Acting as an Agent, Dual Agent or Transaction Broker

Types of Agency Relationships in Missouri

Agent

Licensees are considered agents if a signed agency agreement exists between the licensee and a consumer. With a signed agency agreement, the consumer becomes a **client**, and the agent owes this client a specific set of duties defined by statute.

Most licensees who represent clients are considered **limited agents**, which means that their agency duties relate only to a specific transaction. Limited agents may not bind their clients to a contract or sign documents for clients.

Subagent

Licensees who do not have an agency agreement with a buyer but who are working with the buyer may be considered a subagent (or cooperating agent) of the listing broker. In the absence of any agreement with the buyer, these parties may owe statutory duties to the seller if operating as a subagent for the seller.

For example, suppose you are a licensee affiliated with Ozark Dream Homes. You are working with buyers Candice and Robert, though you do not have an agency agreement with the couple. Candice and Robert ask you to show them a property listed by High Country Realty, another brokerage firm. Without an agency agreement with the buyers, you may work as a subagent for High Country Realty and owe statutory duties to High Country and the listing client, not to Candice and Robert.

Dual agent

Dual agency occurs when the same brokerage firm or a given licensee represents both parties in a single transaction. Licensees must disclose any dual agency relationship, and both principal parties, buyer and seller, must provide consent to dual agency.

As a dual agent, a licensee no longer fully represents either principal party. The dual agent must continue the transaction in good faith and be honest with all parties. Missouri dual agents cannot disclose information which gives one party more bargaining power over the other. In particular, this includes disclosing that the buyer would pay more for the property than the initial offer. or that the seller would take less than the listed price. Dual agents are also prohibited from disclosing either party's motivation for buying or selling the property.

Note that it is impossible for a single licensee to represent the best interests of both the buyer and seller in the same transaction. This conflict of interest can result in complaints to the Commission or even legal action.

Designated agent

As an alternative to dual agency, Missouri brokerage firms are permitted to offer designated agency. If a situation arises in which both the buyer and seller are to be represented by the same firm, *the firm's broker may designate one agent to represent the buyer and another to represent the seller*. No other agents in the firm, including the broker, represent either client. This permits the agents to fully represent their clients without the conflicts presented by dual agency.

Transaction broker

Transaction brokerage is considered a non-agency relationship. A transaction broker does not represent or advocate for either the buyer or the seller but instead simply assists the party in transferring documents and completing the necessary steps to get to the transaction's closing. Therefore, the party to whom the licensee renders transaction brokerage services is not a client; instead, this party is considered a customer.

It is important to understand that a Missouri licensee will be considered a transaction broker unless a written agency agreement exists with a client.

Dual Agency

Informed consent

Licensees may act as dual agents only after explaining the limitations of a dual agency transaction and obtaining written consent from all parties to the transaction. Dual agents operate as limited agents for both the buyer and seller or tenant and landlord.

Confidentiality

As dual agents, licensees may disclose confidential information to one client that the licensee learns from the other client if the information is material to the transaction. However, dual agents may not disclose the following information without the client's consent:

- that a buyer or tenant is willing to pay more than the offered price
- that a landlord or seller is willing to accept less than the asking price
- what factors are motivating the client's purchase, sale, or lease
- that a client will agree to financing options other than those offered
- the terms of any previous offers or counter-offers made by any party

Licensees are permitted to disclose confidential information about one client to the other client in a few situations, notably the following:

- the disclosure is legally required
- where failure to disclose would be considered misrepresentation
- where disclosure is necessary to defend the licensee against wrongful conduct actions

II. Obligations of Agents to Clients and Customers

Agency Duties and Responsibilities

Duties to all parties

Missouri licensees owe reasonable skill, care, and diligence to all parties to a transaction . They owe additional duties to clients and customers for whom they are serving as a transaction broker.

Duties to seller or landlord clients

Licensees who represent a seller or landlord do so as a limited agent with a particular set of duties and obligations. These are as follows.

- perform all terms of the written brokerage agreement
- exercise reasonable skill and care for the client
- promote the client's interests with good faith, loyalty, and fidelity
- negotiate a sales price and contract terms acceptable to the client; (note that licensees do not have to seek additional offers if a property is already under contract or lease)
- present all offers and counteroffers in a timely fashion
- disclose all known adverse material facts to the client
- advise clients to seek expert advice (attorney, accountant) regarding issues that are beyond the licensee's expertise
- promptly account for all money or property received
- abide by all related real estate statutes and rules, as well as federal, state, and local laws and rules
- maintain client confidentiality unless a legal requirement to disclose exists

A licensee who is representing a seller or landlord owes no duties to customers except to disclose adverse material facts. Licensees are not required to independently inspect properties, discover adverse material facts for customers, or verify the accuracy or completeness of any statement that a client or any independent inspector makes.

Licensees acting as subagents are subject to the same duties required when representing clients.

Duties to buyer or tenant clients

Licensees who represent a buyer or tenant do so as a limited agent with a certain set of duties and obligations. These are as follows:

- perform all terms of the written brokerage agreement
- exercise reasonable skill and care for the client
- promote the client's interests with good faith, loyalty, and fidelity
- negotiate a purchase price and contract terms acceptable to the client; note that licensees do not have to search for additional properties if a property is already under negotiation

- present all offers and counteroffers in a timely fashion
- disclose all known adverse material facts to a client
- advise clients to seek expert advice (attorney, accountant) about issues that are beyond the licensee's expertise
- promptly account for all money or property received
- abide by all related real estate statutes and rules, as well as federal, state, and local laws and rules
- maintain client confidentiality unless a legal requirement to disclose exists

A licensee who is representing a buyer or tenant owes no duties to customers except to disclose adverse material facts. Licensees are not required to independently inspect the client's finances for a customer's benefit or to verify the accuracy or completeness of any statement that a client or any independent inspector makes.

Licensees are allowed to show properties to competing buyers or tenants until the property is under contract or lease.

Transaction broker duties and obligations

As stated previously, a real estate licensee who provides real estate services to any party without an agency relationship with either party is called a transaction broker.

Transaction brokers do not owe the typical statutory duties to parties in a transaction brokerage relationship. Licensees do, however, owe the following duties to those parties:

- perform all terms of any written or oral agreement
- exercise reasonable skill, care, and diligence
- present all offers and counteroffers promptly
- suggest parties seek expert advice on issues beyond licensee's scope of expertise or transaction brokerage service parameters
- account for all money or property received from the parties
- disclose to all parties any known adverse material facts
- assist the parties in complying with the contract's terms and conditions
- keep the following information confidential
    - that a buyer or tenant will pay more than the offered price
    - that a seller or landlord will accept less than the listed price
    - the motivating factors for any party's purchase, sale, or lease
    - that either party will agree to financing terms besides those offered
- point out that licensees must disclose information where failure to do so would constitute fraud or dishonest dealing

Transaction brokers are not expected to perform an inspection or investigation to reveal adverse material facts or to inspect the buyer's financial ability to complete the transaction.

A transaction brokerage agreement permits the broker to perform tasks for other customers and clients, including the following:

- showing properties other than the seller's property to buyers
- listing competing properties for sale
- showing properties in which a buyer or tenant has expressed interest to other potential buyers or tenants
- acting in an agency capacity for the same or different parties in other real estate transactions

Transaction brokers who cooperate with other brokers do not become subagents of the other broker.

Disclosure of Agency

Seller's/landlord's agent or subagent

Licensees who act as agents or subagents for a seller or landlord must disclose their status as an agent to any unrepresented buyer or tenant no later than the first property showing.

If the buyer or tenant is represented, licensees must disclose their agency status to the buyer, tenant, or agent upon first contact with any of these parties.

Disclosure by a subagent of a seller's or landlord's agent serves as disclosure by the agent.

A seller's or landlord's agent who cooperates with a buyer's or tenant's transaction broker must provide agency disclosure to both the buyer or tenant and the transaction broker upon first contact with the parties.

In a situation where a landlord's agent is acting as a property manager for the landlord, unlicensed office staff are permitted to make the agency disclosure as a representative of the landlord's agent.

Buyer's/tenant's agent or subagent

Licensees who act as a buyer's or tenant's agent or subagent must disclose their agency status to any unrepresented seller before showing the seller's property.

If the seller is represented, licensees for the buyer or tenant can make the disclosure to the seller or landlord upon first contact with the seller, landlord, or agent, whichever occurs first.

If the buyer's or tenant's agent is working with a subagent licensee, disclosure by the subagent also serves as disclosure by the agent.

Suppose a licensee has no contact with the seller, landlord, agent, or transaction broker. In that case, the buyer's/tenant's agent must establish first contact with the seller's/landlord's agent and make the proper agency disclosure before submitting an offer.

If the landlord's agent or transaction broker is acting as a property manager for the landlord, unlicensed staff members are permitted to receive an agency disclosure on behalf of the landlord's agent or transaction broker.

Dual agent

Dual agency often occurs after a single-agent brokerage agreement is already in place. Suppose a buyer signs a brokerage agreement with a firm and then wishes to make an offer on one of the firm's listings. The firm must disclose the dual agency situation and obtain consent from the buyer and the seller.

When a designated broker who becomes a dual agent does not represent any parties in the transaction, the broker is not required to disclose agency status.

Transaction broker assisting seller/landlord

A licensee who is serving as a transaction broker for a seller or landlord must disclose this status before showing any property to an unrepresented buyer or tenant.

If a buyer or tenant is represented, the transaction broker for the seller or landlord may provide disclosure on first contact with the buyer, tenant, or agent.

A licensee with no transaction brokerage agreement with a seller or landlord must disclose the licensee's transaction brokerage status to the seller or landlord when the parties establish a relationship without a written brokerage agreement.

When both the licensee working with the seller or landlord and the licensee working with the buyer or tenant are transaction brokers, the seller's/landlord's transaction broker must disclose the transaction brokerage status to the buyer or tenant, and the buyer's/tenant's transaction broker.

Suppose the licensee has no contact with the buyer/tenant, the agent, or the transaction broker. In that case, the seller's/landlord's transaction broker must disclose the brokerage relationship status to the buyer's/tenant's agent or transaction broker at the first substantive contact.

A landlord's transaction broker who is also serving as a property manager may permit unlicensed office staff to provide a brokerage disclosure on the landlord's behalf.

Transaction broker assisting buyer/tenant

The timing of transaction brokerage disclosure depends on the licensee's relationship with the buyer or tenant and the brokerage relationship status of the landlord or tenant.

A licensee assisting a buyer or tenant as a transaction broker must disclose the broker relationship to an unrepresented seller or landlord before showing the seller's property.

If the seller or landlord is represented, the licensee must disclose the brokerage relationship on the first contact with the seller/landlord or their agent, whichever happens first.

If the licensee does not have a written transaction brokerage agreement with the buyer or tenant, the licensee must disclose the transaction broker status to the buyer or tenant upon forming the transaction broker relationship.

Suppose a licensee is working as a transaction broker in a cooperative sale or lease transaction with a seller who is also working with a transaction broker. The buyer's broker must disclose the relationship status to the seller or landlord and the licensee assisting those parties upon first contact with each party.

When a buyer or tenant shows interest in purchasing or leasing property but has not yet made contact with the seller/landlord or the agent, the licensee should disclose the brokerage relationship status before presenting any offers to purchase or lease a property.

Finally, if the landlord's agent or transaction broker is providing property management services, unlicensed office staff are permitted to receive the brokerage relationship disclosure on behalf of the agent or transaction broker.

III. Missouri Broker Disclosure Form

Brokerage Service Agreements

A brokerage service agreement may be either an agreement to lease or sell an owner's property or to find a property for a buyer or tenant.

A **listing agreement** is a contract between a seller and a brokerage firm to list and lease or sell real estate. A **buyer/tenant agency agreement** is a contract between a buyer or tenant and a brokerage firm to locate a property the party will purchase or lease. Licensees may also form written or verbal **transaction brokerage agreements** with buyers, sellers, lessees, and lessors.

While these agreements differ in whom they serve, they share a detailing of all appropriate contract terms, including compensation and the licensee's responsibilities. The agreements authorize the brokerage firm and the agent to perform specific tasks only after the signed written agreement is in place. For example, licensees cannot market a property until a listing agreement is in place.

Before soliciting a brokerage agreement from a party, licensees must ensure no exclusive agreement with another agent is already in place. Sometimes called "sign crossing," or "broker interference," working with a party already subject to an exclusive representation agreement violates licensing laws.

As an exception, if an already represented party initiates the discussion with another licensee, such licensee may legitimately negotiate an agreement that will become effective when the current agreement expires.

In any case, all parties must initialize any additional documents or authorizations attached to or included with the agency agreement. These include addenda, riders, attachments, endorsements, or other changes to the agreement or permissions granted to the licensee.

Cannot assign. Brokerage service agreements may not be sold, assigned, or transferred to another broker without the written consent of all parties to the original agreement. These agreements must have a defined end date and may not include automatic renewal provisions.

Finally, licensees must provide a legible copy of all written agreements when all signatures are in place. Each signing party must receive such a copy.

Broker Disclosure Form

In a residential real estate transaction, the designated broker or affiliated licensee must provide the seller, landlord, buyer, or tenant a written copy of the current Broker Disclosure Form prescribed by the Commission if that party has not already entered into a written agreement for services with another designated broker.

This form must be delivered at the earliest practicable opportunity during or following the first substantial contact of licensee with prospect. If the party has already entered into a written agreement for services with a designated broker, this disclosure is not required.

The form describes the different kinds of brokerage relationship available in Missouri and the duties owed the client under each relationship.

The purpose of the disclosure, as stated on the form, is to enable a prospective buyer, seller, tenant or landlord of real estate to make an informed choice about representation before working with a real estate licensee.

Listing Agreements

Licensees may enter into a listing agreement or a transaction brokerage agreement with sellers or landlords. Listing agreements must be in writing.

Licensees may not advertise or place a sign on a property without the owner's consent. A clause in the listing agreement typically grants or denies this consent.

Licensees may not show residential property to buyers or tenants without an agency agreement, transaction brokerage agreement, or other written authorization to show the property.

All residential listing or transaction broker agreements must contain the following information:

- financial details, including price, commissions, and bonuses, if applicable
- the licensee's duties and responsibilities
- a definite beginning and expiration date (The parties may negotiate a new agreement.)
- consent or denial of consent for the designated broker to cooperate and share compensation with other designated brokers, including buyer's agents or transaction brokers
- a statement confirming that the seller or lessor received the prescribed Broker Disclosure Form before signing the listing agreement or before the licensee receives any personal or financial information
- the signature of all owners or landlords and the listing broker or agent
- the listing type
- the property's legal description or complete address
- any additional terms or conditions related to the agreement

In addition, a listing agreement must include a statement permitting or forbidding the following:

- subagency
- dual agency (if authorized, include dual agent's duties and responsibilities)
- transaction brokerage (if authorized, include transaction broker's responsibilities)

All parties must initial any additional documents or authorizations attached to or included with the agency agreement, including addenda, riders, attachments, endorsements, or other changes to the agreement or permissions granted to the licensee.

Licensees must provide a legible copy of all written brokerage agreements to the parties when signed.

Missouri statutes prohibit net listings (a listing in which the listing or transaction broker would receive any funds in excess of the sales price set by the seller).

Buyer/Tenant Agency Agreements

Licensees may enter into brokerage agreements with buyers or tenants. All written buyer/tenant agreements must include the following information:

- description of desired property
- compensation, including any bonuses
- licensee's duties and responsibilities
- a definite beginning and expiration date (The parties may negotiate a new agreement when the original one expires.)
- consent or denial of consent for the designated broker to cooperate with and compensate others, including seller's agents or transaction brokers
- a statement confirming that the buyer or tenant received the prescribed Broker Disclosure Form before signing the agency agreement or before the licensee received any personal or financial information
- the signature of all buyers or tenants and the listing broker or agent
- agreement type
- any additional terms or conditions related to the agreement

In addition, a buyer's agency agreement must include a statement permitting or forbidding the following:

- subagency
- dual agency (if permitted, include dual agent's duties and responsibilities)
- transaction brokerage (if permitted, include transaction broker's duties and responsibilities)

Seller/Lessor Transaction Agreements

A transaction brokerage agreement may be verbal or written. Often, a transaction brokerage arrangement begins with a single-agency brokerage agreement and then is converted to a transaction brokerage agreement when a listing agent comes across a buyer client for a listed property or a buyer's agent lists a seller's property in which the buyer might be interested.

Every written transaction brokerage agreement with a seller or landlord must include the following information:

- property price
- compensation, including bonuses
- definite beginning and end date
- licensee's duties and responsibilities
- signature of all owners and the broker or affiliated licensee
- agreement type
- legal description or complete street address
- all other terms and conditions of the listing and sale
- approval or denial of the broker's authority to work with and compensate cooperating brokers

- verification that the seller or lessor received the Broker Disclosure form in a timely fashion

Buyer/Lessee Transaction Agreements

Every written transaction brokerage agreement with a buyer or tenant must include the following information:

- description of property type
- compensation, including bonuses
- definite beginning and end date
- licensee's duties and responsibilities
- signature of all buyers or tenants and the broker or affiliated licensee
- agreement type
- all other terms and conditions of the listing and sale
- confirmation or denial of cooperating with and compensating buyer's brokers
- verification that the seller or lessor received the Broker Disclosure form in a timely fashion
- approval or rejection of broker's authority to work with and compensate cooperating brokers

Other Written Authorizations

Most real estate brokerage relationships are authorized using one of the agreements previously covered. However, a licensee who does not have an agency or transaction brokerage agreement with an owner or landlord may still show a specific property to a buyer or tenant by creating an "other written authorization" with the seller or landlord.

Much like the other brokerage agency agreements, a **written authorization** must include a beginning and expiration date. It must also identify the property to be shown by either a complete legal description or street address.

The authorization permits a licensee to enter and show the property and contains compensation information and other terms or conditions noted by the owner or landlord. By signing the authorization, the parties confirm that they received the Broker Disclosure Form before signing the authorization or before receiving personal or financial information.

All parties must initial any additional documents or changes to the authorization.

Property Management Agreements

Property owners may employ licensees to act as property managers. A written property management agreement or other written authorization must document such arrangements before a licensee can provide brokerage services to the landlord. The management agreement must identify the property to be managed. It should also include a defined beginning date, detail the compensation structure, and specify who will hold tenant security deposits. It must also outline terms for agreement termination by either party and provide a detailed description of the licensee's duties and responsibilities.

As with the other agreement types, a property management agreement must include a statement permitting or forbidding subagency, dual agency, and transaction brokerage.

Property management agreements must address broker cooperation and the Broker Disclosure Form, all parties must sign the agreement, and all parties must initial any additional documents or changes.

The licensee must provide a legible copy of the signed property management agreement or other written authorization to the owner or the owner's authorized agent. Brokers must also retain a copy of any property management agreement and related documents for at least three years.

A licensee who acts as a property manager must obtain a signed listing agreement before listing a managed property for sale.

Disclosure of Licensee's License Status and Ownership Interest in Transaction

Licensed status

Real estate licensees hold a significant knowledge advantage over unlicensed consumers. To lessen this disadvantage to the consumer, Missouri laws require real estate licensees to provide written disclosure of their licensed status before participating in any real estate transaction for the licensee's own benefit. As an added protection, rules prevent licensees from discouraging parties to the transaction from seeking legal advice.

Ownership interest

Licensees must also disclose, in writing, any ownership interest in a property that is the subject of a transaction involving the licensee.

Directed or controlled business

Federal laws and the Real Estate Settlement Procedures Act (RESPA), in particular, strictly regulate real estate settlement practices to protect consumers from fraudulent charges. Settlement services include mortgage origination and financing assistance, inspections, title work, title insurance, property insurance, and attorney services.

A logical expansion of a broker's business is often to become affiliated in some way with one or more settlement service providers. For example, a broker may purchase an ownership interest in a title company. This ownership interest is considered a controlled business arrangement.

If this same licensee directly or indirectly refers real estate clients to the title company, the licensee must disclose the controlled business arrangement to the client. To avoid any suggestion of unfair dealing, some firms automatically provide these disclosures at the beginning of every transaction, whether or not they refer clients to the other business. As can be expected, licensees are prohibited from requiring consumers to use a specific service provider.

IV: Termination of Brokerage Relationships

Missouri brokerage relationships end in a variety of ways. The goal is always an amicable conclusion that protects the client, the licensee, and the brokerage. Understanding when and how agency terminates — and what obligations survive termination — is essential knowledge for every Missouri licensee.

Ways Agency Can Be Terminated

Successful closing

The preferred conclusion to any agency relationship is a successful closing. When the licensee secures a suitable price and terms for the seller or finds the right property for the buyer, the transaction closes and the agency relationship ends naturally. A satisfied client is also the best source of future referrals.

Expiration of the agreement

Both listing agreements and buyer representation agreements include a specific end date. If the agreement expires without a completed transaction, the agency ends automatically unless both parties agree in writing to extend it. Missouri licensees are expected to maintain consistent communication with clients throughout the term of any agreement — sellers who receive regular updates are far more likely to agree to an extension when needed.

Reasonable time

When no written end date exists — such as in an oral or open listing — agency may end after a "reasonable time" has passed. What is reasonable is determined by a court based on the specific facts. Missouri license law requires listing and buyer representation agreements to include a defined start and end date, which eliminates this issue in nearly all standard transactions.

Mutual rescission

When both the client and the broker agree to end the relationship before its natural conclusion, the agency may be terminated by mutual rescission. Because all clients belong to the broker, the salesperson must consult the broker before agreeing to any early termination. Mutual rescission is often appropriate when a client faces a serious illness, job relocation, or significant change in financial circumstances.

Revocation by the client

A client may revoke the agency relationship at any time, but may not have the legal right to do so without consequences. If a client terminates the relationship before the agreed end date without cause, Missouri courts recognize the broker's right to seek compensation for actual damages, particularly when a commission would otherwise have been earned.

Broker renunciation

A broker may also choose to end the relationship, even when the client wishes to continue. This is known as renunciation. Good cause is required, and proper written notice must be given. Acceptable grounds for renunciation include:

- A client who is verbally abusive or harassing toward brokerage staff
- Repeated missed appointments without notice
- Refusal to negotiate in good faith
- Instructions to violate Missouri's fair housing laws

Renunciation without legitimate cause may expose the broker to legal liability and must always be documented in writing.

Death or incapacity

The death or legal incapacity of either the client or the broker terminates the agency relationship. When a broker dies, all agency relationships in the brokerage end, since client listings legally belong to the broker. Affiliated licensees should coordinate with the Missouri Real Estate Commission to protect all parties in any pending transactions.

Additional grounds for termination

The following events also terminate the agency relationship:

- Bankruptcy of the seller — control of the property transfers to the bankruptcy court
- Foreclosure — the seller no longer holds title once the lender or a third party takes ownership
- Destruction of the property — fire, flood, or other event destroys the improvement; the original listing is considered terminated even if land remains
- Broker's breach of fiduciary duties — such as improperly disclosing confidential client information

Termination paperwork

All terminations should be documented in writing and signed by the relevant parties, even when the original agency agreement was verbal. Missouri licensees must use the correct form for the correct purpose: a termination form ends the relationship, while an amendment modifies the existing agreement (such as changing the listing price or extending the end date). Using the wrong form can create confusion or legal complications.

Confidentiality survives termination

Confidentiality is the one fiduciary duty that does not end when the agency relationship ends. Any information a licensee learned while representing a client must remain confidential indefinitely unless the client provides explicit written permission to share it. Protected information includes:

- The seller's reason for selling or motivation
- The lowest price the seller would accept
- The highest price the buyer would offer
- Pending divorce, job loss, or financial hardship

- A pending foreclosure
- Previous offers that did not result in a contract
- What the buyer would be willing to spend on other properties

Disclosing protected information without authorization — even after the agency has ended — may result in disciplinary action by the Missouri Real Estate Commission, up to and including suspension or revocation of the license.

Actions that DO NOT terminate agency

Not every change in circumstances ends the agency relationship. Missouri licensees should be aware of the following:

- A salesperson changing brokerages does not transfer clients to the new brokerage firm. Clients belong to the broker, not the individual licensee. The departing salesperson may not take clients without the broker's consent.
- A client's marriage after signing a listing agreement does not terminate the agreement. Property that was separate property before the marriage remains separate property, and the listing stays in effect.
- A client's divorce is more complex. The licensee should maintain communication with both parties, avoid taking sides, and consult the broker for guidance on how to proceed.

MODULE 1 SNAPSHOT REVIEW: MISSOURI AGENCY RELATIONSHIPS & AGENCY DISCLOSURE

I: Acting as an Agent, Dual Agent or Transaction Broker

Missouri recognizes the following types of brokerage relationships:

- **Agent** — signed agency agreement exists; consumer becomes a client; licensee owes statutory duties
- **Subagent** — licensee works with a buyer without an agency agreement; may owe duties to the seller/listing broker instead
- **Dual agent** — same firm or licensee represents both parties; requires written disclosure and consent from all parties
- **Designated agent** — firm assigns one agent to represent the buyer and a separate agent to represent the seller, avoiding dual agency conflicts
- **Transaction broker** — non-agency relationship; licensee assists with the transaction but does not represent or advocate for either party; this is the default agency relationship in Missouri in the absence of a written agreement

Dual Agency Key Rules:

- Written informed consent required from all parties before acting as a dual agent
- Dual agents **may not disclose**: willingness to pay more or accept less, motivating factors, agreement to alternative financing terms, or prior offer terms
- Disclosure is permitted only when legally required, when failure would constitute misrepresentation, or to defend against wrongful conduct claims

II: Obligations of Agents to Clients and Customers

Duties owed to ALL parties: reasonable skill, care, and diligence

Duties to seller/landlord clients include:

- Perform all terms of the brokerage agreement
- Promote client interests with good faith, loyalty, and fidelity
- Present all offers and counteroffers in a timely fashion
- Disclose all known adverse material facts
- Maintain client confidentiality
- Advise clients to seek expert advice when issues exceed licensee expertise

Duties to buyer/tenant clients include:

- Same core duties as seller representation
- Negotiate purchase price and contract terms acceptable to the client
- Licensees may show properties to competing buyers until a property is under contract

Transaction broker duties include:

- Exercise reasonable skill, care, and diligence
- Present all offers and counteroffers promptly
- Disclose known adverse material facts to all parties

- Keep confidential: willingness to pay more or accept less, motivating factors, and alternative financing terms
- A transaction broker **does not** become a subagent when cooperating with other brokers

III: Missouri Broker Disclosure Form & Brokerage Service Agreements

- A brokerage service agreement authorizes the licensee to act on a client's behalf and may cover selling, leasing, buying, or tenant representation
- Licensees **cannot** market a property, show residential property, or solicit a new agreement if an exclusive agreement with another broker is already in place
- Brokerage agreements **cannot** be assigned or transferred to another broker without written consent of all parties
- Agreements must have a **defined end date** and may not include automatic renewal provisions
- The **Missouri Broker Disclosure Form** must be provided at the earliest practicable opportunity during or following the first substantial contact with a prospect
- The form explains the types of brokerage relationships available in Missouri and the duties owed under each
- All residential listing agreements must include: price and compensation details, licensee duties, a definite start and end date, cooperation and compensation consent, Broker Disclosure Form confirmation, signatures, listing type, and property address
- All buyer/tenant agency agreements must include: property description, compensation, licensee duties, definite dates, cooperation consent, Broker Disclosure Form confirmation, and signatures
- **Net listings are prohibited** in Missouri
- Property management agreements must be in writing, identify the property, detail compensation, address security deposits, and be retained by the broker for **at least three years**
- Licensees must **disclose in writing** their licensed status before participating in any transaction for their own benefit
- **Controlled business arrangements** must be disclosed; licensees may not require consumers to use a specific service provider

IV: Termination of Brokerage Relationships

Agency can be terminated by:

- **Successful closing** — the preferred and most rewarding conclusion to any agency relationship
- **Expiration** of the listing or buyer representation agreement
- **Reasonable time** — relevant only when no written end date exists; determined by a court
- **Mutual rescission** — both the client and broker agree in writing to end the relationship
- **Revocation by the client** — clients have the power to revoke at any time, though wrongful termination may result in liability for damages
- **Broker renunciation** — broker may end the relationship for good cause with proper notice; must be documented in writing
- **Death or incapacity** of either the client or the broker
- **Bankruptcy of the seller**, foreclosure, destruction of the property, or broker's breach of fiduciary duties

What does NOT terminate agency:

- A salesperson leaving one brokerage for another (clients belong to the broker)
- A client getting married
- A change in personal circumstances unless it directly affects the ability to perform

MODULE 1 QUIZ: MISSOURI AGENCY RELATIONSHIPS & AGENCY DISCLOSURE

1. In Missouri, a licensee will automatically be considered which type of brokerage relationship if no written agency agreement exists with a client?

a. Transaction broker
b. Subagent
c. Designated agent
d. Dual agent

2. The Missouri Broker Disclosure Form must be provided to a prospective client at what point in the relationship?

a. Only after a brokerage agreement has been signed
b. At the earliest practicable opportunity during or following the first substantial contact
c. Before the first property showing, but not before
d. Within 24 hours of the first contact with the prospect

3. Which of the following is a required element of all residential listing agreements in Missouri?

a. A statement permitting the licensee to automatically renew the agreement
b. A definite beginning and expiration date
c. A guaranteed minimum commission amount
d. The names of all prospective buyers the licensee plans to contact

4. A Missouri licensee affiliated with Ozark Dream Homes is working with buyers Marcus and Dana, but has no written agency agreement with them. The couple asks to see a property listed by River Bluff Realty. In this situation, the licensee most likely owes statutory duties to whom?

a. Marcus and Dana as buyer clients
b. River Bluff Realty and the listing client
c. Both parties equally as a dual agent
d. Neither party, since no agreement exists

5. Which of the following information is a Missouri dual agent prohibited from disclosing without client consent?

a. That the seller would accept less than the listed price
b. Known adverse material facts about the property
c. The property's listing price
d. The property's legal description

6. A licensee representing a seller discovers that the roof has a known leak. Under Missouri law, what is the licensee's obligation regarding this information?

a. Disclose all known adverse material facts to the client
b. Disclose it to the seller but keep it confidential from all buyers
c. Disclose it only if the buyer directly asks about the roof
d. Refer the buyer to an independent inspector and say nothing

7. What is the primary purpose of designated agency in Missouri?

a. To allow one licensee to represent both parties and collect a full commission
b. To permit the firm's broker to personally oversee all dual agency transactions
c. To allow two agents within the same firm to each fully represent their respective clients without dual agency conflicts
d. To create a non-agency relationship when both parties are represented by the same firm

8. Under Missouri license law, which of the following actions constitutes "sign crossing" or broker interference?

a. Placing a For Sale sign on a property after obtaining written consent
b. Negotiating a commission split with a cooperating broker
c. Showing a listed property to a competing buyer
d. Soliciting a brokerage agreement from a party already under an exclusive agreement with another broker

9. Which of the following correctly describes when a Missouri agency relationship is terminated by expiration?

a. The listing expires only if the seller submits a written cancellation request
b. The listing cannot expire if the broker has incurred marketing expenses
c. The listing expires only after the broker provides written notice to the seller
d. The listing automatically expires at the end date unless both parties agree in writing to extend it

10. A broker chooses to end an agency relationship even though the client wants to continue. This is known as:

a. Mutual rescission
b. Revocation
c. Renunciation
d. Expiration

11. After an agency relationship ends in Missouri, which fiduciary duty continues indefinitely?

a. Loyalty
b. Obedience
c. Accounting
d. Confidentiality

12. A salesperson leaves her brokerage and joins a competing firm. What happens to the agency relationships she had with her seller clients?
a. The agency relationships transfer with the salesperson to the new brokerage
b. All agency relationships are immediately terminated upon her departure
c. The agency relationships remain with the original broker, since clients belong to the broker
d. The clients must choose whether to follow the salesperson or stay with the original broker

MODULE 1 CASE STUDY:

Missouri Agency Relationships & Agency Disclosure

THE SITUATION

Marcus is a newly licensed Missouri real estate salesperson affiliated with Gateway Properties. He receives a call from a woman named Diane, who says she found his name online and is interested in selling her home. Marcus is excited about the potential listing and drives over to meet Diane that afternoon.

During the visit, Diane mentions that she and her husband are going through a divorce and need to sell quickly. She also shares that they owe $210,000 on the home and cannot afford to take less than that at closing. Marcus tours the property, takes notes, and tells Diane he will put together a pricing analysis and get back to her soon.

Over the next two weeks, Marcus and Diane exchange several phone calls and text messages. Marcus begins researching comparable sales in the neighborhood and drafting a marketing plan. He informally tells Diane he thinks the home will sell quickly and that he is confident he can get her the price she needs.

Before any paperwork is signed, Marcus gets a call from a buyer client he is already working with, Todd. Marcus mentions the conversation with Diane and shares that the seller is motivated by a divorce and cannot go below $210,000. Todd asks to see the property, and Marcus schedules a showing.

After the showing, Todd makes an offer of $205,000. Marcus presents the offer to Diane, who is upset that the offer is below what she needs. When Marcus mentions he has been working with the buyer as well, Diane is blindsided. She had no idea Marcus was representing the buyer and never signed any agreement with Marcus in the first place.

DISCUSSION QUESTIONS

1. What brokerage relationship, if any, existed between Marcus and Diane at the time he shared her confidential information with Todd? What should Marcus have done differently before the first visit?

____

____

____

____

2. What disclosure violations occurred in this scenario, and at what point were they triggered under Missouri law?

3. By sharing Diane's motivation for selling and her minimum acceptable price with Todd, what duty did Marcus violate, and does it matter that no written agreement was ever signed?

4. If Marcus ultimately represents both Diane and Todd in the same transaction, what Missouri brokerage relationship would apply, and what steps are legally required before that can occur?

5. What practical lessons from Module 1 would have prevented every problem in this scenario?

Module 2: MISSOURI SELLER REPRESENTATION

I. Listing a Property
II. Real Property Valuation
III. Role of the Appraiser

Module 2 Learning Objectives

Listing a Property

1. Identify effective prospecting strategies Missouri licensees use to generate listing opportunities.
2. Describe the key elements of a successful listing presentation.
3. Distinguish between the types of seller listing agreements used in Missouri.
4. Explain the broker's responsibilities during the pre-closing period.

Real Property Valuation

1. Explain how supply, demand, and the four determinants of value influence real estate market prices.
2. Define market value and describe the criteria required to validate it, distinguishing between market value, market price, and a broker's opinion of value.
3. Apply the sales comparison approach to estimate residential property value.

Role of the Appraiser

1. Explain the role of the licensed appraiser in a Missouri real estate transaction.
2. Distinguish between appraised value and listing price, and explain why Missouri listing agents must educate sellers on the relationship between the two to reduce transaction risk.

I. Listing a Property

Listings are the traditional source of a broker's income. By obtaining a listing, a broker obtains a share of the commission generated whenever a cooperating broker finds a buyer. By contrast, in working with a buyer, it is not so certain that the effort will produce income. In the absence of an exclusive buyer representation agreement, a buyer may move from one agent to another without making any commitment. Agents can spend considerable time with a buyer and earn nothing. Hence the special value of an exclusive listing with a seller: it is likely to generate revenue.

As of August 17, 2024, new rules were implemented due to the National Association of REALTORS® (NAR) settlement, which prohibits offers of buyer agent compensation on MLS and requires written buyer agency agreements.

The National Association of REALTORS® policies on buyer agent commissions require that brokers clearly communicate to sellers and buyers that broker compensation is fully negotiable and not set by law. Although buyer agent commission may not be shown in the MLS, they may be communicated via marketing materials or other means.

Prospecting

Prospecting is any activity designed to generate listing prospects: parties who intend to sell or lease property and who have not yet committed to a broker. Prospecting activities include mailing newsletters and flyers, selling directly and person-to-person, advertising, and selling indirectly via community involvement.

The goal of prospecting is to reach a potential seller or landlord, make that person aware of the agent's and brokerage's services, and obtain permission to discuss the benefits of listing, often in the form of a formal selling presentation.

Prospecting strategies

There are numerous ways to find listings and the most profitable options depend on the market and personality of the listing agent. If an agent is familiar with a particular neighborhood or they have a large network of colleagues, then focusing on marketing to these spheres of influence would be the most profitable way to find clients. This can be done with face-to-face meetings, phone calls, or handwritten cards.

When buyers and sellers are looking for a Realtor, they typically ask their friends first. This is why a referral-based lead generation objective is the most fruitful and sustainable. The leads are already "warm" and comfortable with being approached. Most agents strive to reach this stage of maturity in their business where they do not have to actively market to "cold" leads and can focus on their friends, family and past clientele.

Expireds and FSBOs.

If the agent has yet to establish a network or a presence in their local market, then their efforts are better focused on direct outreach to build a database filled with future clients. Some of the more popular methods include cold calling expired listings and For Sale By Owners, or FSBOs.

Expired listings are homes that have had trouble selling with their original real estate agent. These listings are a great target because they are actively looking to sell. When calling expired listings it is important to come from a helpful angle and suggest what could be done differently in order to sell the home. There are paid services out there that offer the phone numbers and addresses of expired listings daily, and some brokerages offer these services to their agents.

Reaching out to FSBOs also requires some preparation and familiarity with common scripts. For Sale By Owners are typically people who are trying to save as much money as possible and believe they can handle everything themselves. These prospects can be found by driving around or by searching online or on social media.

Farming

Besides cold-calling expired listings and FSBOs, agents can also build their network by "farming" a specific neighborhood with mailers and door-knocking, hosting open houses for other agents, purchasing leads through online platforms like Zillow and Realtor.com and utilizing social media such as Facebook and Instagram.

When choosing a neighborhood to "farm", it is important to research the hottest areas. Where are most of the homes selling? Which neighborhoods have the largest turnover rates? The turnover rate can be calculated by adding up all of the sold homes in the last 12 months, and dividing it by the total number of homes. Depending on the market, this rate should be around 7 to 8%. But, before committing to a neighborhood, it is vital to check if there are other agents heavily farming that area or consistently listing homes. If there are a few agents with whom each listing is sold with, then that neighborhood will take longer and more effort to convert. Consider farming neighborhoods that do not have a preference for a given Realtor. One of the ways to find this out is by door-knocking a neighborhood and speaking with some of the current residents.

Once a neighborhood is picked, the agent has to develop a consistent marketing plan in order to see any results. By incorporating regular mailers (postcards, community event calendars, recipes, handwritten letters, market trends), door-knocking, door hangers, and special promotions, the agent will become accepted and trusted by the whole neighborhood. Farming takes consistent effort and time before showing results.

Open houses

An agent does not have to rely on their own listings in order to host an open house. The key to running a successful open house is picking one in a popular neighborhood where the leads are easy to convert. The busiest open houses are ones that have been aggressively pre-marketed for at least one week prior. Pre-marketing an open house can be done through posting on social media, delivering flyers to the neighbors, and door-knocking the surrounding homes with invites to the open house. Open houses are typically held on weekends between the hours of 11-4pm in order to allow for maximum traffic.

When hosting an open house, the goal is to capture the emails and phone numbers of the attendees with a sign-in sheet in order to follow-up with them in the future. The attendees rarely purchase the actual listing, but they are active buyers that literally come knocking on your door.

Open house leads usually take about 3-6 months to convert so it is important to stay on top of following up through phone calls, text messages, and emails.

In the current period, it is very common for agents to also utilize online platforms to build their pipelines. This can be done through social media or by purchasing leads through platforms like Zillow and Realtor.com. These platforms allow buyers to request showings directly through their websites and phone applications. The platform then captures the buyer's information and sends it to local agents who are purchasing leads for that particular zip code. These particular leads have to be responded to almost immediately and converted with a quick phone call or a text message.

Listing Presentations

The listing presentation is a chance for the listing agent to tour the home and showcase why the seller should list with them. Chances are, the seller will be interviewing multiple agents so it is important to be professional.

Preparations

The agent should come prepared with an estimated net sheet, a detailed marketing plan, and all of the necessary listing paperwork. During the property tour, the agent should ask specific questions about any upgrades the seller may have done, and the age of the major systems (AC, roof, plumbing, and electrical). Some listing appointments can be casual, for example during a happy hour, whereas others require a top-notch, formal presentation. The key is to adjust to the style of the owner. By mirroring the clients preferences, the agent can quickly adapt and make a better impression.

Optimize the property

During the listing presentation, the agent should discuss how to outshine other active listings. Present the property at its full potential. If possible, the sellers should add a fresh coat of paint and spruce up the landscaping for maximum curb appeal. During the listing presentation it is also vital to highlight the importance of a de-cluttered and clean home. Staging the property and providing professional photography will greatly impact the amount of traffic the listing will have. There are staging companies out there who focus on real estate listings, and there are also staging kits that can be purchased online with minor items to spruce up the showing potential of the home.

Elements of Seller Agency Agreements

The most common way of creating an agency relationship between a broker and a seller is through a listing agreement. A listing agreement is a legally enforceable real estate agency agreement between a real estate broker and a client, authorizing the broker to perform a stated service for compensation. It is the foundational document that puts a broker in business on behalf of a seller, and it is governed both by agency law and by contract law.

In Missouri, all exclusive listing agreements must be in writing to be enforceable. While an open listing may be oral, best practice, and the standard expectation of the Missouri Real Estate Commission, is that any agency relationship with a seller be documented in a written agreement before any services are rendered.

Scope of authority

A listing agreement is customarily a special agency, or limited agency, agreement. This means the broker's authority is limited to specific activities, generally those that generate customers and facilitate the transaction. A special agency agreement does not authorize the broker to obligate the seller to a contract as a principal party unless the agreement expressly grants that authority or the seller has executed a power of attorney. A listing broker in Missouri may not, for example, tell a prospective buyer that the seller will accept an offer regardless of its terms. Doing so would exceed the scope of authority granted and could expose both the broker and the seller to liability.

Types of Listing Agreements

There are three primary types of seller listing agreements used in Missouri:

The *exclusive right-to-sell* is the most widely used. Under this agreement, the seller contracts exclusively with a single broker. If a buyer is procured during the listing period, the broker is entitled to a commission regardless of who is the procuring cause, whether that is the listing broker, a cooperating broker, or even the seller themselves. This provides the listing broker with the greatest assurance of compensation for their marketing efforts.

The *exclusive agency* listing also authorizes a single broker to sell the property, but it preserves the seller's right to sell the property on their own without owing a commission. If any party other than the seller is the procuring cause of a completed transaction, the broker has earned their commission. If the seller finds the buyer independently, no commission is owed.

The *open listing* is a non-exclusive authorization that a seller may offer to any number of brokers simultaneously. Under an open listing, only the broker who is the first to produce a ready, willing, and able buyer is entitled to a commission. If the seller closes without a participating broker, no commission is payable. Open listings are rare in residential transactions in Missouri due to the lack of guaranteed compensation and the increased potential for commission disputes.

Missouri law does not permit net listings, which are agreements in which the seller sets a minimum net amount and the broker retains everything above that figure as commission. Net listings are considered unprofessional and create an inherent conflict of interest, as the broker benefits by encouraging the seller to set the lowest possible acceptable price rather than acting in the seller's best financial interest.

Beyond the type of agreement, every listing agreement should clearly define the listing price, the duration of the agreement, the compensation structure, the broker's authorized marketing activities, and the responsibilities of both parties. A well-constructed listing agreement protects the seller, the broker, and the integrity of the transaction from beginning to end.

Listing Benchmarks

Once a listing has been procured, it must be fulfilled. To this end, the essential benchmarks in the listing process are pricing, marketing the listing, selling the buyer prospect, obtaining offers, and presenting and finalizing the offer.

Determining a price

It is almost always necessary for an agent seeking a listing to suggest a listing price or price range for the property. It is important to make a careful estimate, because underpricing a property is not in the best interests of the seller, and overpricing it often prevents a transaction altogether. In brief, an agent usually relies on an analysis of comparable properties which have recently sold in the same neighborhood. By making adjustments for the differences between the subject property and the comparables, the agent arrives at a general price range. Agents must be careful to caution sellers that they are not appraisers, and that the suggested price range is not an expert opinion of market value. If a more precise estimate of market value is desired, the seller should hire a licensed appraiser.

Marketing listings

The process of marketing a listed property leads to the desired end of a completed sale contract. During this process, there are critical skills an agent must master during the key phases of marketing plan implementation, selling the buyer prospect, and obtaining an accepted offer.

After the broker formalizes the listing agreement, the agent initiates a marketing plan for the property. An ideal marketing plan is a cohesive combination of promotional and selling activities directed at potential customers. The best combination is one that aims to have maximum impact on the marketplace in relation to the time and money expended.

Professional photography of a home will help garner more attention. Besides photography, professional videos can be filmed, and a Matterport camera can be used in order to share the floorplan with potential buyers.

Once the listing is on the market, the true work begins. Besides “shouting from the rooftops” that a listing is live, there are actual strategies to share a listing with the local market. Broker’s opens are open houses geared towards agents only so they can preview the home to see if it is a good fit for their buyers. These are common with luxury listings. Besides broker’s opens, cold calling local agents, delivering door hangers to the neighbors, hosting open houses and running social media advertisements will help get more eyes on the listing as well. Real estate is a numbers game, and the sooner a listing is seen by a majority of agents, the faster it will sell.

Selling the buyer prospect

When marketing activities produce prospects, the agent's marketing role becomes more interpersonal. An agent must now:

- qualify prospects' plans, preferences, and financial capabilities
- show properties that meet the customer's needs

- elicit the buyer's reactions to properties
- report material results to the seller or listing agent

At the earliest appropriate time, an agent must make certain disclosures to a prospective customer. An agent is required to disclose the relevant agency relationship, the property's physical condition, and the possible presence of hazardous materials.

Obtaining offers

If a buyer is interested in purchasing a property, an agent obtains the buyer's offer of transaction terms, including price, down payment, desired closing date, and financing requirements. An agent must be extremely careful at this point to abide by statutory obligations to the client, whoever that party may be. Discussions of price are particularly delicate: whether the client is buyer or seller, the agent's duty is to uphold the client's best interests. Thus, it is not acceptable to suggest to a customer what price the client will or will not accept. With pricing and other issues, it is always a good practice to understand what role the client wants the agent to assume in the offering phase of the transaction; in other words, exactly how far the agent may go in developing terms on the client's behalf.

When a buyer or tenant makes an offer, the agent must present it to the seller or landlord at the earliest possible moment. If the terms of the offer are unacceptable, the agent may assist the seller in developing a counteroffer, which the agent would subsequently submit to the customer or customer's agent. The offering and counteroffering process continues until a meeting of the minds results in a sale contract.

Multiple offers

Multiple offer situations are common in seller's markets. If a listing is priced well, in good condition and in a hot area, then it will sell quickly and may result in a bidding war. Multiple offers can be difficult to organize, but one strategy is to call for a "highest and best" offer from all of the agents. This will save time from going back and forth with each agent and ensure that the offers are the strongest option a buyer is willing to make.

Presenting offers

Once all of the new offers are in, organizing the important terms in an Excel sheet is a helpful way to present the offers to the sellers.

The important terms to organize are as follows:

- purchase price
- earnest money deposit
- financing type (cash, conventional, FHA, VA,)
- downpayment amount
- length of inspection period
- closing date
- incentives (are the buyer's asking for any closing cost assistance?)
- miscellaneous additional terms

Once these essential listing benchmarks are achieved, the transaction moves into the pre-closing period where all involved parties satisfy the various terms, conditions and contingencies of the accepted agreement, or sales contract.

Pre-Closing Activities

Hopefully, the marketing plan, prospect selling and offer presentations generate an executed contract. At this point, between the execution of the sale contract and the closing of the transaction, the property is "under contract" or "contract pending." During this period, buyer and seller have certain things to do to achieve a successful closing. The buyer often needs to arrange financing and dispose of other property; the seller may need to clear up title encumbrances and make certain property repairs. The sale contract should specify all such required tasks. The time period between contracting and closing is referred to as the contingency period, or pre-closing period.

Broker responsibilities

As dictated by custom and the circumstances of a transaction, an agent has a range of duties and responsibilities during the pre-closing period. An agent's foremost duty following acceptance of an offer is to submit the contract and the earnest money to the managing broker without delay. In Missouri, earnest money must be deposited promptly after the time of acceptance of a sales contract.

The agent must also complete their due diligence in the listing. This refers to verifying the accuracy of the statements in the listing regarding the property, the owner, and the owner's representations. Especially important facts for a broker to verify are:

- the property condition
- ownership status
- the client's authority to act

Failure to perform a reasonable degree of due diligence may increase an agent's exposure to liability in the event that the property is not as represented or that the client cannot perform as promised.

Other responsibilities are:

- assisting the buyer in obtaining financing
- recommending inspectors, appraisers, attorneys, and title companies
- assisting in communications between principals
- assisting in the exchange of transaction documents

Waiting for the inspection and appraisal results is one of the most stressful times in a real estate transaction. There are so many moving parts and these two reports can completely alter the trajectory of the transaction. An inspection period is the time the buyers have to complete their due diligence and review any inspections that have been ordered for the home. Oftentimes, buyers will request repairs to be completed that are not necessary for insurance purposes so a listing agent's job is to negotiate with the buyers and keep their sellers from completing any unnecessary repairs. A buyer's agents job is to fight for the buyers and negotiate for any repairs they deem necessary.

Not all inspection results are positive, and sometimes a deal has to fall through due to the buyers wanting to move on from the property. In this case, a contract cancellation addendum should be sent to all parties to sign.

The appraisal could also lead to some stress. A third party completes the appraisal by picking comparable properties, and ensuring the safety and condition of the home. Different financing types have different appraisal criteria so it is important to let both the inspector and appraiser know what financing is being used.

If an appraisal comes in below the purchase price with required repairs (i.e. a piece of wood rot was found), then all parties have to come together and work through the issues. Either the buyer will have to come to the closing table with cash to cover the difference or the seller will have to lower the price. Another option is that the seller and buyer split the difference amongst themselves. In regards to any property damage that needs to be fixed for an appraisal, that will have to be negotiated between both parties as well. Once everything is agreed upon and fixed, then a re-appraisal occurs to confirm that the necessary repairs have been made.

The culmination of the pre-closing period -- and all its diligence activities -- is a successful closing where the parties exchange consideration and title, and the transaction is consummated. At this point the sale contract is successfully extinguished.

Impacts of the NAR Lawsuit on Seller Representation

As of August 17, 2024, significant changes to how buyer agent compensation is handled took effect across the country as a result of the National Association of REALTORS® (NAR) settlement. These changes have meaningful implications for Missouri sellers and the licensees who represent them.

Prior to the settlement, it was standard practice for a seller's listing agreement to include an offer of compensation to a buyer's agent, and that offer was routinely published in the Multiple Listing Service (MLS). The NAR settlement prohibits offers of buyer agent compensation from being included in MLS listings. This represents a fundamental shift in how the real estate industry has historically operated and requires sellers and their agents to approach compensation conversations differently than before.

Under the new rules, buyer agent compensation may no longer be advertised through the MLS. However, sellers are still permitted to offer compensation to a buyer's agent through other channels, such as marketing materials, direct communication between brokers, or as a term within the purchase contract itself. Missouri sellers should understand that offering buyer agent compensation, even outside the MLS, remains entirely legal and may, in many cases, be a strategic decision that makes a property more attractive to a broader pool of buyers.

What has changed most significantly for sellers is the need for transparency and intentional decision-making regarding compensation. Missouri licensees are required to clearly communicate to both sellers and buyers that broker compensation is fully negotiable and is not set by law. There is no standard or mandated commission rate, and sellers should feel empowered to discuss compensation terms openly with their listing broker.

Additionally, the NAR settlement requires that buyers have a **written buyer agency agreement in place before a broker can show them property**. This means that buyers entering the market are now formally committing to their representation arrangement upfront, which in turn brings compensation expectations to the surface earlier in the process. Sellers may encounter buyers whose agents have negotiated a specific compensation arrangement with their clients, and those buyers may request that the seller cover some or all of that compensation as part of their offer terms.

For Missouri sellers, the practical takeaway is this: compensation is now more openly negotiated, more visible during in the offer and acceptance process, and more directly tied to the terms of each individual transaction. Listing agents in Missouri have a responsibility to fully explain these changes to their seller clients so they can make informed decisions about how to price and position their property in today's market.

II. Real Property Valuation

The American Market System

The valuation of real property is one of the most fundamental activities in the real estate business. Its role is particularly critical in the transfer of real property since the value of a parcel establishes the general price range for the principal parties to negotiate.

In understanding value and pricing, it is important to appreciate the underlying determinants of value: supply and demand. These are the fundamental economic forces interacting in the market that drive the upward and downward movement of prices.

Supply and demand

The goal of an economic system is to produce and distribute a supply of goods and services to satisfy the demand of its constituents. Economic activity therefore centers on the production, distribution and sale of goods and services to meet consumer demand.

- **Supply** is the quantity of a product or service available for sale, lease, or trade at any given time.
- **Demand** is the quantity of a product or service that is desired for purchase, lease, or trade at any given time.

The interplay of supply and demand is what makes an economy work: consumers demand goods and services; suppliers and sellers produce and distribute the goods and services for a negotiated price.

Price and Value

The price mechanism

In addition to supply and demand, the other critical component of an economic system is the price mechanism, or simply, price. A price is the amount of money or other asset that a buyer has agreed to pay and a seller has agreed to accept to complete the exchange of a good or service. It is a quantification of the value of an item traded.

Price in this context means the final trading price; it is not the preliminary asking price of the seller nor the initial bidding price of the purchaser. Asking and bidding prices are pricing positions in a negotiation between the parties prior to the exchange. The true price of an item or service is the final number the parties agree to.

Value and value determinants

Price is not something of value in itself. It is only a number that quantifies value. The economic issue underlying the interplay of supply and demand is, how do trading parties arrive at the value of a good or service as indicated by the price?

Consider consumer demand for air conditioners. Why do air conditioners have value? How do they command the price they do?

The value of something is based on the answers to four questions:

- How much do I desire it?
- How useful is it?
- How scarce is it?
- Am I able to pay for it?

Desire

One determinant of value is how dear the item is to the purchaser. Returning to the air conditioner example, the question becomes "how much do I desire to be cool, dry, and comfortable?" To a person who lives in the tropics, it is safe to say that air conditioning is more valuable than a heating system. It is also safe to say the opposite is true for residents of northern Alaska.

Utility

The second determinant of value is the product's ability to do the job. Can the air conditioner satisfy my need to stay cool? How cool does it make my house? Does it even work properly? Of course, I won't pay as much if it is old or ineffectual.

Scarcity

The third critical element of value is a product's availability in relation to demand. The air conditioner is quite valuable if there are only five units in the entire city and everyone is hot. On the other hand, the value of an air conditioner goes down if there are ten thousand units for sale in a 500-person market.

Purchasing power

A fourth component of value is the consumer's ability to pay for the item. If one cannot afford to buy the air conditioner, the value of the air conditioner is diminished, since it is financially out of reach. If all air conditioners are too expensive, consumers are forced to consider alternatives such as ceiling fans.

In the marketplace, the relative presence or absence of the four elements of value is constantly changing due to innumerable factors. Since price is a reflection of the total of all value factors at any time, changes in the underlying factors of value trigger changes in price.

Real Estate Market Dynamics

As an economic commodity, real estate is bought, sold, traded, and leased as a product within a real estate market.

Economic characteristics of real estate

Real estate, like other products and services, is:

- subject to the laws of supply and demand
- governed in the market by the price mechanism
- influenced by the producer's costs to bring the product to market
- influenced by the determinants of value: utility, scarcity, desire, and purchasing power

Distinguishing features

In comparison with other economic products and services, real estate has certain unique traits. These include:

- **Inherent product value**

  Land is a scarce resource as well as a required factor of production. Like gold and silver, it has both inherent value and utility value.

- **Unique appeal of product**

  Since no two parcels of real estate can be alike (each has a different location), every parcel of real property has its own appeal. Likewise, no two parcels of real estate can have exactly the same value, except by coincidence.

- **Demand must come to the supply**

  Since real property cannot be moved, real property investors and users must come to the supply. This creates risk, because if demand drops, the supply cannot be transported to a higher demand market.

- **Illiquid**

  Real estate is a relatively illiquid economic product, meaning it cannot always be readily sold for cash. Since it is a large, long-term investment that has no exact duplicate, buyers must go through a complex process to evaluate and purchase the right parcel of real estate.

- **Slow to respond to changes**

  Real estate is relatively slow to respond to market imbalances. Because new construction is a large-scale, time-consuming process, the market is slow to respond to increases in demand. The market is similarly slow to respond to sharp declines in demand, since the product cannot be moved and sold elsewhere. Instead, owners must wait out slow periods and simply hope for the best.

- **Decentralized, local market**

  A real property cannot be shipped to a large, central real estate marketplace. Real estate markets are thus local in nature and highly susceptible to swings in the local economy.

Real estate supply and demand

Supply. In real estate, supply is the amount of property available for sale or lease at any given time. The units of supply used to quantify the amount of property available differ for different categories of property. These supply units, by property type, are:

- residential: dwelling units
- commercial and industrial: square feet
- agricultural: acreage

Factors influencing supply. In addition to the influences of demand and the underlying determinants of value, real estate supply responds to

- development costs, particularly labor
- availability of financing
- investment returns
- a community's master plan
- government police powers and regulation

Demand. Real estate demand is the amount of property buyers and tenants wish to acquire by purchase, lease or trade at any given time. Units of demand, by property classification, are:

- residential: households
- commercial and industrial: square feet
- agricultural: acreage

Supply and demand interaction. Real estate supply and demand, like supply and demand for other economic products, interact in the marketplace to produce price movements.

Real Estate Supply-Demand Cycle

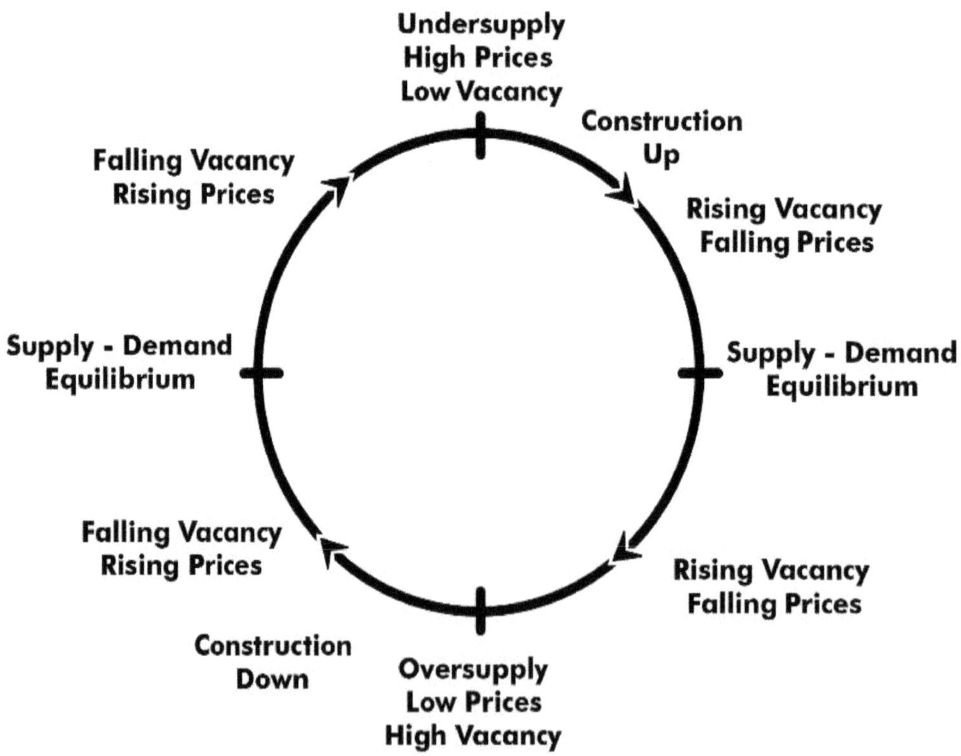

Appraising Market Value

Market value

Understanding market economics and supply and demand interaction gives the licensee a solid foundation for estimating market value and pricing residential properties. The complexity in valuation, however, is that there are numerous types of value – leasehold, insured, book value, mortgage value, depreciated value – to name a few. What we are after in this context of residential valuation is the type of value referred to as market value. "Market value" is the quantification that residential licensees are after in valuing properties and understanding prices in a market.

Market value validity criteria. There is a specific set of criteria for defining and validating market value, as follows:

Market value is an opinion of the price that a willing seller and willing buyer would probably agree on for a property at a given time if:

- the transaction is a cash transaction
- the property is exposed on the open market for a reasonable period
- buyer and seller have full information about market conditions and about potential uses
- there is no abnormal pressure on either party to complete the transaction
- buyer and seller are not related (it is an "arm's length" transaction)
- title is marketable and conveyable by the seller
- the price is a "normal consideration," that is, it does not include hidden influences such as special financing deals, concessions, terms, services, fees, credits, costs, or other types of consideration.

Market price

The market price, as opposed to market value, is what a property actually sells for. Market price should theoretically be the same as market value if all the conditions essential for market value were present. Market price, however, may not reflect the analysis of comparables and of investment value that an estimate of market value includes.

Broker's opinion of value (BPO)

A broker's opinion of value may resemble an appraisal, but it differs from an appraisal in that it is not necessarily performed by a disinterested third party or licensed professional and it generally uses only a limited form of one of the three appraisal approaches. In addition, the opinion is not subject to regulation, nor does it follow any particular professional standards.

Value principles underlying residential valuation

To identify residential market value, appraisers and brokers principally rely on two principles of value: ***substitution and contribution***.

Substitution. According to the principle of substitution, a buyer will pay no more for a property than the buyer would have to pay for an equally desirable and available substitute property. For example, if three houses for sale are essentially similar in size, quality and location, a potential buyer is unlikely to choose the one that is priced significantly higher than the other two. This principle is actively applied in developing a broker's competitive market analysis, or CMA. Numerous properties are compared to the subject property using the assumption that buyers will not pay more for a given property than they would for a similar property located elsewhere.

Contribution. The principal of contribution focuses on the degree to which a particular improvement affects market value of the overall property. In essence, the contribution of the improvement is equal to the change in market value that the addition of the improvement causes.

For example, adding a bathroom to a house may contribute an additional $15,000 to the appraised value. Thus, the contribution of the bathroom is $15,000. Note that an improvement's contribution to value has little to do with the improvement's cost. The foregoing bathroom may have cost $5,000 or $20,000. Contribution is what the market recognizes as the change in value, not what an item cost.

If continuous improvements are added to a property, it is possible that, at some point, the cost of adding improvements to a property no longer contributes a corresponding increase in the value of the property. When this occurs, the property suffers from diminishing marginal return, where the costs to improve exceed contribution.

Estimating Residential Property Value

The sales comparison approach, also known as the market data approach, is used for almost all properties. It also serves as the basis for a broker's opinion of value. As stated previously, it is based on the principle of substitution-- that a buyer will pay no more for the subject property than would be sufficient to purchase a comparable property-- and contribution-- that specific characteristics add value to a property.

The sales comparison approach is widely used because it takes into account the subject property's specific amenities in relation to competing properties. In addition, because of the currency of its data, the approach incorporates present market realities.

Steps in the approach

The sales comparison approach consists of comparing sale prices of recently sold properties that are comparable with the subject, and making dollar adjustments to the price of each comparable to account for competitive differences with the subject. After identifying the adjusted value of each comparable, the appraiser weighs the reliability of each comparable and the factors underlying how the adjustments were made. The weighting yields a final value range based on the most reliable factors in the analysis.

Steps in the Sales Comparison Approach

1. ***Identify comparable sales.***
2. ***Compare comparables to the subject and make adjustments to comparables.***
3. ***Weight values indicated by adjusted comparables for the final value estimate of the subject.***

Identifying comparables

To qualify as a comparable, a property must:

- resemble the subject in size, shape, design, utility and location
- have sold recently, generally within six months of the appraisal
- have sold in an arm's-length transaction

An appraiser considers three to six comparables, and usually includes at least three in the appraisal report.

Appraisers have specific guidelines within the foregoing criteria for selecting comparables, many of which are set by secondary market organizations such as FNMA. For example, to qualify as a comparable for a mortgage loan appraisal, a property might have to be located within one mile of the subject. Or perhaps the size of the comparable must be within a certain percentage of improved area in relation to the subject.

The time-of-sale criterion is important because transactions that occurred too far in the past will not reflect appreciation or recent changes in market conditions.

An arm's length sale involves objective, disinterested parties who are presumed to have negotiated a market price for the property. If the sale of a house occurred between a father and a daughter, for example, one might assume that the transaction did not reflect market value.

Principal sources of data for generating the sales comparison are tax records, title records, and the local multiple listing service.

Adjusting comparables

The appraiser must adjust the values of the comparables to account for competitive differences with the subject property. Note that the sale prices of the comparables are known, while the value and price of the subject are not. Therefore, adjustments can be made only to the comparables' prices, not to the subject's. Adjustments are made to the comparables in the form of a value deduction or a value addition.

Adding or deducting value. If the comparable is better than the subject in some characteristic, an amount is ***deducted*** from the sale price of the comparable. This accounts for the value discrepancy – if for example the comparable did not have that extra bedroom, it would have sold for less – so make a deduction so that the subject and the comp are equalized.

If the comparable is inferior to the subject in some characteristic, an amount is ***added*** to the price of the comparable. This adjustment equalizes the subject's competitive advantage in this area. Note that the subject is never adjusted!

Key adjustment criteria. The principal factors for comparison and adjustment are time of sale, location, physical characteristics, and transaction characteristics.

- **time of sale**

  An adjustment may be made if market conditions, market prices, or financing availability have changed significantly since the date of the comparable's sale. Most often, this adjustment is to account for appreciation.

- **location**

  An adjustment may be made if there are differences between the comparable's location and the subject's, including neighborhood desirability and appearance, zoning restrictions, and general price levels.

- **physical characteristics**

  Adjustments may be made for marketable differences between the comparable's and subject's lot size, square feet of livable area (or other appropriate measure for the property type), number of rooms, layout, age, condition, construction type and quality, landscaping, and special amenities.

- **transaction characteristics**

  An adjustment may be made for such differences as mortgage loan terms, mortgage assumability, and owner financing.

Weighting comparables.

Adding and subtracting the appropriate adjustments to the sale price of each comparable results in an adjusted price for the comparables that indicates the value of the subject. The last step in the approach is to perform a weighted analysis of the indicated values of each comparable. The appraiser, in other words, must identify which comparable values are more indicative of the subject and which are less indicative.

An appraiser primarily relies on experience and judgment to weight comparables. There is no formula for selecting a value from within the range of all comparables analyzed. However, there are three quantitative guidelines: the total number of adjustments; the amount of a single adjustment; and the net value change of all adjustments.

As a rule, *the fewer the total number of adjustments, the smaller the adjustment amounts, and the less the total adjustment amount, the more reliable the comparable.*

Broker's comparative market analysis

A broker or associate who is attempting to establish a listing price or range of prices for a property uses a scaled-down version of the appraiser's sales comparison approach called a comparative market analysis, or **CMA** (also called a competitive market analysis). While the CMA serves a useful purpose in setting general price ranges, brokers and agents need to exercise caution in presenting a CMA as an appraisal, which it is not. Two important distinctions between the two are objectivity and comprehensiveness.

First, the broker is not unbiased: he or she is motivated by the desire to obtain a listing, which can lead one to distort the estimated price. Secondly, the broker's CMA is not comprehensive: the broker does not usually consider the full range of data about market conditions and comparable sales that the appraiser must consider and document. Therefore, the broker's opinion will be less reliable than the appraiser's.

The following is a case illustration of a comparative market analysis. A broker is estimating market value for a certain house. Four comparables are adjusted to find an indicated value for the subject. The grid which follows the property and market data shows the adjustments for the differences between the four comparables and the subject.

CMA Case Illustration:

Data

Subject property:

8 rooms-- 3 bedrooms, two baths, kitchen, living room, family room; 2,000 square feet of gross living area; 2-car attached garage; landscaping is good. Construction is frame with aluminum siding.

Comparable A:

Sold for 1,000,000 within previous month; conventional financing at current rates; located in subject's neighborhood with similar locational advantages; house approximately same age as subject; lot size smaller than subject; view similar to subject; design less appealing than subject's; construction similar to subject; condition similar to subject; 7 rooms-- two bedrooms, one bath; 1,900 square feet of gross living area; 2-car attached garage; landscaping similar to subject.

Comparable B:

Sold for 1,200,000 within previous month; conventional financing at current rates; located in subject's neighborhood with similar locational advantages; house six years newer than subject; lot size smaller than subject; view is better than the subject's; design is more appealing than subject's; construction (brick and frame) better than subject's; better condition than subject; 10 rooms-¬four bedrooms, three baths; 2,300 square feet of gross living area; 2-car attached garage; landscaping similar to subject.

Comparable C:

Sold for 1,150,000 within previous month; conventional financing at current rates; located in subject's neighborhood with similar locational advantages; house five years older than subject; lot size larger than subject; view similar to subject; design and appeal similar to subject's; construction similar to subject; condition similar to subject; 8 rooms-- three bedrooms, two baths; 2,000 square feet of gross living area; 2-car attached garage; landscaping similar to subject.

Comparable D:

Sold for 1,090,000 within previous month; conventional financing at current rates; located in a neighborhood close to subject's, but more desirable than subject's; house approximately same age as subject; lot size same as subject; view similar to subject; design less appealing than subject's; construction (frame) poorer than subject's; poorer condition than subject; 7 rooms-- two bedrooms, one and one half baths; 1,900 square feet of gross living area; 2-car attached garage; landscaping similar to subject.

Sales Comparison Approach Illustration:

Adjustments

	Subject	A	B	C	D
Sale price		1,000,000	1,200,000	1,150,000	1,090,000
Financing terms		standard	standard	standard	standard
Sale date	NOW	equal	equal	equal	equal
Location		equal	equal	equal	-20,000
Age		equal	-12,000	+10,000	equal
Lot size		+10,000	+10,000	-10,000	equal
Site/view		equal	-10,000	equal	equal
Design/appeal		+10,000	-12,000	equal	+5,000
Construction quality	good	equal	-30,000	equal	+10,000
Condition	good	equal	-50,000	equal	+20,000
No. of rooms	8				
No. of bedrooms	3	+5,000	-5,000	equal	+5,000
No. of baths	2	+10,000	-15,000	equal	+5,000
Gross living area	2,000	+10,000	-20,000	equal	+10,000
Other space					
Garage	2 car/attd.	equal	equal	equal	equal
Other improvements					
Landscaping	good	equal	equal	equal	equal
Net adjustments		+45,000	-144,000	0	+35,000
Indicated value	1,120,000	1,045,000	1,056,000	1,150,000	1,125,000

Sales Comparison Approach Illustration:

Analysis and Reconciliation

Analysis

For comparable A, the appraiser has made additions to the lot value, design, number of bedrooms and baths, and for gross living area. This accounts for the comparable's deficiencies in these areas relative to the subject. A total of five adjustments amount to $45,000, or 4.5% of the purchase price.

For comparable B, the appraiser has deducted values for age, site, design, construction quality, condition, bedrooms, baths, and living area. This accounts for the comparable's superior qualities relative to the subject. The only addition is the lot size, since the subject's is larger. A total of nine adjustments amount to $144,000, or 12% of the sale price.

For comparable C, the appraiser has added value for the age and deducted value for the lot size. The two adjustments offset one another for a net adjustment of zero.

For comparable D, one deduction has been made for the comparable's superior location. This is offset by six additions reflecting the various areas where the comparable is inferior to the subject. A total of seven adjustments amount to $35,000, or 3.2% of the sale price.

Reconciliation

In view of all adjusted comparables, the appraiser developed a final indication of value of $1,120,000 for the subject. Underlying this conclusion is the fact that Comparable C, since it only has two minor adjustments which offset each other, it is by far the best indicator of value. Comparable D might be the second-best indicator, since the net adjustments are very close to the sale price. Comparable A might be the third best indicator, since it has the second fewest number of total adjustments. Comparable B is the least reliable indicator, since there are numerous adjustments, three of which are of a significant amount. In addition, Comparable B is questionable altogether as a comparable, since total adjustments alter the sale price by 12%.

III. ROLE OF THE APPRAISER

When a Missouri seller is preparing to list a property, one of the most important concepts for both the seller and their agent to understand is the role of the professional appraiser. While a listing agent is responsible for determining a competitive listing price through a comparative market analysis, the appraiser serves a distinct and legally defined function in the real estate process. Understanding the difference between these two roles, and knowing when and why an appraisal matters, is essential knowledge for any licensee engaged in seller representation.

What is an Appraisal?

An appraisal is an objective, professional estimate of a property's market value performed by a licensed or certified appraiser. Unlike a comparative market analysis prepared by a real estate agent, a formal appraisal is a regulated professional opinion that carries legal weight in transactions involving mortgage financing. Lenders rely on appraisals to confirm that the collateral securing a loan, the property itself, is worth at least as much as the amount being borrowed. In a residential sale, if the buyer is financing the purchase, an appraisal ordered by the lender is almost always a required step before the transaction can close.

It is important for Missouri sellers and their agents to understand that an appraiser is an independent third party. The appraiser does not represent the buyer, the seller, or either agent. Their obligation is to the accuracy and integrity of their opinion of value, conducted in accordance with established professional standards.

Regulation of Appraisal Practice

The appraisal profession is federally regulated. In 1989, Congress passed the Financial Institutions Reform, Recovery and Enforcement Act (FIRREA) in response to the savings and loan crisis. Title XI of FIRREA requires that competent individuals whose professional conduct is properly supervised perform all appraisals used in federally-related transactions. Such appraisals must be performed only by state-certified appraisers, individuals who have passed the necessary examinations and competency standards established by each state in conformance with federal standards under FIRREA and the Uniform Standards of Professional Appraisal Practice (USPAP). The criteria for certification must, at a minimum, follow those established by the Appraiser Qualifications Board of the Appraisal Foundation.

In Missouri, appraisers are licensed and regulated through the Missouri Real Estate Appraisers Commission. Buyers, sellers, and their agents can verify an appraiser's credentials through this body to confirm they are working with a properly certified professional.

Professional Standards: USPAP

The Uniform Standards of Professional Appraisal Practice (USPAP) is the set of standards, guidelines, and provisions that governs the appraisal industry nationwide. It resulted from the cooperation of nine national appraisal organizations in 1985 and establishes the ethical and performance requirements all appraisers must follow.

Among the key provisions of USPAP is the competence requirement, which requires appraisers to assess whether they have the necessary knowledge and experience to perform a specific assignment. If they do not, they must disclose this fact to the client. There is also a departure provision, which permits appraisers under certain circumstances to perform an appraisal that does not meet all USPAP guidelines, provided they have informed the client of the limitations and the partial appraisal will not be misleading. The standards address recognized appraisal methods, the definition of due diligence, how appraisal results are reported, required disclosures and assumptions, and appraisal review procedures, among other matters.

For Missouri seller agents, understanding that appraisers operate under these strict professional standards helps explain why an appraiser's conclusions may sometimes differ from what a seller, or even an agent, expects.

Professional Associations and Designations

Prior to the establishment of state certification programs, the primary indication of professional competence for an appraiser was membership in and designation by one of the national appraisal associations. These associations continue to provide education and professional recognition. The organizations that jointly formed the Appraisal Foundation in 1987 include the American Society of Appraisers, the American Society of Farm Managers and Rural Appraisers, the International Association of Assessing Officers, and several others. The American Institute of Real Estate Appraisers and the Society of Real Estate Appraisers have since merged to become the Appraisal Institute, which today offers widely recognized designations such as the MAI and SRA credentials. Missouri agents working with sellers on higher-value or complex properties may encounter appraisers holding these designations, which signal advanced training and experience.

Appraised Value is Not the Same as Listing Price

One of the most important distinctions a Missouri listing agent must communicate to a seller is that appraised value and listing price are not the same thing, and they serve different purposes.

A listing price is a strategic market decision. It is based on recent comparable sales, current competition, local market conditions, and the seller's goals and timeline. A skilled listing agent will prepare a thorough comparative market analysis and recommend a price range designed to attract qualified buyers while maximizing the seller's net proceeds. The listing price is set before a buyer is involved and before any lender has ordered an appraisal.

The appraised value, by contrast, is determined after a purchase contract has been executed. It is ordered by the buyer's lender and reflects the appraiser's independent conclusion of what the property is worth in the current market based on USPAP-compliant methodology. If the appraised value comes in at or above the purchase price, the transaction typically proceeds without complication. If the appraisal comes in below the purchase price, the transaction faces a challenge, the lender will generally only lend based on the appraised value, leaving the buyer, seller, or both parties to negotiate a resolution.

For this reason, Missouri listing agents should price properties thoughtfully and realistically from the beginning. An aggressive listing price that attracts a buyer but fails to appraise can cause deals to fall apart, waste valuable time, and ultimately result in a lower final sale price than a more accurately priced listing might have achieved. Educating sellers on the relationship between listing price, market value, and appraised value is one of the most valuable services a Missouri seller's agent can provide.

MODULE 2 SNAPSHOT REVIEW: MISSOURI SELLER REPRESENTATION

I: Listing a Property

Prospecting

- Prospecting is any activity designed to generate listing prospects who have not yet committed to a broker
- Referral-based lead generation is the most sustainable strategy — warm leads from friends, family, and past clients convert most reliably
- Expired listings and FSBOs are effective targets for agents building a new database; both require prepared scripts and a helpful approach
- Farming a neighborhood requires consistent mailers, door-knocking, and marketing over time; choose areas with a turnover rate of approximately 7 to 8% and limited agent competition
- Open houses should be aggressively pre-marketed at least one week in advance; the goal is capturing contact information, not just selling the listing
- Online platforms such as Zillow and Realtor.com generate leads that must be responded to almost immediately

The Listing Presentation

- Come prepared with an estimated net sheet, a detailed marketing plan, and all listing paperwork
- Ask the seller about upgrades and the age of major systems during the property tour
- Adapt presentation style to the seller's preferences and personality
- Recommend fresh paint, improved curb appeal, decluttering, professional staging, and professional photography to maximize showing potential

Elements of Seller Agency Agreements

- A listing agreement is a legally enforceable contract governed by both agency law and contract law
- All exclusive listing agreements in Missouri must be in writing to be enforceable
- A listing agreement creates a special agency, meaning the broker's authority is limited to specific activities and does not authorize the broker to obligate the seller
- The three primary types of listing agreements in Missouri are the exclusive right-to-sell, the exclusive agency listing, and the open listing
- The exclusive right-to-sell is the most widely used and provides the broker the greatest assurance of compensation
- Net listings are prohibited in Missouri as they create an inherent conflict of interest

Listing Benchmarks and Pre-Closing

- Key benchmarks include pricing, marketing, working with buyer prospects, obtaining offers, and presenting and finalizing offers
- Agents must caution sellers that a CMA is not an appraisal and does not constitute an expert opinion of market value
- In multiple offer situations, calling for a highest and best offer from all buyers is an effective strategy
- During the pre-closing period, the agent must submit the contract and earnest money to the managing broker without delay, verify due diligence, and assist all parties in satisfying contract conditions

- A low appraisal or inspection issues can derail a transaction; the listing agent's role is to negotiate repairs and guide parties toward resolution

NAR Settlement Impacts on Seller Representation

- As of August 17, 2024, buyer agent compensation offers may no longer be published in the MLS
- Sellers may still offer buyer agent compensation through other channels, including marketing materials, direct broker communication, or purchase contract terms
- Missouri licensees must communicate clearly to all parties that broker compensation is fully negotiable and not set by law
- Buyers are now required to have a written buyer agency agreement before being shown property, which brings compensation discussions to the surface earlier in the transaction

II: Real Property Valuation

Supply, Demand, and Value

- Supply is the quantity of a product available at any given time; demand is the quantity desired for purchase
- The four determinants of value are desire, utility, scarcity, and purchasing power
- Real estate has unique economic characteristics: inherent land value, no two identical parcels, illiquidity, slow market response, and a decentralized local market structure

Market Value

- Market value is an opinion of the price a willing buyer and willing seller would agree on in an arm's length transaction with full information and no abnormal pressure
- Market price is what a property actually sells for, which may or may not equal market value
- A broker's opinion of value (BPO) differs from an appraisal in that it is not performed by a regulated third party and does not follow professional appraisal standards

Valuation Principles and the Sales Comparison Approach

- The principle of substitution states that a buyer will pay no more for a property than the cost of an equally desirable substitute
- The principle of contribution measures how much a specific improvement adds to overall market value, regardless of the improvement's cost
- The sales comparison approach is the most widely used method for residential valuation and forms the basis of the CMA
- Steps: identify comparable sales, adjust comparable prices for differences with the subject, and weight adjusted values to reach a final estimate
- Adjustments are made only to the comparables, never to the subject property; if the comparable is superior, deduct from its price; if inferior, add to its price
- The fewer the adjustments and the smaller the adjustment amounts, the more reliable the comparable
- A CMA is less objective and less comprehensive than a formal appraisal and should never be presented as one

III: Role of the Appraiser

- An appraisal is an objective, regulated professional estimate of market value performed by a licensed or certified appraiser

- Appraisers are independent third parties and do not represent the buyer, seller, or either agent
- FIRREA (1989) requires that all appraisals used in federally related transactions be performed by state-certified appraisers
- In Missouri, appraisers are licensed and regulated through the Missouri Real Estate Appraisers Commission
- USPAP governs the appraisal profession nationally and requires competence, proper disclosure, and adherence to established methods and reporting standards
- The Appraisal Institute offers the MAI and SRA designations, which signal advanced professional training
- Listing price and appraised value are not the same: listing price is a strategic pre-contract decision; appraised value is an independent post-contract determination ordered by the lender
- If the appraisal comes in below the purchase price, the lender will generally only lend up to the appraised value, requiring negotiation between buyer and seller
- Missouri listing agents should price realistically from the start to reduce the risk of appraisal-related transaction failures

MODULE 2 QUIZ - MISSOURI SELLER REPRESENTATION

1. Which of the following best describes prospecting in real estate?

   a. Any activity designed to generate listing prospects who have not yet committed to a broker
   b. Preparing a comparative market analysis for an active seller client
   c. Submitting an offer to purchase on behalf of a represented buyer
   d. Hosting an open house for a property that is already under contract

2. Which type of lead generation strategy is considered the most sustainable and productive for a Missouri licensee?

   a. Referral-based lead generation from friends, family, and past clients
   b. Purchasing zip code leads through Zillow or Realtor.com
   c. Cold calling expired listings from a paid daily service
   d. Door-knocking a different neighborhood each week

3. When farming a neighborhood, a healthy annual turnover rate in most markets is approximately:

   a. 7 to 8%
   b. 4 to 5%
   c. 2 to 3%
   d. 12 to 15%

4. The primary goal of capturing attendee contact information at an open house is to:

   a. Follow up with active buyers who may be in the market even if they do not purchase that particular listing
   b. Register buyers with the MLS before they tour other properties
   c. Provide the seller with a list of all parties who toured the home
   d. Verify that each attendee has a pre-qualification letter before showing the property

5. Which of the following should a listing agent bring to a listing presentation?

   a. A signed purchase agreement from a pre-qualified buyer
   b. A written appraisal from a licensed Missouri appraiser
   c. An estimated net sheet, a detailed marketing plan, and all necessary listing paperwork
   d. A pre-printed commission disclosure signed by the managing broker

6. In Missouri, a listing agreement is best described as what type of agency?

   a. Special or limited agency, restricting the broker's authority to specific transaction-related activities
   b. General agency, authorizing the broker to act on the seller's behalf in all matters
   c. Universal agency, permitting the broker to sign documents and bind the seller to any contract
   d. Dual agency, since the broker represents both the seller and prospective buyers

7. Under an exclusive right-to-sell listing agreement, the listing broker is entitled to a commission if a buyer is procured by:

a. The listing broker only
b. A cooperating broker only
c. Only brokers who are members of the local MLS
d. Any party, including the listing broker, a cooperating broker, or the seller themselves

8. Under an exclusive agency listing, no commission is owed to the broker if:

a. The property sells below the listed price
b. The seller finds the buyer independently without the broker's involvement
c. The listing expires before a buyer is found
d. A cooperating broker brings the buyer to the transaction

9. Net listings are prohibited in Missouri because they:

a. Prevent the seller from receiving any net proceeds at closing
b. Require the broker to pay all closing costs out of pocket
c. Are not recognized by the National Association of REALTORS
d. Create an inherent conflict of interest by incentivizing the broker to encourage the seller to set the lowest possible price

10. When a listing receives multiple offers, one effective strategy for managing the situation efficiently is to:

a. Accept the first offer received regardless of price or terms
b. Call for a highest and best offer from all buyers to save time and ensure the strongest possible terms
c. Present all offers to the seller only after the listing period ends
d. Reject all offers and relist the property at a higher price

11. After a purchase offer is accepted, the agent's most immediate duty is to:

a. Order a home inspection on behalf of the seller
b. Contact the buyer's lender to initiate the appraisal process
c. Submit the contract and earnest money to the managing broker without delay
d. Begin marketing the property to backup buyers in case the deal falls through

12. As of August 17, 2024, what specific practice is prohibited under the NAR settlement rules?

a. Sellers offering buyer agent compensation in any form or through any channel
b. Buyers entering into written buyer agency agreements before touring properties
c. Brokers discussing commission amounts with their seller clients
d. Offers of buyer agent compensation being published or advertised in the MLS

13. Under the NAR settlement, Missouri licensees are required to communicate to clients that broker compensation is:

a. Set by the Missouri Real Estate Commission at a standardized rate
b. Determined annually by the local MLS board
c. Fully negotiable and not established or mandated by law
d. Always divided equally between the listing broker and the cooperating broker

14. The four determinants of value that apply to all economic goods and services, including real estate, are:

a. Supply, demand, price, and competition
b. Location, condition, age, and financing
c. Desire, utility, scarcity, and purchasing power
d. Appreciation, depreciation, income, and equity

15. Market value is best described as:

a. The price a property actually sold for in its most recent closed transaction
b. The assessed value established by the county for ad valorem tax purposes
c. The listing price recommended by a broker after completing a competitive market analysis
d. An opinion of the price a willing buyer and willing seller would agree on in an arm's length transaction with full information and no abnormal pressure

16. According to the principle of substitution, a buyer will:

a. Always pay a premium for a property with no comparable alternatives on the market
b. Pay no more for a property than the cost of an equally desirable and available substitute
c. Substitute their financing type when interest rates change during the contract period
d. Accept a lower-quality property if the asking price is close to market value

17. In the sales comparison approach, if a comparable property is superior to the subject in a given characteristic, the appraiser should:

a. Add value to the comparable's sale price to reflect its competitive advantage
b. Ignore the difference if it represents less than 5% of the sale price
c. Deduct value from the comparable's sale price to equalize it with the subject
d. Adjust the subject property's value upward to match the comparable

18. Which of the following correctly describes the difference between a listing price and an appraised value?

a. A listing price is set after the appraisal is completed; the appraised value is established before the buyer makes an offer
b. A listing price is a strategic pre-contract market decision; the appraised value is an independent post-contract determination ordered by the buyer's lender
c. Missouri law requires the listing price and appraised value to be the same amount before a property can be marketed
d. A listing price is determined by the appraiser; the appraised value is determined by the listing broker's CMA

MODULE 2 CASE STUDY:

Missouri Seller Representation

THE SITUATION

Patricia is a newly licensed Missouri salesperson affiliated with Heartland Realty Group. She receives a referral from a past client and meets with Frank and Gloria, a married couple looking to sell their home of 22 years in a popular suburban neighborhood. Frank and Gloria are motivated — they have already found a new home and need to close on the sale within 90 days.

During the listing appointment, Patricia tours the home and is impressed. The couple recently remodeled the kitchen, adding new appliances and custom cabinetry. They paid $45,000 for the renovation and are confident it added at least that much to the value of the home. Based on their own research on a popular home-search website, Frank and Gloria believe the home is worth $375,000 and tell Patricia they will not list it for less.

Patricia has not yet completed her comparative market analysis. Wanting to secure the listing and not disappoint her referral, she verbally agrees that $375,000 sounds reasonable and tells the couple she will get the paperwork together. She also mentions that she has a buyer client who might be interested and suggests she could represent both parties if that buyer makes an offer, which would make the transaction move faster. Frank and Gloria agree without fully understanding what that means.

Patricia writes up an exclusive right-to-sell agreement with a 90-day term but does not include any discussion of dual agency or what it would require. She also does not present or discuss the Broker Disclosure Form. The listing is entered into the MLS the following day.

Three weeks later, Patricia's buyer client, David, tours the home and wants to make an offer. Patricia assists David in preparing an offer of $362,000. She presents it to Frank and Gloria without disclosing that David has told her privately that he would go up to $380,000 if needed. Frank and Gloria accept the offer. During the pre-closing period, the lender orders an appraisal, which comes back at $348,000, well below the purchase price.

DISCUSSION QUESTIONS

1. Patricia agreed to a $375,000 listing price without completing a CMA and without cautioning the sellers that she is not an appraiser. What obligations did she fail to meet, and what risks does this create for the transaction and for her license?

____

____

____

____

2. Patricia mentioned dual agency casually without explaining its limitations or obtaining written informed consent. What are the Missouri requirements for dual agency, and what should Patricia have done differently before David ever toured the property?

3. When presenting David's offer, Patricia knew he was willing to pay up to $380,000 but said nothing to Frank and Gloria. Whose interests was she protecting in that moment, and what fiduciary duty did she potentially violate?

4. The appraisal came in at $348,000, which is $14,000 below the accepted offer price. What are the possible outcomes for the transaction at this point, and what role should Patricia play in helping the parties reach a resolution?

5. Looking back at the listing presentation, what are the three most significant things Patricia should have done differently to protect her clients, herself, and the integrity of the transaction?

Module 3: Missouri Buyer Representation

I. Missouri Buyer Representation

Module 3 Learning Objectives

Missouri Buyer Representation

1. **Distinguish between a buyer as a client and a buyer as a customer.**
2. **Identify the types of buyer representation agreements used in Missouri.**
3. **Describe the required elements of a Missouri buyer representation agreement.**
4. **Explain the impact of the August 2024 NAR settlement on Missouri buyer representation practice.**

I. Missouri Buyer Representation

Before buyer agency became widely practiced, brokers generally treated buyers as customers rather than clients. A customer receives basic assistance including property showings, information about listings, help scheduling appointments, but does not receive the full set of fiduciary duties that an agent owes to a client. As the real estate industry evolved and consumers became more sophisticated, it became clear that buyers could benefit significantly from the same quality of representation that sellers had long enjoyed. Today, buyer agency is a standard and expected feature of the Missouri real estate landscape, and Missouri licensees must have a thorough understanding of how to create it, document it, and fulfill it, especially in the post-NAR settlement environment that took effect in August 2024.

Buyer agency exists when a broker represents the buyer exclusively in a real estate transaction. When a buyer becomes a client rather than a customer, the broker owes that buyer the full set of fiduciary duties: loyalty, confidentiality, disclosure, obedience, reasonable care, and accounting. The most important practical consequence of this relationship is negotiating power. When a buyer is a client, the licensee actively works to negotiate the lowest possible price and the most favorable contract terms on the buyer's behalf. When a buyer is merely a customer, there is no such advocacy, no advice, no opinions, no negotiating skill working in the buyer's corner. Any buyer who understands this distinction will seek client representation before they ever begin touring homes.

Missouri licensees also benefit from formalizing the buyer relationship. In the days before buyer agency, buyers would float from agent to agent without any sense of loyalty or obligation. An agent could spend weeks showing properties, answering questions, and doing research, only to have the buyer work with a different licensee at the moment of purchase. A properly executed buyer representation agreement changes that dynamic entirely, creating a mutual commitment that benefits both parties and gives the licensee a reasonable assurance of compensation for their efforts.

Types of Buyer Agency Agreements

Just as there are different types of listing agreements on the seller side, there are different frameworks under which a buyer agency relationship can be structured. Missouri licensees should understand each type and be able to explain them clearly to prospective buyer clients.

Exclusive buyer representation agreement

This is the most widely used and most strongly recommended form of buyer agency agreement in Missouri. Under an exclusive buyer representation agreement, the buyer commits to working solely with one broker for a defined period of time within a defined geographic area. In return, the broker commits the full scope of their fiduciary duties to that buyer. The broker is entitled to compensation if the buyer purchases any property within the scope of the agreement during its term, regardless of how the property was found, whether through the MLS, a For Sale By Owner, or any other source.

The exclusive agreement gives the buyer the strongest possible representation and gives the broker the greatest assurance of compensation. It is the buyer-side equivalent of the exclusive right-to-sell listing agreement. Under post-NAR settlement rules in Missouri, this is the agreement that must be in place before a licensee shows a buyer any property. The agreement must clearly state the compensation the buyer's agent will seek, how that compensation will be paid, and under what circumstances the buyer may be responsible for covering all or part of that compensation if the seller does not agree to pay it.

Exclusive agency buyer representation agreement

An exclusive agency buyer representation agreement authorizes one broker to represent the buyer but preserves the buyer's right to find a property on their own without owing a commission. If the buyer independently locates and purchases a property without the broker's involvement, no compensation is owed. If the broker is the procuring cause of the transaction, the broker has earned their fee. This type of agreement is less common in residential practice because it creates uncertainty around compensation and can lead to disputes about procuring cause.

Non-exclusive or open buyer representation agreement

Under a non-exclusive arrangement, the buyer is not committed to any single broker. The buyer may work with multiple agents simultaneously, and compensation is generally owed only to the agent who is the procuring cause of the ultimate purchase. While this arrangement exists in practice, it offers the buyer the least protection and the broker the least security. Missouri licensees working under a non-exclusive arrangement have limited ability to advocate fully for a buyer's interests, and they carry significant risk of working without compensation. In the current environment, non-exclusive agreements are generally discouraged in residential transactions.

Oral buyer representation

A buyer agency relationship can technically be created verbally or through the implied actions of the licensee. However, in Missouri's post-NAR settlement environment, an oral agreement is no longer a viable option in practice. The NAR settlement requires that a written buyer representation agreement be in place before a broker shows a buyer any property. This requirement effectively eliminates oral buyer agency as a practical starting point for a representation relationship, even though the legal concept still exists. Missouri licensees should never rely on an implied or oral agreement and should always begin the relationship with a written, signed document.

Geographic and property scope

Regardless of the type of agreement used, the buyer representation agreement in Missouri should clearly define the geographic territory covered and the type of property being sought. A buyer might initially want to search within a single county or zip code, and that limitation should be written into the agreement. If the buyer's search area later expands, the agreement should be amended in writing and initialed by both parties to reflect the change. Similarly, the agreement should specify the type of property, residential, commercial, land, so that the scope of the relationship is clearly understood by both the buyer and the broker.

Elements of Buyer Agency Agreements

A well-constructed buyer representation agreement is the foundation of a productive and protected relationship between a Missouri buyer and their broker. Every licensee should be comfortable explaining each element of the agreement to a prospective buyer client and obtaining signatures with full transparency and mutual understanding.

Parties to the agreement

The agreement must identify the broker and the buyer client by name. Because clients belong to the broker, not the individual salesperson, the agreement is technically between the buyer and the brokerage, with the salesperson acting as the broker's representative. All adult parties who will be purchasing property together should be identified and should sign the agreement.

Duration of the agreement

The buyer representation agreement must include a start date and an end date. Unlike a listing agreement, which may run for several months to a year, a buyer representation agreement is often written for a shorter period of time. If the buyer and broker are productive and the relationship is working well, the agreement can be renewed or extended by mutual written agreement. The duration should be long enough to give the broker a fair opportunity to find suitable property, but not so long that a buyer feels trapped if the relationship is not functioning well.

Geographic territory and property description

As discussed above, the agreement should define the area in which the broker is authorized to work on the buyer's behalf and the type of property being sought. This protects both parties by clearly defining the scope of the relationship and reduces the potential for disputes about whether a particular property falls within the agreement.

Scope of authority and fiduciary duties

A buyer representation agreement establishes the broker's authority to act on behalf of the buyer. This is a special agency agreement, meaning the broker is authorized to locate properties, negotiate terms, and advise the buyer, but the broker does not have authority to bind the buyer to a contract without the buyer's explicit consent. The agreement should also make clear that the broker owes the buyer the full set of fiduciary duties: loyalty, confidentiality, disclosure, obedience to lawful instructions, reasonable care and diligence, and proper accounting of all funds.

Compensation

One of the most important elements of a Missouri buyer representation agreement in the post-NAR settlement era is the compensation section. The agreement must clearly and specifically state the compensation the buyer's broker is seeking, expressed as a dollar amount or a percentage of the purchase price, and must explain how that compensation will be obtained. Missouri licensees are required to communicate clearly to buyers that broker compensation is fully negotiable and is not set by law.

The agreement should explain that the buyer's agent compensation may be paid by the seller, by the buyer, or by a combination of both. Most buyers will prefer that the seller pay the buyer's agent compensation, and in many transactions sellers will agree to do so, either voluntarily as an incentive to attract buyers or as a term negotiated within the purchase offer. However, the agreement must also make clear that if the seller declines to pay the buyer's agent compensation, or if the seller's offer of compensation is less than the amount stated in the buyer representation agreement, the buyer may be responsible for paying the difference. Missouri buyers should understand this possibility before they sign and should discuss it openly with their agent.

Pre-qualification and financial readiness.

While not always a formal element of the written agreement itself, Missouri licensees should make it a standard practice to have buyer clients meet with a lender and obtain a pre-qualification or pre-approval letter before investing significant time in property showings. Understanding a buyer's financial capacity helps the licensee focus the search appropriately, protects both parties from wasted effort, and strengthens the buyer's position when it comes time to make an offer. A buyer who is not financially prepared to purchase is not yet ready for a formal buyer representation relationship.

Termination provisions

The agreement should address how the relationship can be ended before the expiration date. Either party may wish to end the relationship in certain circumstances, and having clear termination language in writing protects both the buyer and the broker. Any termination should be documented in writing. If the buyer attempts to end the agreement without cause before its expiration, the broker may have grounds to seek compensation for services already rendered.

Impacts of the NAR Lawsuit on Buyer Representation

The changes that took effect on August 17, 2024, as a result of the National Association of REALTORS® settlement have fundamentally reshaped how buyer representation is practiced in Missouri and across the country. For Missouri buyer's agents, understanding these changes is not optional, it is a core professional requirement.

The written agreement requirement

The most immediate and operationally significant change for buyer's agents is the requirement that a written buyer representation agreement must be in place before a broker shows a buyer any property. This is a departure from prior practice, in which many agents would work informally with buyers for weeks or even months before any written agreement was signed, or in some cases, without ever formalizing the relationship at all.

In Missouri today, a licensee may not show a property to a buyer without first having a signed buyer representation agreement that clearly discloses the compensation the buyer's agent is seeking. This requirement applies whether the buyer found the property on Zillow, drove by a for-sale sign, or was referred to the agent by a friend. There are no exceptions for a single showing or a casual conversation about a listing. The written agreement must be in place first.

This change has required Missouri buyer's agents to become more direct and comfortable discussing representation and compensation at the very first point of contact with a prospective buyer. The days of indefinitely deferring the compensation conversation are over. Buyers should expect to be asked to sign a representation agreement before they ever walk through a front door, and licensees have a professional obligation to explain that agreement clearly and obtain a knowing, voluntary signature.

Compensation is no longer advertised in the MLS

Prior to the NAR settlement, it was standard industry practice for a seller's listing agreement to include an offer of compensation to the buyer's agent, and that offer was published directly in the MLS for all cooperating brokers to see. A buyer's agent could look at any listing and know in advance exactly how much they would be paid if their client purchased that property. That practice is now prohibited.

Under the new rules, offers of buyer agent compensation may no longer appear in MLS listings. This does not mean that sellers cannot offer to pay buyer agent compensation, they absolutely still can, and many will. However, that offer must now be communicated outside the MLS, such as through direct broker-to-broker communication, in the purchase contract, or through other marketing materials. For Missouri buyer's agents, this means that compensation from any given transaction is less predictable upfront, and the discussion of how the buyer's agent will be paid must happen in direct negotiation around the transaction itself.

Compensation is a negotiated transaction term

In practical terms, the shift away from MLS-advertised buyer agent compensation means that in many Missouri transactions, the buyer's agent compensation will be negotiated as part of the purchase offer. A buyer may make an offer on a property that includes a request for the seller to pay the buyer's agent compensation as a concession. The seller can agree to that request, counter it, or decline it entirely, just as they would with any other term of the offer.

This dynamic places Missouri buyer's agents in a position where they must help their clients understand that including a request for seller-paid buyer agent compensation in an offer is a legitimate and common negotiating tool, not an unusual or inappropriate ask. At the same time, buyers need to understand that in competitive markets or multiple-offer situations, asking the seller to cover buyer agent compensation may affect how their offer is perceived. The buyer's agent must be able to counsel their client on how to approach compensation strategically within the context of the overall offer.

Transparency and client education essential

Perhaps the most lasting impact of the NAR settlement on Missouri buyer representation is the cultural shift toward full transparency about compensation. Missouri licensees are required to communicate clearly that broker compensation is fully negotiable and not set by law. There is no standard rate, no mandatory split, and no assumed arrangement. Every aspect of how the buyer's agent will be paid must be discussed openly, agreed upon in writing, and executed before the representation relationship begins in earnest.

For Missouri buyers, this transparency is ultimately a benefit. Buyers who understand how their agent is compensated, what services they will receive in return, and what their potential financial obligations are can make informed decisions about who to work with and how to structure their home purchase. For Missouri licensees, the ability to clearly explain the value of buyer representation, and to have that conversation confidently at the very beginning of the relationship, is now a foundational professional skill. The agents who adapt to this environment, embrace transparency, and demonstrate their value to buyer clients will build stronger, more productive, and more sustainable practices as a result.

MODULE 3 SNAPSHOT REVIEW: MISSOURI BUYER REPRESENTATION

I. Missouri Buyer Representation

Client vs. Customer

- A customer receives basic assistance but no fiduciary duties; a client receives the full set of agency protections
- The six fiduciary duties owed to a buyer client are loyalty, confidentiality, disclosure, obedience, reasonable care, and accounting
- The most important practical benefit of buyer agency is negotiating power — the licensee actively works to secure the lowest price and best terms on the buyer's behalf
- Formalizing the buyer relationship through a written agreement creates mutual commitment and gives the licensee reasonable assurance of compensation

Types of Buyer Agency Agreements

- The exclusive buyer representation agreement is the most widely used and strongly recommended — the buyer commits to one broker, and the broker owes the full scope of fiduciary duties in return
- The exclusive agency buyer representation agreement preserves the buyer's right to find a property independently without owing a commission, but creates uncertainty around compensation
- The non-exclusive or open buyer representation agreement allows the buyer to work with multiple agents simultaneously — it offers the least protection and is generally discouraged in residential practice
- Oral buyer representation is legally possible but is no longer viable in Missouri following the NAR settlement, which requires a written agreement before any property is shown
- The agreement should define both the geographic territory and the type of property being sought, and any changes to scope must be amended in writing

Elements of a Buyer Agency Agreement

- The agreement must identify all parties by name; all adult buyers who will purchase together must sign
- A definite start and end date is required; duration should be long enough for the broker to work effectively but not so long that a buyer feels unable to exit a non-functioning relationship
- The agreement establishes a special agency — the broker may locate properties and negotiate terms but may not bind the buyer to a contract without explicit consent
- The compensation section must clearly state the amount or percentage the buyer's broker is seeking and explain how it will be obtained
- The agreement must disclose that compensation may be paid by the seller, the buyer, or both, and that if the seller pays less than the stated amount, the buyer may be responsible for the difference
- Pre-qualification is not a formal agreement element but is a recommended standard practice before investing significant time in property showings
- Termination language should address how either party may exit the relationship before its expiration date, with any termination documented in writing

NAR Settlement Impacts on Buyer Representation

- Effective August 17, 2024, a written buyer representation agreement must be in place before a licensee shows a buyer any property — there are no exceptions for a single showing

- Licensees must be prepared to discuss representation and compensation at the very first point of contact with a prospective buyer client
- Offers of buyer agent compensation may no longer be published in the MLS — sellers may still offer compensation but must do so through other channels such as direct broker communication, marketing materials, or the purchase contract
- Buyer agent compensation is now a negotiated transaction term — buyers may include a request for seller-paid compensation as part of their offer, and sellers may agree, counter, or decline
- Missouri licensees must communicate clearly that broker compensation is fully negotiable and is not set by law
- Transparency about compensation is now a core professional skill — agents who embrace this environment and demonstrate their value clearly will build stronger and more sustainable practices

MODULE 3 QUIZ QUESTIONS: MISSOURI BUYER REPRESENTATION

1. Which of the following best describes the difference between a buyer client and a buyer customer in Missouri?

a. A client receives the full set of fiduciary duties from the broker, while a customer receives only basic assistance without advocacy or negotiating representation
b. A client pays a higher commission than a customer
c. A customer has more legal protections than a client because the relationship is informal
d. A client and a customer receive the same services but sign different forms

2. Which of the following is one of the six fiduciary duties a Missouri broker owes to a buyer client?

a. Confidentiality
b. Indemnification
c. Subrogation
d. Arbitration

3. Under an exclusive buyer representation agreement, the broker is entitled to compensation if the buyer purchases a property that was found:

a. Only through the MLS during the agreement term
b. Only through the broker's direct referral
c. Through any source during the agreement term, including the MLS, a For Sale By Owner, or any other channel
d. Only if the listing broker agrees to cooperate and share compensation

4. An exclusive agency buyer representation agreement differs from an exclusive buyer representation agreement in that it:

a. Requires the buyer to work with multiple brokers simultaneously
b. Preserves the buyer's right to find a property independently without owing a commission
c. Eliminates the broker's fiduciary duties to the buyer
d. Does not require a start date or end date

5. Why is oral buyer representation no longer a viable option in Missouri's current real estate environment?

a. Missouri license law has always required buyer representation to be in writing
b. Oral agreements are not recognized under Missouri contract law
c. The NAR settlement requires a written buyer representation agreement to be in place before a broker shows a buyer any property
d. Oral agreements are only permitted when the buyer is purchasing commercial property

6. In a Missouri buyer representation agreement, the broker's authority is best described as:

a. General agency, authorizing the broker to act on the buyer's behalf in all financial matters
b. Universal agency, permitting the broker to sign contracts and bind the buyer without additional consent
c. Transaction brokerage, which requires the broker to remain neutral and not advocate for either party
d. Special agency, authorizing the broker to locate properties, negotiate terms, and advise the buyer but not to bind the buyer to a contract without explicit consent

7. Regarding compensation in a post-NAR settlement buyer representation agreement, which of the following statements is correct?

a. The compensation amount is set by the Missouri Real Estate Commission and must appear in the agreement
b. The agreement must clearly state the compensation being sought and explain that the buyer may be responsible for paying the difference if the seller offers less than that amount
c. The buyer's agent compensation is always paid by the seller and does not need to be discussed with the buyer
d. Compensation may not be expressed as a percentage of the purchase price under the new NAR rules

8. Which of the following best explains why Missouri licensees should recommend that buyer clients obtain a pre-qualification or pre-approval letter before beginning property showings?

a. Missouri law requires a pre-qualification letter before a buyer representation agreement can be signed
b. It allows the broker to collect a retainer fee before investing time in the search
c. It satisfies the written agreement requirement under the NAR settlement
d. It helps focus the property search, avoids wasted effort, and strengthens the buyer's position when making an offer

9. Under the post-NAR settlement rules, a Missouri licensee who wants to show a buyer a property the buyer found through an online listing service must:

a. Show the property first and then obtain a written agreement within 24 hours
b. Have a signed written buyer representation agreement in place before showing the property, with no exceptions
c. Only show the property if it is listed in the MLS by a cooperating broker
d. Obtain verbal consent from the buyer and document it in a follow-up email

10. In the post-NAR settlement environment, buyer agent compensation is best described as:

a. A fixed percentage of the purchase price published in the MLS for all cooperating brokers to see
b. A standardized amount set by the local real estate board and disclosed at closing
c. A negotiated transaction term that may be included as a request in the buyer's purchase offer and which the seller may agree to, counter, or decline
d. Always paid directly by the buyer to the broker outside of the purchase transaction

MODULE 3 CASE STUDY:

Missouri Buyer Representation

Jordan is a Missouri licensee affiliated with Performance Programs Real Estate. He receives a call on a Tuesday afternoon from a woman named Simone, who explains that she and her husband Terrence are ready to start looking for their first home. They have been researching neighborhoods online, have a budget in mind, and are eager to get started as soon as possible. Simone tells Jordan that a friend referred him and that they are excited to work with someone they can trust.

Jordan is equally excited. He schedules a showing for that Saturday at a property Simone found on Zillow that they love. He plans to bring the buyer representation agreement paperwork to the showing and go over it with the couple at the house before they tour it.

On Saturday, Simone and Terrence arrive at the property and are clearly enthusiastic. Jordan quickly pulls out the buyer representation agreement and begins explaining it at the front door. The couple feels a little rushed and uncomfortable. Terrence asks why they have to sign paperwork before even going inside. Jordan explains it is just a formality. Simone notices that the agreement states a compensation rate of 3% but does not explain who pays it or what happens if the seller does not agree to that amount. She asks Jordan about it. Jordan tells her not to worry, that sellers always cover it, and that it will not cost them anything. The couple signs and they tour the home.

Two weeks later, Simone and Terrence find another property they love that is listed as a For Sale By Owner. They contact the seller directly to schedule a showing, not realizing their signed agreement with Jordan covers any property purchase within their county during the 90-day term. When Jordan finds out, he reminds them they are still under contract with him and that his compensation would be owed even on a FSBO purchase. The couple is surprised and upset. They feel they were never clearly told this.

DISCUSSION QUESTIONS

1. Jordan planned to present and sign the buyer representation agreement at the front door of the first property. What did he do wrong, and what should the process have looked like under Missouri's current requirements?

____

____

____

____

2. When Simone asked about the compensation section, Jordan told her sellers always cover it and not to worry. What specific obligation did Jordan fail to meet, and what should he have told the couple instead?

____

____

____

____

3. Simone and Terrence were surprised to learn their agreement covered FSBO purchases within the county. Whose responsibility was it to ensure they understood the geographic scope and property coverage of the agreement, and what practical steps should Jordan have taken to prevent this dispute?

Module 4: Completing the Transaction

I. The Contract for Sale
II. Offer and acceptance
III. Qualification
IV. Earnest Money
V. Estimating Closing Costs
VI. Types of Financing

Module 4 Learning Objectives

The Contract for Sale

1. Identify the legal characteristics and enforceability requirements of a Missouri real estate sale contract
2. Explain the consequences of buyer and seller default under a Missouri sale contract

Offer and acceptance

1. Explain the offer and acceptance process in Missouri real estate contracts
2. Describe the legal boundaries of contract preparation for Missouri licensees

Qualification

1. Identify the key components of borrower analysis used in Missouri mortgage qualification
2. Explain the federal ability-to-repay requirements and Qualified Mortgage standards

Earnest Money

1. Explain Missouri's trust fund requirements for earnest money, including deposit timelines, prohibitions on commingling and conversion, and the broker's responsibilities when disputes arise over escrow fund disbursement

Estimating Closing Costs

1. Describe the closing event and the roles of the parties involved
2. Explain the requirements of the Real Estate Settlement Procedures Act (RESPA),
3. Distinguish between debits and credits on a closing statement, and identify which costs are typically paid by the buyer and which are paid by the seller in a Missouri real estate transaction.

4. **Calculate prorated closing costs using both the 12-month/30-day method and the 365-day method, applying the correct approach to items paid in advance and items paid in arrears.**
5. **Identify the five pages of the H-25 Closing Disclosure form and the information each page contains.**

Types of Financing

1. **Distinguish between conventional, FHA-insured, and VA-guaranteed loans**
2. **Identify common loan structures used in Missouri real estate transactions**
3. **Explain the purpose and characteristics of special-purpose loans**

I. The Contract for Sale

Contract for Sale

A real estate sale contract is a binding and enforceable agreement wherein a buyer, the **vendee**, agrees to buy an identified parcel of real estate, and a seller, the **vendor**, agrees to sell it under certain terms and conditions. It is the document that is at the center of the transaction.

The conventional transfer of real estate ownership takes place in three stages. First, there is the negotiating period where buyers and sellers exchange offers in an effort to agree to all transfer terms that will appear in the sale contract. Second, when both parties have accepted all terms, the offer becomes a binding sale contract and the transaction enters the pre-closing stage, during which each party makes arrangements to complete the sale according to the sale contract's terms. Third is the closing of the transaction, when the seller deeds title to the buyer, the buyer pays the purchase price, and all necessary documents are completed. At this stage, the sale contract has served its purpose and terminates.

Other names for the sale contract are *agreement of sale, contract for purchase, contract of purchase and sale*, and *earnest money contract.*

Legal Characteristics of the Contract for Sale

Executory contract

A sale contract is *executory:* the signatories have yet to perform their respective obligations and promises. Upon closing, the sale contract is fully performed and no longer exists as a binding agreement.

Signatures

All owners of the property should sign the sale contract. If the sellers are married, both spouses should sign to ensure that both spouses release homestead, dower, and curtesy rights to the buyer at closing. Failure to do so does not invalidate the contract but can lead to encumbered title and legal disputes.

Enforceability criteria

To be enforceable, a sale contract must:

- be validly created (mutual consent, consideration, legal purpose, competent parties, voluntary act)
- be in writing
- identify the principal parties
- clearly identify the property, preferably by legal description
- contain a purchase price
- be signed by the principal parties

Written vs. oral form

A contract for the sale of real estate is enforceable only if it is in writing. A buyer or seller cannot sue to force the other to comply with an oral contract for sale, even if the contract is valid.

Assignment

Either party to a sale transaction can assign the sale contract to another party, subject to the provisions and conditions contained in the agreement.

Who may complete

A broker or agent may assist buyer and seller in completing an offer to purchase, provided the broker represents the client faithfully and does not charge a separate fee for the assistance. It is advisable, and legally required in most states, for a broker to use a standard contract form promulgated by state agencies or real estate boards, as such forms contain generally accepted language. This relieves the broker of the dangers of creating new contract language, which can be construed as a practice of law for which the broker is not licensed.

Contract Creation

Offer and acceptance

A contract of sale is created by full and unequivocal acceptance of an offer. Offer and acceptance may come from either buyer or seller. The offeree must accept the offer without making any changes whatsoever. A change terminates the offer and creates a new offer, or counteroffer. An offeror may revoke an offer for any reason prior to communication of acceptance by the offeree.

Equitable title

A sale contract gives the buyer an interest in the property that is called equitable title, or *ownership in equity*. If the seller defaults and the buyer can show good faith performance, the buyer can sue for specific performance, that is, to compel the seller to transfer legal title upon payment of the contract price.

Earnest Money Escrow

The buyer's earnest money deposit fulfills the consideration requirements for a valid sale contract. In addition, it provides potential compensation for damages to the seller if the buyer fails to perform. The amount of the deposit varies according to local custom. It should be noted that the earnest money deposit is not the only form of consideration that satisfies the requirement.

The sale contract provides the *escrow instructions* for handling and disbursing escrow funds. The earnest money is placed in a third party trust account or escrow. A licensed escrow agent employed by a title company, financial institution, or brokerage company usually manages the escrow. An individual broker may also serve as the escrow agent.

The escrow holder acts as an impartial fiduciary for buyer and seller. If the buyer performs under the sale contract, the deposit is applied to the purchase price.

Strict rules govern the handling of earnest money deposits, particularly if a broker is the escrow agent. For example, state laws direct the broker when to deposit the funds, how to account for them, and how to keep them separate from the broker's own funds.

Contract Contingencies

A sale contract often contains contingencies. A contingency is a condition that must be met before the contract is enforceable.

The most common contingency concerns financing. A buyer makes an offer contingent upon securing financing for the property under certain terms on or before a certain date. If unable to secure the specified loan commitment by the deadline, the buyer may cancel the contract and recover the deposit. An appropriate and timely loan commitment eliminates the contingency, and the buyer must proceed with the purchase.

It is possible for both buyers and sellers to abuse contingencies in order to leave themselves a convenient way to cancel without defaulting. To avoid problems, the statement of a contingency should:

- be explicit and clear
- have an expiration date
- expressly require diligence in the effort to fulfill the requirement

A contingency that is too broad, vague, or excessive in duration may invalidate the entire contract on the grounds of insufficiency of mutual agreement.

Default

A sale contract is bilateral, since both parties promise to perform. As a result, either party may default by failing to perform. Note that a party's failure to meet a contingency does not constitute default, but rather entitles the parties to cancel the contract.

Buyer default

If a buyer fails to perform under the terms of a sale contract, the breach entitles the seller to legal recourse for damages. In most cases, the contract itself stipulates the seller's remedies. The usual remedy is forfeiture of the buyer's deposit as **liquidated damages**, provided the deposit is not grossly in excess of the seller's actual damages. It is also customary to provide for the seller and broker to share the liquidated damages. The broker may not, however, receive liquidated damages in excess of what the commission would have been on the full listing price.

If the contract does not provide for liquidated damages, the seller may sue for damages, cancellation, or specific performance.

Seller default

If a seller defaults, the buyer may sue for specific performance, damages, or cancellation.

II. Offer and Acceptance

The mutual consent required for a valid contract is reached through the process of offer and acceptance: The **offeror** proposes contract terms in an **offer** to the **offeree**. If the offeree accepts all terms without amendment, the offer becomes a contract. The exact point at which the offer becomes a contract is when the offeree gives the offeror notice of the acceptance.

Offer

An offer expresses the offeror's intention to enter into a contract with an offeree to perform the terms of the agreement in exchange for the offeree's performance. In a real estate sale or lease contract, the offer must clearly contain all intended terms of the contract in writing and be communicated to the offeree.

If an offer contains an expiration date and the phrase "time is of the essence," the offer expires at exactly the time specified. In the absence of a stated time period, the offeree has a "reasonable" time to accept an offer.

Acceptance

An offer gives the offeree the power of accepting. For an acceptance to be valid, the offeree must manifestly and unequivocally accept all terms of the offer without change, and so indicate by signing the offer, preferably with a date of signing. The acceptance must then be communicated to the offeror. If the communication of acceptance is by mail, the offer is considered to be communicated as soon as it is placed in the mail.

Counteroffer

By changing any of the terms of an offer, the offeree creates a counteroffer, and the original offer is void. At this point, the offeree becomes the offeror, and the new offeree gains the right of acceptance. If accepted, the counteroffer becomes a valid contract provided all other requirements are met.

For example, a seller changes the expiration date of a buyer's offer by one day, signs the offer and returns it to the buyer. The single amendment extinguishes the buyer's offer, and the buyer is no longer bound by any agreement. The seller's amended offer is a counteroffer which now gives the buyer the right of acceptance. If the buyer accepts the counteroffer, the counteroffer becomes a binding contract.

Revocation of an Offer

An offer may be revoked, or withdrawn, at any time before the offeree has communicated acceptance. The revocation extinguishes the offer and the offeree's right to accept it.

For example, a buyer has offered to purchase a house for the listed price. Three hours later, a family death radically changes the buyer's plans. She immediately calls the seller and revokes the offer, stating she is no longer interested in the house. Since the seller had not communicated acceptance of the offer to the buyer, the offer is legally cancelled.

If the offeree has paid consideration to the offeror to leave an offer open, and the offeror accepts, an option has been created which cancels the offeror's right to revoke the offer over the period of the option.

Termination of an Offer

Any of the following actions or circumstances can terminate an offer:

- acceptance: the offeree accepts the offer, converting it to a contract
- rejection: the offeree rejects the offer
- revocation: the offeror withdraws the offer before acceptance
- lapse of time: the offer expires
- counteroffer: the offeree changes the offer
- death or insanity of either party

Assignment of a Contract

A real estate contract that is not a personal contract for services can be assigned to another party unless the terms of the agreement specifically prohibit assignment.

Listing agreements, for example, are not assignable, since they are personal service agreements between agent and principal. Sales contracts, however, are assignable, because they involve the purchase of real property rather than a personal service.

Contract Preparation

State laws define the extent to which real estate brokers and agents may legally prepare real estate contracts. Such laws, referred to as "broker-lawyer accords," also define what types of contracts brokers and agents may prepare. In some states, brokers and agents may not draft contracts, but they may use standard promulgated forms and complete the blanks in the form.

As a rule, a broker or agent who completes real estate contracts is engaging in the unauthorized practice of law unless the broker is a party to the agreement, such as a in a listing agreement or sales contract. Brokers and agents may not complete leases, mortgages, contracts for deed, or promissory notes to which they are not a party.

Agents must be fully aware of what they are legally allowed to do and not do in preparing and interpreting contracts for clients. In addition to practicing law without a license, agents expose themselves to lawsuits from clients who relied on a contract as being legally acceptable.

III. Qualification

Borrower Analysis

Borrower analysis is a critical component of the mortgage loan origination process. Its purpose is to verify and validate the accuracy of information provided in the loan application and to assess the borrower's overall financial and creditworthiness. While the exact steps may vary by lender, the process generally includes reviewing the loan application for completeness and accuracy, preparing and delivering required initial disclosures, conducting a credit check, and submitting the completed file to underwriting for formal risk assessment.

Evaluation of assets and liabilities

A key element of borrower analysis is the evaluation of **assets**, which demonstrate the borrower's ability to meet financial obligations such as down payment, closing costs, and monthly payments, as well as the maintenance of escrow accounts, if applicable. Common asset types include funds in checking or savings accounts, money market accounts, certificates of deposit, retirement accounts, business accounts, stocks and bonds, proceeds from the sale of real estate or other assets, financial gifts, and down payment assistance programs.

Lenders typically categorize assets as either **liquid (current)**—those that can be readily converted to cash—or **fixed (non-current)**—those not easily converted. Moreover, the concept of seasoning is important; lenders often require that funds be in the borrower's account for at least 60 days to confirm legitimacy and rule out undisclosed borrowing. Verifying that the reported assets are both accurate and appropriately documented is a critical part of this analysis.

The borrower's **liabilities** are also carefully examined, as they directly affect the borrower's capacity to repay the mortgage loan. Common liabilities include existing mortgage obligations, installment loans such as auto, personal, or student loans, revolving credit accounts (e.g., credit cards), court-ordered payments such as alimony and child support, and any legal judgments or tax liens. **Contingent liabilities**, such as co-signed loans, are generally excluded from underwriting consideration if the lender can document that the primary borrower has made timely payments from their own funds over the past 12 months.

Check Your Understanding

Which of the following would typically be considered a liquid asset?

A. Land owned in another state
B. Funds in a savings account
C. A rental property
D. Income from a second job

If you selected Option B, that's correct. Liquid assets are those that can be easily converted to cash—such as checking or savings account funds.

Income analysis

Another central component of the loan application is **income analysis**. Lenders verify income documents such as recent pay stubs, W-2s, and tax returns to determine the stability and reliability of income streams. Most programs require that income be verifiable for at least two years, and when income varies—such as commissions or bonuses—a two-year average is often used.

Income with a defined expiration date, such as child support, long-term disability, or alimony, must be reasonably expected to continue for at least three years following the closing date.

Acceptable income sources, provided they are documented appropriately, include salaried and hourly employment, self-employment, rental income, retirement benefits, investment income, alimony, and non-taxable sources such as Social Security or permanent disability benefits.

Unemployment income may be accepted if it is part of a consistent seasonal work cycle and documented with two years of tax returns. However, unemployment benefits received due to layoff or termination cannot be used as qualifying income.

Some income, particularly non-taxable income, may be **grossed up** by multiplying it by 115% to 125%, depending on the lender's policy, to reflect its tax-free nature.

Self-employed borrowers must typically submit two years of federal income tax returns, including Form 1040 with Schedule C for sole proprietors, or relevant business tax returns for partnerships or corporations. If the borrower has experienced an employment gap, further explanation may be required. In cases where the gap is fewer than six months, current employment verification is usually sufficient. For gaps exceeding six months, the borrower may need to demonstrate at least six months of continuous full-time employment before qualifying.

Check Your Understanding

What must be true for child support or alimony income to be counted in mortgage qualification?

A. It must be received monthly for at least six months.
B. It must be court-ordered.
C. It must be expected to continue for at least three years after closing.
D. It must be untaxed.

Option C is correct. For qualifying purposes, income with a defined expiration must be expected to continue at least three years post-closing.

Credit requirements

The **credit report** is a vital tool used in conjunction with other financial documents to evaluate the borrower's creditworthiness. Credit reports are obtained from one or more of the three national credit reporting agencies: Equifax, Experian, and TransUnion. These reports contain detailed records of the borrower's credit accounts, including payment histories, account balances, and any derogatory remarks.

Credit scores, such as the FICO Score or VantageScore, are calculated based on this data and typically range from 320 to 850. Higher scores reflect stronger creditworthiness and lower risk to the lender. Key factors influencing the score include on-time payments (35%), credit utilization (30%), account age (15%), credit mix (10%), and recent inquiries (10%). **Derogatory credit**, such as late payments, delinquencies, charge-offs, foreclosures, or bankruptcies, can significantly affect the borrower's ability to qualify.

Undisclosed debt

When a credit report reveals a substantial debt that the borrower failed to disclose on the mortgage application, the loan originator must follow up by requesting a written explanation for the omission. It is the originator's duty to investigate and ensure the borrower is not deliberately omitting financial obligations in an effort to appear more creditworthy or to qualify for the loan under false pretenses. Identifying and addressing such discrepancies is a critical part of responsible lending practices.

Qualifying ratios

Lenders rely on **qualifying ratios** to evaluate the borrower's ability to manage monthly mortgage obligations. These include the **Housing Ratio** (front-end ratio) and the **Debt-to-Income (DTI)** Ratio (back-end ratio).

The **Housing Ratio compares the borrower's gross monthly income to their total monthly housing expense**, which includes principal, interest, property taxes, homeowners insurance (PITI), and any applicable homeowners association fees. This ratio generally should not exceed **28% to 31% of gross monthly income**, depending on the loan program. However, this benchmark may be exceeded if the borrower presents compensating factors such as strong credit or substantial reserves. The formula for calculating the housing ratio is:

Housing Ratio = PITI on Primary Residence ÷ Gross Monthly Income

The DTI Ratio represents the percentage of gross monthly income that is allocated toward all monthly debt obligations, including PITI, installment debts, revolving debts, alimony, and child support. This ratio generally should not exceed **33% to 43%** of gross monthly income, although some lenders may allow higher ratios under certain circumstances. The DTI calculation excludes non-debt-related expenses such as utilities, groceries, education costs (excluding student loans), childcare (unless court-ordered), and insurance premiums. The formula for DTI is:

DTI Ratio = Total Recurring Monthly Debt ÷ Gross Monthly Income

The LTV ratio

Another essential financial measure is the **loan-to-value (LTV) ratio**, which compares the loan amount to either the appraised value or purchase price of the property—whichever is lower. This ratio helps assess whether the property's value adequately supports the requested loan. A higher LTV suggests a smaller down payment and therefore greater risk to the lender, while a lower LTV implies a larger down payment and less lender exposure.

LTV requirements vary by loan program. Government-backed loans such as FHA and VA loans typically allow for higher LTV ratios. For conventional loans, an LTV exceeding 80% usually requires the borrower to obtain private mortgage insurance (PMI). The formula used to calculate LTV is:

LTV Ratio = Loan Amount ÷ Property Value

To ensure responsible lending practices, federal law requires lenders to evaluate a borrower's ability to repay (ATR) the loan. These rules, established by the Consumer Financial Protection Bureau (CFPB) under the Dodd-Frank (12 U.S.C. §5301 et seq.) Wall Street Reform and Consumer Protection Act, mandate a comprehensive financial review. Lenders must document and verify key factors, including income, employment status, assets, housing costs, debt obligations, and credit history.

Qualified mortgages

If the loan qualifies as a **Qualified Mortgage (QM)**, the lender is presumed to be in compliance with ATR requirements. QM loans offer certain legal protections, such as the **Safe Harbor**, which applies when the borrower's DTI does not exceed 43% and other strict criteria are met. The **Rebuttable Presumption** applies to higher-DTI loans that meet QM standards but allow the borrower greater ability to challenge a lender's compliance. The ATR rules prohibit high-risk features such as balloon payments, negative amortization, no-documentation loans, and interest-only payments beyond the first five years. However, these rules do not apply to home equity lines of credit (HELOCs), reverse mortgages, timeshare loans, short-term bridge loans, or loans for business purposes.

Refinance analyses

When evaluating refinance transactions, lenders must ensure that the borrower will receive **a tangible net benefit** from the new loan. This may include:

- reducing interest rate or monthly payments
- shortening the loan term
- converting from an adjustable-rate to a fixed-rate mortgage
- eliminating private mortgage insurance
- consolidating debt

In some cases, borrowers may refinance to access home equity for other financial needs. Lenders must document and validate that such benefits exist. If a loan is refinanced repeatedly without a clear benefit to the borrower, this practice—known as **loan flipping** or **churning**—may constitute a form of loan fraud and can subject the lender to regulatory penalties.

IV. Earnest Money

Definition and Responsibility

Trust funds (AKA escrow funds) in the real estate industry generally fall under one of two types: earnest money deposits and lease security deposits. However, some firms may also manage prepaid rent, loan proceeds, and other funds paid for or by parties to the transaction. Missouri regulations strictly enforce rules regarding how licensees handle such trust funds.

The designated broker and branch office manager(s) are responsible for managing all trust or escrow accounts and must ensure that the firm and all affiliated licensees comply with the state's trust fund regulations.

Deposit Requirements

Licensees must promptly deliver all trust funds they receive for purchase or lease transactions to the broker. The broker must deposit these funds in the firm's trust account within ten banking days of the date when all parties have signed and initialed the contract unless the contract provides other instructions.

Brokers may also deposit earnest money that a licensee accepts before a contract is written or signed in the firm's escrow account with written permission from the person(s) providing the funds.

The Commission permits brokerage firms to establish a trust account as a checking account at a bank, savings and loan, or credit union. If the account bears interest, the broker must provide written disclosure to all parties to the transaction that the funds were deposited in an interest-bearing account. The disclosure must note who is to receive the interest earned.

Brokerage firms that offer property management services as well as sales services must maintain a separate escrow account for the deposit of current rents and any other funds received from the owner or on the owner's behalf. Firms must establish and maintain a separate escrow account to hold security deposits.

Commingling and Conversion

Brokerage firms may not commingle personal or operating funds with trust funds except to deposit funds necessary to cover service charges and minimum balance requirements. Licensees are also forbidden to convert trust funds for personal or operating purposes (conversion).

Prepaid commissions deposited to the trust account must be disbursed at closing. Interest earned on the account must be disbursed no more than ten banking days after receiving the next bank statement.

Disbursements

Checks written on an escrow account must clearly identify the associated transaction. Checks written on the account to pay commissions may be made payable to the licensee or the firm's operating account for disbursement to the appropriate licensee.

Disputes

Most earnest money deposits are cash-based, but on rare occasions, a buyer may wish to provide earnest money in the form of a promissory note or some other type of property. Licensees may not accept an earnest money deposit of this type without the seller's permission.

If, after a transaction terminates and before any trust account disbursals, the parties dispute the earnest money's disposition, the broker should retain the deposit until all parties have signed a written release or someone files a civil action. In the latter instance, the broker may remit the funds directly to the court.

If the broker does not receive a written release or notice of a civil action, the broker may disburse escrow funds after 60 days from the date of the dispute to either party to the transaction. Such disbursement must be based on a good-faith decision by the broker that the opposite party is in breach of contract. Before disbursing funds under this condition, the broker must give all parties 15 days' written notice.

V. Estimating Closing Costs

The Closing Event

The setting

The closing event is the culmination of the real estate transaction. During this event, the buyer pays the purchase price and receives title to the purchased real estate. At the same time, the buyer completes financing arrangements, and buyer and seller pay all required taxes, fees, and charges.

Customary Practices. Procedures and customary practices for conducting real estate closings vary from state to state. For example, it is common in some states for sellers to pay title insurance, while in other states the buyer and seller might share this expense. Students should refer to supplemental state materials to ascertain prevailing practices in their state.

Time. The sale contract sets the date of the closing, usually within sixty days of signing. The time period between signing and closing is expected to be sufficient for the removal of any contingencies, such as the buyer's obtaining of financing, the performance of inspections, and the correction of identified physical defects. Failure of either buyer or seller to perform pre-closing actions specified in the contract can delay or terminate the transaction. If the contract includes a statement that "time is of the essence," all parties agree to meet the time limitations exactly as stated. If both parties consent, however, they can re-schedule the closing date.

Location. Closings occur at various locations, such as the office of the title company, the lender, the escrow agent, one of the attorneys, the broker, or the county recorder. The sale contract specifies the location.

Parties at closing. The primary parties at the closing are normally buyer, seller, and a closing agent or escrow officer. Other parties who might be present include the title officer, attorneys, brokers or agents, and the lender's representative. It is not actually necessary for any of these parties to attend the meeting. The closing agent can complete the transaction, provided all documents have been duly executed in advance.

The closing process

The closing process consists of buyer and seller verifying that each has fulfilled the terms of the sale contract. If they have, then the mortgage loan, if any, is closed, all expenses are apportioned and paid, the consideration is exchanged for the title, final documents are signed, and arrangements are made to record the transaction according to local laws.

The Closing Process

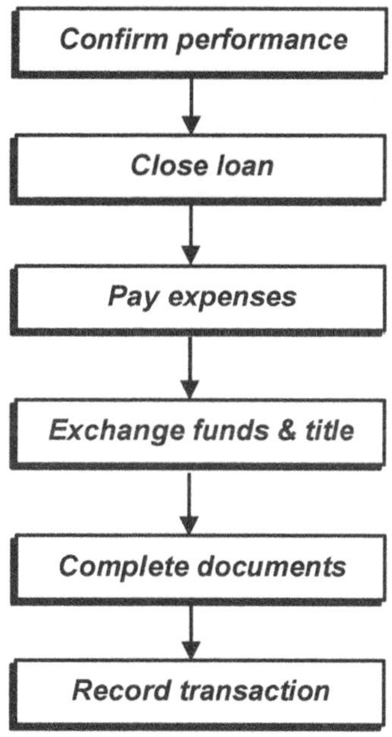

Transfer of title

The seller must produce evidence of marketable title, such as a commitment for title insurance by a title insurer. Before making a title commitment, a title company performs a title search to discover any liens, encumbrances, restrictions, conditions, or easements attaching to the title.

If there are any encumbrances or liens that damage the title, the seller is expected to remove these prior to the date specified in the contract. The most common title cloud is an unpaid lien.

The seller may also be asked to execute an affidavit of title stating that, since the date of the original title search, the seller has incurred no new liens, judgments, unpaid bills for repairs or improvements, no unrecorded deeds or contracts, no bankruptcies or divorces that would affect title, or any other defects the seller is aware of.

The purchaser, purchaser's lender, or title company may require a survey to verify the location and size of the property. The survey also identifies any easements, encroachments, or flood plain hazard.

The buyer should inspect the property to make certain that the property is in the condition in which the seller states that it is, and that any repairs or other required actions have been performed. A final inspection, called a **buyer's walk-through**, should be conducted as close to the closing date as possible.

If the seller's mortgage lien(s) are to be satisfied at closing, the lender will provide a **payoff statement**, also called an **offset statement**, specifying the amount of unpaid principal and any interest due as of the closing date, plus fees that will be due the lender and any credits or penalties that may apply. The holder of a note secured by a trust deed will provide a similar statement, called a **beneficiary statement**, to show any unpaid balance. Even if the buyer is assuming the seller's mortgage loan, the buyer will want to know the exact amount of the unpaid balance as of the closing date.

Finally, the seller produces and/or deposits with the escrow agent the deed that conveys the property to the buyer.

Transfer of purchase funds

The buyer usually produces and/or deposits with the escrow agent the following:

- earnest money
- loan funds and documents
- any other cash needed to complete the purchase

Escrow procedures

If the closing occurs "in escrow" rather than face-to-face, the principal parties deposit funds and documents with the appointed escrow agent, and the escrow agent disburses funds and releases documents to the appropriate parties when all the conditions of the escrow have been met. If for any reason the transaction cannot be completed, for instance if the buyer refuses the title as it is offered, or the buyer fails to produce the necessary cash, the escrow instructions usually provide a mechanism for reconveying title to the seller and funds to the buyer. In such a case, both parties return to their original status as if no sale had occurred.

Lender closing requirements

A lender is concerned about the quality of the collateral a borrower is providing in return for the mortgage loan. The collateral would be endangered by defects in the title, by liens that would take precedence over the mortgage lien, such as a tax lien, and by physical damage to the property which is not repaired. Consequently, the lender typically requires a survey; a property inspection; hazard insurance; a title insurance policy; a reserve account for taxes and insurance; and possibly, private mortgage insurance. In some cases the lender may also require a *certificate of occupancy* verifying that any new construction performed complies with local building codes.

Broker's role

A broker usually continues to provide service between the signing of the sale contract and the closing by helping to make arrangements for pre-closing activities such as inspections, surveys, appraisals and repairs and generally taking steps to ensure that the closing can proceed as scheduled.

A broker may conduct proceedings at the closing meeting, or may have no further role in the transaction after the sale contract is signed, depending on local practices and the transaction in question. In many states, the broker is charged with the responsibility for accuracy and timely delivery of the closing documents to the principal parties. A broker may also have the responsibility for reporting the transaction to the Internal Revenue Service.

Finally, if the seller of the property is a non-resident alien, U.S. law may require the broker to withhold and transmit to the Internal Revenue Service a portion of the sale proceeds to cover the alien seller's income tax liability. There are also special reporting requirements when the transaction involves a non-resident alien.

Real Estate Settlement Procedures Act (RESPA)

The Real Estate Settlement Procedures Act (RESPA) is a consumer protection statute enacted in 1974. Its purpose is to clarify settlement costs and to eliminate kickbacks and fees that increase settlement costs. RESPA specifies certain closing procedures when a purchase:

- involves a residential property, including one- to four-family residences, cooperatives and condominiums;
- involves a first or second mortgage lien; and
- is being financed by a "federally-related" mortgage loan, which includes loans made by a federally-insured lender; loans insured or guaranteed by the VA or FHA, loans administered by HUD, and loans intended to be sold to FNMA, FHLMC, or GNMA.

RESPA regulations do not apply to transactions being otherwise financed except in the case of an assumption in which the terms of the assumed loan are modified or the lender's charges for the assumption are greater than $50.

RESPA is directed at lenders and settlement companies, but licensees should be familiar with requirements and changes implemented as of January, 2014. The Dodd-Frank Act of 2010 granted rule-making authority under RESPA to the Consumer Financial Protection Bureau (CFPB) and generally granted the CFPB authority to supervise and enforce compliance with RESPA and its implementing regulations. In 2013, the CFPB made substantive and technical changes to the existing regulations. Substantive changes included modifying the servicing transfer notice requirements and implementing new procedures and notice requirements related to borrowers' error resolution requests and information requests. The amendments also included new provisions related to escrow payments, force-placed insurance, general servicing policies, procedures, and requirements, early intervention, continuity of contact, loss mitigation and the relation of RESPA's servicing provisions to State law. These RESPA amendments went into effect on January 10, 2014.

TRID

Effective October 3, 2015, a TILA/RESPA Integrated Disclosure Rule (TRID) integrates the disclosure requirements of RESPA and Truth-in-Lending, replacing the old Good Faith Estimate form and HUD-1 Uniform Settlement Statement a new Loan Estimate form and Closing Disclosure form, respectively.

Information booklet

A lender subject to RESPA must give loan applicants the CFPB booklet, "Your Home Loan Toolkit," within three days of receiving a loan application. This booklet describes loans, closing costs, and the Closing Disclosure form.

Loan estimate

A lender must give the applicant, at the time of application or within three business days of application, a Loan Estimate (H-24) of likely settlement costs. This estimate is usually based on comparable transactions completed in the area. The terms stated in the Closing Disclosure must agree with those of the Loan Estimate within certain limits.

Mortgage servicing disclosure

The lender must disclose to the buyer whether the lender intends to service the loan or convey it to another lender for servicing. This disclosure must also be accompanied by information as to how the buyer can resolve complaints.

Closing disclosure

Under CFPB rules, a lender must use the Closing Disclosure (H-25) to disclose settlement costs to the buyer. This form covers all costs that the buyer will have to pay at closing, whether to the lender or to other parties. Use of this form enforces RESPA's prohibitions against a lender's requiring a buyer to deposit an excessive amount in the tax and insurance escrow account or to use a particular title company for title insurance. The consumer must receive the completed form not later than three business days before closing and has the right to inspect a revised form one business day before closing. A description and example of this form are provided later in this chapter.

Disclosures after settlement

Loan servicers must provide borrowers with an annual escrow statement which summarizes all inflows and outflows in the prior 12-month period. The statement must also disclose shortfalls or overages in the account, and how the discrepancies will be resolved.

Limits on escrow accounts

Section 10 of RESPA limits the amounts lenders can require borrowers to place in escrow for purposes of paying taxes, hazard insurance, and other property-related expenses. The limitation applies to the initial deposits as well as deposits made over the course of the loan's term.

Referral fees and kickbacks

RESPA prohibits the payment of fees as part of a real estate settlement when no services are actually rendered. This prohibition includes referral fees for such services as title searches, title insurance, mortgage loans, appraisals, credit reports, inspections, surveys, and legal services.

Business relationships and affiliations among real estate firms, mortgage brokers, title insurance firms and other such companies that are involved in a transaction are permitted, provided the relationships are disclosed in writing to the consumer, the consumer is free to go elsewhere for the relevant service, and the companies do not exchange fees for referrals.

Financial Settlement of the Transaction

Settlement process

The process of settlement consists of five basic steps:

1. Identify selling terms and closing costs.
2. Determine non-prorated debits and credits.
3. Determine prorated debits and credits.
4. Complete the closing statement.
5. Disburse funds.

Selling terms and closing costs

Selling terms are the price of the property, the buyer's deposit and downpayment, and the terms and amounts of the buyer's financing arrangements. Closing costs are final expenses that buyer or seller must pay at closing to complete the transaction. The sale contract identifies all selling terms and who pays which costs. The apportionment of expenses is subject to negotiation, and in the absence of a specific agreement, is determined by custom. Closing costs include such items as brokerage fees, mortgage-related fees, title-related expenses, and real estate taxes.

Debits and credits

The closing statement accounts for the debits and credits of the buyer and seller to settle and complete the transaction. A debit is an amount that one party must pay at closing or has already paid prior to closing. A credit is an amount that a party must receive at closing or that has already been received prior to closing.

The excess of the buyer's debits over the buyer's credits is the amount the buyer must bring to the closing. The excess of the seller's credits over the seller's debits is the amount the seller will receive at closing.

An individual expense item that one party owes to a party unrelated to the transaction, such as an attorney or the state, is treated as *a debit to that party only*. An income or expense item that affects both parties is apportioned, or **prorated**, to each party to reflect the proper amount that each owes or should receive. A prorated item is treated as *a debit to one party and a credit to the other party for the same amount.*

Buyer's debits and credits

To determine how much money the buyer owes at closing, the buyer's debits are totaled and compared with the total of the buyer's credits. The excess of debits over credits is the amount the buyer must bring to the closing, usually in the form of a cashier's check or certified check. The items typically debited and credited to the buyer are illustrated in the following exhibit.

Buyer's Credits and Debits

Buyer's Credits

earnest money

loan amount (borrowed or assumed)

Buyer's Debits

purchase price

expenses (per agreement or custom)

Seller's credits and debits

To determine how much the seller will receive at closing, the same procedure is followed for the seller's debits and credits. The excess of credits over debits is what the seller will receive. The items typically debited and credited to the seller are illustrated in the following exhibit.

Seller's Debits and Credits

Seller's Debits

expenses (per agreement or custom)

seller's share of prorated items the buyer will

Seller's Credits

purchase price

buyer's share of prorated items prepaid by

Non-prorated items

Non-prorated items are costs *incurred by one party only.* Items not prorated include those listed in the next exhibit.

Non-Prorated Items

Buyer usually pays	Seller usually pays
Mortgage recording fees Documentary stamp tax Intangible tax on mortgage Mortgage-related fees: appraisal, credit, survey, loan Impound reserves: insurance, taxes Attorney fees	Stamp tax on deed Title insurance Brokerage fee Inspection fees Title-related expenses Attorney fees

Prorated items

Many of the items to be settled at the closing are partly the responsibility of the buyer and partly of the seller. Some are expense items that the seller has *paid in advance*, where the buyer owes the seller part of the expense. Some are income items that the seller received in advance, and the seller owes the buyer a part of the income. Others are items the buyer will have to pay *in arrears*, and the seller owes the buyer part of the expense. The method of dividing financial responsibility for such items is **proration**. With a prorated item, there is always a debit to one party and a corresponding credit for the same amount to the other party.

Items paid in advance

At the time of closing, the seller has paid some items in advance that cover a period of time that goes beyond the closing date. In effect, the seller has prepaid some of the buyer's expenses, and the buyer must reimburse the seller. Heating oil and natural gas are typical items. By the same token, the seller of a rental property may have received rent or rental deposits in advance, and must reimburse the buyer for the part that belongs to the buyer.

For an expense the seller paid in advance, *the buyer receives a debit and the seller receives a credit.*

For income the seller received in advance, *the buyer receives a credit and the seller receives a debit.*

Items paid in arrears

At the time of closing, the seller has incurred certain expenses that have not been billed or paid at the time of closing and that the buyer will have to pay later. A typical item is real estate taxes.

For an item the buyer will pay in arrears, *the buyer receives a credit and the seller receives a debit.*

Items Paid in Arrears and Advance

	arrears	advance
real estate taxes	x	
mortgage interest	x	
rents received by seller		x
utilities	x	

Charging shares

If the seller has paid the buyer's share of an item, *charge the buyer for the buyer's share of the period.* If the buyer will pay the seller's share of an item, *charge the seller for the seller's share of the period.* If the seller has received the buyer's share of an income item, *charge the seller for the buyer's share of the period.*

Who Gets Charged

Seller paid for the year: charge buyer for buyer's share

Annual expense – closing August 7											
Jan	Feb	Mar	Apr	May	Jun	Jul	Aug	Sep	Oct	Nov	Dec
							7 | 8				
Seller's share							Buyer's share				

Buyer will pay for the month: charge seller for seller's share

Monthly expense – closing August 7							
August							
1	2	3	4	5	6	7	8-31
Seller's share							Buyer's share

Computing Prorations

The primary methods of calculating prorations are the 360/30-day method, which computes prorations on the basis of a 360-day year and 30-day month, and the 365-day method, which computes prorations on the basis of a 365-day year. The 360/30-day method is commonly used for prorating mortgage interest. Either method may be used for real estate taxes, depending on local practice.

It is customary in most states that the seller owns the property up to and including the day of closing unless stated otherwise in the contract. Thus the closing day is apportioned to the seller in computing prorations. The method of prorating, if not specified in the contract, will follow local custom.

12-month / 30 day method (also, 360-day method)

The 12-month/30-day method determines an average daily rate of payment for an item to be prorated *based on a 30-day month and a 360-day year*. The method consists of the following steps for annual and monthly items.

Annual items

1. Identify the total amount to be prorated.
2. Divide this amount by 12 to obtain an average monthly rate.
3. Divide the monthly rate by 30 to obtain an average daily rate.
4. Multiply the monthly amount times the seller's number of months of ownership in the year of the sale up to the month of closing. For the month of closing, multiply

the seller's number of days of ownership times the daily amount and add the result to the previous result. The final result is the seller's pro rata share of this item.

5. The buyer's pro rata share of an item is the total amount less the seller's pro rata share.

Monthly items

1. Identify the total amount to be prorated.
2. Divide this amount by 30 to obtain the average daily amount.
3. Multiply the daily amount times the seller's number of days of ownership. The result is the seller's pro rata share of this item.
4. The buyer's pro rata share of an item is the total amount less the seller's pro rata share.

Prorating Annual Item: Real Estate Tax
12-month/30-day Method

A sale transaction on a single-family house closes on March 2. County taxes for the previous year, to be paid in arrears, amount to $1,730. The seller owns the house through the day of closing. What are the seller's and buyer's prorated shares of this item?

Total amount due:		=	$ 1,730.00
Monthly amount:	1,730 ÷ 12	=	$ 144.17
Daily amount:	144.17 ÷ 30	=	$ 4.81
Seller's share:	144.17 x 2	=	$ 288.34
	4.81 x 2 days	=	$ 9.62
	288.34 + 9.62	=	$ 297.96
Buyer's share	1,730 - 297.96	=	$ 1,432.04

Closing statement entries. The seller will be charged for the seller's share of the proration; an amount of $297.96 will be entered as a debit to the seller and a credit to the buyer because the buyer will have to pay the seller's share when the tax bill is received.

Prorating Monthly Item: Rent Received
12-month/30-day Method

The house in the previous example has been rented during the listing and selling period at a rate of $1800 per month. Rent for the month of March was paid to the seller on March 1. What is the buyer's prorated share of this rent? The day of closing, March 2, belongs to the seller.

Total received:		=	$ 1,800.00
Daily amount:	1800 ÷ 30	=	$ 60.00
Seller's share:	60.00 x 2 days	=	$ 120.00
Buyer's share	1800.00 – 120.00	=	$ 1,680.00

Closing statement entries. The seller will be charged for the buyer's share of the proration; an amount of $1,680.00 will be debited to the seller's account and credited to the buyer's account because the seller has received rent that belongs to the new owner after closing.

365-day method

The 365-day method uses the actual number of days in the calendar. The steps in the calculation are the same for annual and monthly prorations. The steps are:

1. Identify the total annual or monthly amount to be prorated.
2. For an annual proration, divide the total amount by 365 to obtain a daily amount (366 in a Leap Year). For a monthly proration, divide the total amount by the actual number of days in the month to obtain the daily amount.
3. Multiply the daily amount times the seller's number of days of ownership. The result is the seller's pro rata share of the item.
4. The buyer's pro rata share of an item is the total amount less the seller's pro rata share.

Prorating an Annual Tax Bill, 365-day Method

The seller in the previous example has a $1,730 tax bill, paid annually in arrears on December 31. Closing is on March 2, and the seller owns the day of closing. What is the seller's prorated share of this item?

Total amount due:		=	$ 1.730.00
Daily amount:	1730 ÷ 365	=	$ 4.74
Seller's share:	61 days x 4.75	=	$ 289.14
Buyer's share:	1730 - 289.14	=	$ 1,440.86

Closing statement entries. The seller will be charged for the seller's share of the proration; an amount of $289.14 will be debited to the seller's account and credited to the buyer's account because the buyer will have paid the seller's share of the tax bill in arrears.

Taxes Due at Closing

Certain transfer taxes that are due in connection with the closing appear and are accounted for on the closing statement. These include state taxes relating to the deed and to the buyer's mortgage. In addition to state-imposed taxes, counties and municipalities may also impose a tax on the real estate transfer.

State taxes on the deed

Most states impose a **transfer tax** when real estate is conveyed. The tax is usually paid when the deed is recorded, often in the form of **documentary stamps** purchased from the recorder where the deed is recorded. The stamps must be attached to deeds and conveyances before they are recorded.

Tax rates are specific to each state. Methods of stating the transfer tax due include quoting the tax as a percentage of the taxable consideration and as a dollar rate per $100.00 of total selling price. If the number of 100's is not a whole number, it must be rounded up to the next 100. For instance, if a property sells for $350,120 and the tax rate is $.55 per $100.00 "or any fraction thereof," the tax stamps will cost:

350,120 ÷ 100.00	=	3,501.20
3,501.20 *rounded up*	=	3,502
3,502 x $.55	=	$1,926.10

State taxes on the mortgage

Some states also impose a tax on instruments that contain promises to pay money, such as mortgages, notes, and contracts. Such taxes may be paid by the purchase of documentary stamps from the agency which will record the instrument. In addition, some states impose a further tax on the mortgage as an item of intangible personal property.

Taxes on the mortgage are typically paid by the buyer/borrower.

Closing Cost Itemization: Case Illustration

The Closing Disclosure summarizes the financial settlement of a transaction. At closing, the closing agent also generally provides a statement to the buyer and/or seller detailing receipts and disbursements from relevant escrow accounts to which the buyer and seller have contributed funds as part of the transaction. The following illustration shows how some of these cost components are calculated and allocated in a sample transaction.

Selling terms and closing costs

Lawrence and Sandy Binder have accepted an offer on their house located at 928 Elm Street, Littleburg. The buyers, Bill and Dillis Waite, offered $450,000, with earnest money of $70,000 and the remaining $380,000 of the purchase price to come from a new conventional loan from Scepter Mortgage Company. The loan is for 30 years at 5.5% interest, with a monthly principal plus interest payment of $2,158. The lender is charging 1.5 points and a 1% origination fee. Closing is set to occur at Alta Title Company at 4 p.m. on May 10 of the current (non-leap) year.

The Binders have an agreement to pay a broker's commission of 6% to Littleburg Realty. Their unpaid mortgage loan balance as of May 1 will be $184,000. Their monthly interest payments are $613.00. The annual interest rate is 4%. The previous year's county taxes, amounting to $2,572, have been paid by the seller in arrears. The current year's taxes, not yet billed or paid, are assumed to be the same as the previous year's. The parties agree to prorate using the 365-day method, and that the day of closing belongs to the seller. The relevant facts and costs, and who pays them according to the terms of the sale contract, are summarized below.

Selling terms	
Sale price:	$450,000
Deposit/downpayment	$70,000
Loan amount	$380,000
Seller-paid Costs	
Commissions:	6% of sale price (.06)
Real estate taxes:	$2,572, to be prorated
Title insurance:	$900 owner's coverage
Seller's attorney:	$1,500
Record Release Deed:	$25
Survey:	$550
Transfer stamps	
state:	$162
county:	$162
Seller's loan payoff:	$184,000 + 10 days' prorated May interest @ $613/month
Buyer- paid Costs	
Sale price:	$450,000 ($70,000 earnest money already deposited by buyer)
Appraisal fee:	$400 already paid by buyer
Credit report:	$50 already paid by buyer
Closing fee:	$350

Recording fees:	$55
Title insurance:	$250 for lender's coverage
Buyer's attorney:	$1200
Pest inspection:	$100
Buyer's loan:	$380,000; 30-year fixed @ 5.5% (.055) points: 1.5% of loan amount (.015) origination fee: 1.0% of loan amount (.01)
Hazard insurance:	$2,400/year
Real estate taxes:	$2,572.00, to be prorated
Tax and insurance escrow:	8 months' taxes, 4 months' insurance
Prepaid interest:	from day after closing to end of month

Prorations and charges

According to the summarized sale contract, the only cost to be prorated and shared between seller and buyer is the real estate tax. Other costs to be computed are the broker's commission, the seller's unpaid mortgage interest, the buyer's loan fees and points, the buyer's tax and insurance escrows, and the buyer's prepaid mortgage interest.

Commission

The commission paid by the seller is:

$450,000 x 6%	=	$27,000.00

At closing this amount will be charged, or debited, to the seller.

Real estate taxes

Using the 365-day method, the daily amount is $2,572 ÷ 365, or $7.05 (rounded). The total number of days is the number of days in January, February, March and April, plus 10 days in May, or (31+28+31+30+10), or 130 days. At closing, the seller's share of $916.50 is charged to the seller and the buyer is credited with the same amount.

Total amount due:		=	$	2,572.00
Daily amount:	2,572 ÷ 365	=	$	7.05
Seller's share	7.051 x 130	=	$	916.50
Buyer's share:	2,572 – 916.50	=	$	1,655.50

Seller's unpaid mortgage interest

Since mortgage interest is paid in arrears, the seller owes the lender for interest not yet charged for the ten days of the month of closing. This amount is therefore debited to the seller.

Daily amount:	613 ÷ 31 days	=	$	19.77

Seller's charge:	19.77 x 10 days	=	$	197.70

Buyer's loan origination and points

The buyer's debits for loan fees and points are:

Fee:	380,000 x 1%	=	$	3,800
Points:	380,000 x 1.5%	=	$	5,700

Buyer's escrow

The lender requires the buyer to establish an escrow account to cover eight months of real estate taxes and four months of hazard insurance. The debits charged to the buyer are therefore:

Taxes:

Annual amount:		=	$	2,572.00
Monthly amount:	2,572 ÷ 12	=	$	214.33
Amount due:	214.33 x 8 mo.	=	$	1,714.64

Insurance:

Annual amount:		=	$	2400.00
Monthly amount:	2400 ÷ 12	=	$	200.00
Amount due:	200 x 4 mo.	=	$	800.00

Prepaid interest

The lender requires the buyer (borrower) to pay, in advance, the interest on the loan amount disbursed at closing to cover the 21 days of the closing month that would be due in arrears later. Note that the lender is not charging the borrower for interest for the day of closing. The buyer's first mortgage payment, which will cover the month of June, will not be due until July 1. Charged to buyer:

Monthly amount:	380K x 5.5% ÷ 12	=	$	1741.67
Daily amount:	1,741.67 ÷ 31	=	$	56.18
Total prepaid interest	56.18 x 21 days	=	$	1179.78

TILA/RESPA Integrated Disclosure Rule

Forms and procedures

As mentioned earlier, the TILA/RESPA Integrated Disclosures (TRID) rule is in effect as of October 3, 2015. These changes introduce new mandatory forms and procedures to replace the old ones, as follows.

- Lenders must give the consumer a copy of the **booklet**, "Your Home Loan Toolkit" **at the time** of loan application.
- Lenders must deliver or mail the **Loan Estimate** (Form H-24) to the consumer **no later than the third business day** after receiving a loan application. (A "business day" in this context is any day on which the lender's offices are open for business. An "application" exists when the consumer has given the lender or mortgage broker six pieces of information: name; income; Social Security number; property address; estimated value of property; loan amount sought).
- Lenders must provide the **Closing Disclosure** (Form H-25) to the consumer **at least three business days** before consummation of the loan. (A "business day" in this context is any calendar day except a Sunday or the day on which a legal public holiday is observed. "Consummation" refers to the day on which the borrower becomes indebted to the creditor; this may or may not correspond to the day of closing the transaction.)

TILA/RESPA Disclosures

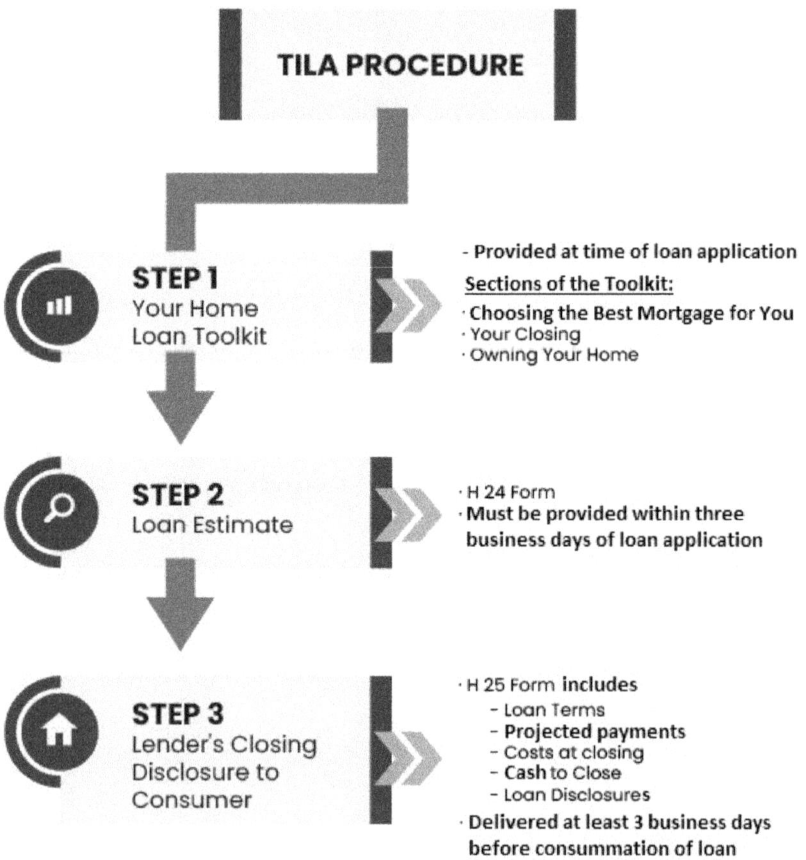

Good faith

Creditors are responsible for ensuring that the figures stated in the Loan Estimate are made in good faith and consistent with the best information reasonably available to the creditor at the time they are disclosed.

Good faith is measured by calculating the difference between the estimated charges originally provided in the Loan Estimate and the actual charges paid by or imposed on the consumer in the Closing Disclosure.

Generally, if the charge paid by or imposed on the consumer exceeds the amount originally disclosed on the Loan Estimate it is not in good faith, regardless of whether the creditor later discovers a technical error, miscalculation, or underestimation of a charge, although there are exceptions.

Types of charges

For certain costs or terms, creditors are permitted to charge consumers more than the amount disclosed on the Loan Estimate without any tolerance limitation.

These charges are:

- prepaid interest; property insurance premiums; amounts placed into an escrow, impound, reserve or similar account
- charges for services required by the creditor if the creditor permits the consumer to shop and the consumer selects a third-party service provider not on the creditor's written list of service providers
- charges paid to third-party service providers for services not required by the creditor (may be paid to affiliates of the creditor)

However, creditors may only charge consumers more than the amount disclosed when the original estimated charge, or lack of an estimated charge for a particular service, was based on the best information reasonably available to the creditor at the time the disclosure was provided.

Charges for third-party services and recording fees paid by or imposed on the consumer are grouped together and subject to a 10% cumulative tolerance ("10% tolerance" charges). This means the creditor may charge the consumer more than the amount disclosed on the Loan Estimate for any of these charges so long as the total sum of the charges added together does not exceed the sum of all such charges disclosed on the Loan Estimate by more than 10%.

For all other charges ("zero tolerance" charges), creditors are not permitted to charge consumers more than the amount disclosed on the Loan Estimate under any circumstances other than changed circumstances that permit a revised Loan Estimate.

If the amounts paid by the consumer at closing exceed the amounts disclosed on the Loan Estimate beyond the applicable tolerance threshold, the creditor must refund the excess to the consumer no later than 60 calendar days after consummation.

Applicable transactions

The Integrated Disclosures rule applies to most closed-end consumer mortgages. It does not apply to:

- home equity lines of credit (HELOCs)
- reverse mortgages
- mortgages secured by a mobile home or by a dwelling that is not attached to real property (i.e., land)
- loans made by persons who are not considered "creditors" by virtue of the fact they make five or fewer mortgages in a year.

However, certain types of loans that used to be subject to TILA but not RESPA are now subject to the TILA-RESPA rule's integrated disclosure requirements, including:

- construction-only loans
- loans secured by vacant land or by 25 or more acres
- credit extended to certain trusts for tax or estate planning

Guides and detailed information about the current TILA-RESPA rule can be found on the Consumer Financial Protection Bureau (CFPB) website at

https://www.consumerfinance.gov/policy-compliance/guidance/tila-respa-disclosure-rule/

The H-25 Closing Disclosure form

The H-25 Closing Disclosure form consists of five pages. Pages 1, 4, and 5 vary, depending on the loan type. To illustrate the form, we use a sample disclosure for a ***30-year fixed rate*** loan that is presented on the CFPB website.

Page 1 has four sections: general information, Loan Terms, Projected Payments, and Costs at Closing.

General information. This section has three columns:

- Closing information –issue date, closing date, disbursement date, settlement agent, file number, property address, and sale price
- Transaction information – names and addresses for borrower, seller and lender
- Loan information – loan term, loan purpose, product type, loan type and loan ID number

Loan Terms. This section states the loan amount, interest rate, and monthly principal and interest payment, and indicates whether any of those amounts can increase after closing. It also gives specifics of any prepayment penalty or balloon payment.

Projected Payment. This section displays the borrower's payment for principal and interest and mortgage insurance, an estimated escrow payment, and the total estimated monthly mortgage payment for years 1-7 and 8-30 of the loan term. It also provides an estimate of monthly tax, insurance, and assessment payments and indicates whether the payments will be held in escrow.

Costs at Closing. The last section of page 1 shows the borrowers' total closing costs (brought forward from page 2) and the total amount of cash the buyer needs to close (brought forward from page 3).

Page 2 details the closing costs. There are two sections divided into four columns:

- Description of the costs—loan costs and other costs
- Costs paid by the borrower – "at closing" or "before closing"
- Costs paid by the seller – "at closing" or "before closing"
- Costs paid by others (in the example, someone other than buyer or seller pays for the appraisal)

Loan Costs. The first section deals with the loan costs:

A. Origination charges, such as points, application fee, and underwriting fee

B. Charges for services the borrower did not shop for - items the lender requires, such as appraisals and credit reports

C. Services the borrower did shop for - items the borrower orders on his own, such as pest inspections, survey fees, and title insurance

D. The total of A, B, and C above

Other Costs. The second section deals with additional transaction-related costs:

E. Taxes and other government fees, such as recording fees and transfer taxes

F. Prepaid items, such as homeowner's insurance, mortgage insurance, prepaid interest, and property taxes to be paid before the first scheduled loan payment

G. Initial escrow payment at closing – an amount the borrower will pay the lender each month to be held in escrow until due, typically for insurance premiums and tax instalments

H. Other costs not covered elsewhere on the disclosure, such as items as association fees, home warranty fees, home inspection fees, real estate commission, and prorated items

I. The total of the costs of E, F, G, and H above

J. The total borrower-paid closing costs from D + I above. This total is carried to the bottom of page 1 as "Costs at Closing – Closing Costs."

Page 3 has two sections, one for calculating cash to close, the other for summarizing the transactions of borrower and seller.

Calculating Cash to Close. The first section compares the final costs of the loan with the lender's original Loan Estimate. This calculation considers costs paid before closing, down payment, deposits, seller credits, adjustments, and other credits. The last line of the calculation is "Cash to close," the amount the borrower needs to produce at closing.

When an amount has changed, the creditor must indicate where the consumer can find the amounts that have changed on the Loan Estimate. For example, if the Seller Credit amount changed, the creditor can indicate that the consumer should "See Seller Credits in Section L." When the increase in Total Closing Costs exceeds the legal limits, the creditor must disclose this fact and the dollar amount of the excess in the “Did this change?” column. A statement directing the consumer to the Lender Credit on page 2 must also be included if the creditor owes a credit to the consumer at closing for the excess amount.

Summaries of Transactions. The second section of page 3 is divided into two columns (or subsections), one to summarize the borrower's transaction and the other for the seller's transaction. The borrower's column includes:

K. amounts due from the borrower at closing, including the sale price and adjustments for items paid by the seller in advance.

L. amounts already paid by or on behalf of the borrower at closing, such as deposit, loan amount, loan assumptions, seller credits, other credits, and adjustments for items unpaid by the seller, such as taxes and assessments.

The calculation at the bottom of the left column subtracts the totals already paid by the borrower (line L) from the total due from the borrower (line K) to derive the Cash to Close due from the borrower at closing. This figure is the same as that at the bottom of page 1 under "Costs at Closing – Cash to Close."

The seller's column of the Summaries section includes:

M. amounts due to the seller at closing, including the sale price of the property and adjustments for items paid by the seller in advance.

N. amounts due from the seller at closing, such as closing costs the seller will pay, payoff of first or second mortgages, seller credit, and adjustments for items unpaid by the seller, such as taxes and assessments.

The calculation at the bottom of the right column subtracts the total due from the seller (line N) from the total due to the seller (line M) to derive the Cash to Seller, which is the amount the seller will receive at closing.

Page 4 provides additional Loan Disclosures:

- Assumption –whether the lender will allow a loan assumption on a future transfer
- Demand feature –whether the lender can require early repayment
- Late payment – the fee the lender will charge for a late payment
- Negative amortization –whether the loan is negatively amortized, which increases loan amount and diminishes the borrower's equity over the term
- Partial payments –whether the lender accepts partial payments and applies them to the loan
- Security interest –identifies the property securing the loan
- Escrow account – itemizes what is included in the escrow account and states the monthly escrow payment

Page 5 provides additional calculations, disclosures, and contact information:

- Loan Calculations –the total amount of all payments on the loan, the dollar amount of the finance charges over the life of the loan, the amount financed, the annual percentage rate (APR), and the total interest percentage (TIP)
- Other Disclosures –other important information for the borrower, including the right to a copy of the appraisal report and an indication of whether the borrower is protected against liability for the unpaid balance in the event of a foreclosure
- Contact Information –names, addresses, license numbers, contact names, email addresses, and phone numbers for persons involved in the transaction.
- Confirm Receipt –the borrowers' signatures confirming receipt of the Closing Disclosure document. **Signing the document does not indicate acceptance of the loan.**

Sample H-25 Closing Disclosure, Page 1

Closing Disclosure

This form is a statement of final loan terms and closing costs. Compare this document with your Loan Estimate.

Closing Information

Date Issued	4/15/2013
Closing Date	4/15/2013
Disbursement Date	4/15/2013
Settlement Agent	Epsilon Title Co.
File #	12-3456
Property	456 Somewhere Ave Anytown, ST 12345
Sale Price	$180,000

Transaction Information

Borrower	Michael Jones and Mary Stone 123 Anywhere Street Anytown, ST 12345
Seller	Steve Cole and Amy Doe 321 Somewhere Drive Anytown, ST 12345
Lender	Ficus Bank

Loan Information

Loan Term	30 years
Purpose	Purchase
Product	Fixed Rate
Loan Type	☒ Conventional ☐ FHA ☐ VA ☐ ________
Loan ID #	123456789
MIC #	000654321

Loan Terms

Loan Terms		Can this amount increase after closing?
Loan Amount	$162,000	NO
Interest Rate	3.875%	NO
Monthly Principal & Interest *See Projected Payments below for your Estimated Total Monthly Payment*	$761.78	NO
		Does the loan have these features?
Prepayment Penalty		YES • **As high as $3,240** if you pay off the loan during the first 2 years
Balloon Payment		NO

Projected Payments

Payment Calculation	Years 1-7	Years 8-30
Principal & Interest	$761.78	$761.78
Mortgage Insurance	+ 82.35	+ —
Estimated Escrow *Amount can increase over time*	+ 206.13	+ 206.13
Estimated Total Monthly Payment	$1,050.26	$967.91

		This estimate includes	In escrow?
Estimated Taxes, Insurance & Assessments *Amount can increase over time* *See page 4 for details*	$356.13 a month	☒ Property Taxes	YES
		☒ Homeowner's Insurance	YES
		☒ Other: Homeowner's Association Dues	NO
		See Escrow Account on page 4 for details. You must pay for other property costs separately.	

Costs at Closing

Closing Costs	$9,712.10	Includes $4,694.05 in Loan Costs + $5,018.05 in Other Costs – $0 in Lender Credits. *See page 2 for details.*
Cash to Close	$14,147.26	Includes Closing Costs. *See Calculating Cash to Close on page 3 for details.*

CLOSING DISCLOSURE PAGE 1 OF 5 • LOAN ID # 123456789

Sample H-25 Closing Disclosure, Page 2

Closing Cost Details

Loan Costs	Borrower-Paid At Closing	Borrower-Paid Before Closing	Seller-Paid At Closing	Seller-Paid Before Closing	Paid by Others
A. Origination Charges	**$1,802.00**				
01 0.25 % of Loan Amount (Points)	$405.00				
02 Application Fee	$300.00				
03 Underwriting Fee	$1,097.00				
04					
05					
06					
07					
08					
B. Services Borrower Did Not Shop For	**$236.55**				
01 Appraisal Fee to John Smith Appraisers Inc.					$405.00
02 Credit Report Fee to Information Inc.		$29.80			
03 Flood Determination Fee to Info Co.	$20.00				
04 Flood Monitoring Fee to Info Co.	$31.75				
05 Tax Monitoring Fee to Info Co.	$75.00				
06 Tax Status Research Fee to Info Co.	$80.00				
07					
08					
09					
10					
C. Services Borrower Did Shop For	**$2,655.50**				
01 Pest Inspection Fee to Pests Co.	$120.50				
02 Survey Fee to Surveys Co.	$85.00				
03 Title – Insurance Binder to Epsilon Title Co.	$650.00				
04 Title – Lender's Title Insurance to Epsilon Title Co.	$500.00				
05 Title – Settlement Agent Fee to Epsilon Title Co.	$500.00				
06 Title – Title Search to Epsilon Title Co.	$800.00				
07					
08					
D. TOTAL LOAN COSTS (Borrower-Paid)	**$4,694.05**				
Loan Costs Subtotals (A + B + C)	$4,664.25	$29.80			

Other Costs	Borrower-Paid At Closing	Borrower-Paid Before Closing	Seller-Paid At Closing	Seller-Paid Before Closing	Paid by Others
E. Taxes and Other Government Fees	**$85.00**				
01 Recording Fees Deed: $40.00 Mortgage: $45.00	$85.00				
02 Transfer Tax to Any State			$950.00		
F. Prepaids	**$2,120.80**				
01 Homeowner's Insurance Premium (12 mo.) to Insurance Co.	$1,209.96				
02 Mortgage Insurance Premium (mo.)					
03 Prepaid Interest ($17.44 per day from 4/15/13 to 5/1/13)	$279.04				
04 Property Taxes (6 mo.) to Any County USA	$631.80				
05					
G. Initial Escrow Payment at Closing	**$412.25**				
01 Homeowner's Insurance $100.83 per month for 2 mo.	$201.66				
02 Mortgage Insurance per month for mo.					
03 Property Taxes $105.30 per month for 2 mo.	$210.60				
04					
05					
06					
07					
08 Aggregate Adjustment	– 0.01				
H. Other	**$2,400.00**				
01 HOA Capital Contribution to HOA Acre Inc.	$500.00				
02 HOA Processing Fee to HOA Acre Inc.	$150.00				
03 Home Inspection Fee to Engineers Inc.	$750.00			$750.00	
04 Home Warranty Fee to XYZ Warranty Inc.			$450.00		
05 Real Estate Commission to Alpha Real Estate Broker			$5,700.00		
06 Real Estate Commission to Omega Real Estate Broker			$5,700.00		
07 Title – Owner's Title Insurance (optional) to Epsilon Title Co.	$1,000.00				
08					
I. TOTAL OTHER COSTS (Borrower-Paid)	**$5,018.05**				
Other Costs Subtotals (E + F + G + H)	$5,018.05				
J. TOTAL CLOSING COSTS (Borrower-Paid)	**$9,712.10**				
Closing Costs Subtotals (D + I)	$9,682.30	$29.80	$12,800.00	$750.00	$405.00
Lender Credits					

Sample H-25 Closing Disclosure, Page 3

Calculating Cash to Close — Use this table to see what has changed from your Loan Estimate.

	Loan Estimate	Final	Did this change?
Total Closing Costs (J)	$8,054.00	$9,712.10	**YES** • See Total Loan Costs (D) and Total Other Costs (I)
Closing Costs Paid Before Closing	$0	– $29.80	**YES** • You paid these Closing Costs **before closing**
Closing Costs Financed (Paid from your Loan Amount)	$0	$0	**NO**
Down Payment/Funds from Borrower	$18,000.00	$18,000.00	**NO**
Deposit	– $10,000.00	– $10,000.00	**NO**
Funds for Borrower	$0	$0	**NO**
Seller Credits	$0	– $2,500.00	**YES** • See Seller Credits in **Section L**
Adjustments and Other Credits	$0	– $1,035.04	**YES** • See details in **Sections K and L**
Cash to Close	$16,054.00	$14,147.26	

Summaries of Transactions — Use this table to see a summary of your transaction.

BORROWER'S TRANSACTION

K. Due from Borrower at Closing		**$189,762.30**
01 Sale Price of Property		$180,000.00
02 Sale Price of Any Personal Property Included in Sale		
03 Closing Costs Paid at Closing (J)		$9,682.30
04		
Adjustments		
05		
06		
07		
Adjustments for Items Paid by Seller in Advance		
08 City/Town Taxes	to	
09 County Taxes	to	
10 Assessments	to	
11 HOA Dues	4/15/13 to 4/30/13	$80.00
12		
13		
14		
15		
L. Paid Already by or on Behalf of Borrower at Closing		**$175,615.04**
01 Deposit		$10,000.00
02 Loan Amount		$162,000.00
03 Existing Loan(s) Assumed or Taken Subject to		
04		
05 Seller Credit		$2,500.00
Other Credits		
06 Rebate from Epsilon Title Co.		$750.00
07		
Adjustments		
08		
09		
10		
11		
Adjustments for Items Unpaid by Seller		
12 City/Town Taxes	1/1/13 to 4/14/13	$365.04
13 County Taxes	to	
14 Assessments	to	
15		
16		
17		
CALCULATION		
Total Due from Borrower at Closing (K)		$189,762.30
Total Paid Already by or on Behalf of Borrower at Closing (L)		– $175,615.04
Cash to Close ☒ From ☐ To Borrower		**$14,147.26**

SELLER'S TRANSACTION

M. Due to Seller at Closing		**$180,080.00**
01 Sale Price of Property		$180,000.00
02 Sale Price of Any Personal Property Included in Sale		
03		
04		
05		
06		
07		
08		
Adjustments for Items Paid by Seller in Advance		
09 City/Town Taxes	to	
10 County Taxes	to	
11 Assessments	to	
12 HOA Dues	4/15/13 to 4/30/13	$80.00
13		
14		
15		
16		
N. Due from Seller at Closing		**$115,665.04**
01 Excess Deposit		
02 Closing Costs Paid at Closing (J)		$12,800.00
03 Existing Loan(s) Assumed or Taken Subject to		
04 Payoff of First Mortgage Loan		$100,000.00
05 Payoff of Second Mortgage Loan		
06		
07		
08 Seller Credit		$2,500.00
09		
10		
11		
12		
13		
Adjustments for Items Unpaid by Seller		
14 City/Town Taxes	1/1/13 to 4/14/13	$365.04
15 County Taxes	to	
16 Assessments	to	
17		
18		
19		
CALCULATION		
Total Due to Seller at Closing (M)		$180,080.00
Total Due from Seller at Closing (N)		– $115,665.04
Cash ☐ From ☒ To Seller		**$64,414.96**

CLOSING DISCLOSURE — PAGE 3 OF 5 • LOAN ID # 123456789

Sample H-25 Closing Disclosure, Page 4

Additional Information About This Loan

Loan Disclosures

Assumption
If you sell or transfer this property to another person, your lender
☐ will allow, under certain conditions, this person to assume this loan on the original terms.
☒ will not allow assumption of this loan on the original terms.

Demand Feature
Your loan
☐ has a demand feature, which permits your lender to require early repayment of the loan. You should review your note for details.
☒ does not have a demand feature.

Late Payment
If your payment is more than *15* days late, your lender will charge a late fee of *5% of the monthly principal and interest payment.*

Negative Amortization (Increase in Loan Amount)
Under your loan terms, you
☐ are scheduled to make monthly payments that do not pay all of the interest due that month. As a result, your loan amount will increase (negatively amortize), and your loan amount will likely become larger than your original loan amount. Increases in your loan amount lower the equity you have in this property.
☐ may have monthly payments that do not pay all of the interest due that month. If you do, your loan amount will increase (negatively amortize), and, as a result, your loan amount may become larger than your original loan amount. Increases in your loan amount lower the equity you have in this property.
☒ do not have a negative amortization feature.

Partial Payments
Your lender
☒ may accept payments that are less than the full amount due (partial payments) and apply them to your loan.
☐ may hold them in a separate account until you pay the rest of the payment, and then apply the full payment to your loan.
☐ does not accept any partial payments.
If this loan is sold, your new lender may have a different policy.

Security Interest
You are granting a security interest in
456 Somewhere Ave., Anytown, ST 12345

You may lose this property if you do not make your payments or satisfy other obligations for this loan.

Escrow Account
For now, your loan
☒ will have an escrow account (also called an "impound" or "trust" account) to pay the property costs listed below. Without an escrow account, you would pay them directly, possibly in one or two large payments a year. Your lender may be liable for penalties and interest for failing to make a payment.

Escrow		
Escrowed Property Costs over Year 1	$2,473.56	Estimated total amount over year 1 for your escrowed property costs: *Homeowner's Insurance* *Property Taxes*
Non-Escrowed Property Costs over Year 1	$1,800.00	Estimated total amount over year 1 for your non-escrowed property costs: *Homeowner's Association Dues* You may have other property costs.
Initial Escrow Payment	$412.25	A cushion for the escrow account you pay at closing. See Section G on page 2.
Monthly Escrow Payment	$206.13	The amount included in your total monthly payment.

☐ will not have an escrow account because ☐ you declined it ☐ your lender does not offer one. You must directly pay your property costs, such as taxes and homeowner's insurance. Contact your lender to ask if your loan can have an escrow account.

No Escrow		
Estimated Property Costs over Year 1		Estimated total amount over year 1. You must pay these costs directly, possibly in one or two large payments a year.
Escrow Waiver Fee		

In the future,
Your property costs may change and, as a result, your escrow payment may change. You may be able to cancel your escrow account, but if you do, you must pay your property costs directly. If you fail to pay your property taxes, your state or local government may (1) impose fines and penalties or (2) place a tax lien on this property. If you fail to pay any of your property costs, your lender may (1) add the amounts to your loan balance, (2) add an escrow account to your loan, or (3) require you to pay for property insurance that the lender buys on your behalf, which likely would cost more and provide fewer benefits than what you could buy on your own.

Sample H-25 Closing Disclosure, Page 5

Loan Calculations

Total of Payments. Total you will have paid after you make all payments of principal, interest, mortgage insurance, and loan costs, as scheduled.	$285,803.36
Finance Charge. The dollar amount the loan will cost you.	$118,830.27
Amount Financed. The loan amount available after paying your upfront finance charge.	$162,000.00
Annual Percentage Rate (APR). Your costs over the loan term expressed as a rate. This is not your interest rate.	4.174%
Total Interest Percentage (TIP). The total amount of interest that you will pay over the loan term as a percentage of your loan amount.	69.46%

Questions? If you have questions about the loan terms or costs on this form, use the contact information below. To get more information or make a complaint, contact the Consumer Financial Protection Bureau at **www.consumerfinance.gov/mortgage-closing**

Other Disclosures

Appraisal
If the property was appraised for your loan, your lender is required to give you a copy at no additional cost at least 3 days before closing. If you have not yet received it, please contact your lender at the information listed below.

Contract Details
See your note and security instrument for information about
- what happens if you fail to make your payments,
- what is a default on the loan,
- situations in which your lender can require early repayment of the loan, and
- the rules for making payments before they are due.

Liability after Foreclosure
If your lender forecloses on this property and the foreclosure does not cover the amount of unpaid balance on this loan,

☒ state law may protect you from liability for the unpaid balance. If you refinance or take on any additional debt on this property, you may lose this protection and have to pay any debt remaining even after foreclosure. You may want to consult a lawyer for more information.

☐ state law does not protect you from liability for the unpaid balance.

Refinance
Refinancing this loan will depend on your future financial situation, the property value, and market conditions. You may not be able to refinance this loan.

Tax Deductions
If you borrow more than this property is worth, the interest on the loan amount above this property's fair market value is not deductible from your federal income taxes. You should consult a tax advisor for more information.

Contact Information

	Lender	Mortgage Broker	Real Estate Broker (B)	Real Estate Broker (S)	Settlement Agent
Name	Ficus Bank		Omega Real Estate Broker Inc.	Alpha Real Estate Broker Co.	Epsilon Title Co.
Address	4321 Random Blvd. Somecity, ST 12340		789 Local Lane Sometown, ST 12345	987 Suburb Ct. Someplace, ST 12340	123 Commerce Pl. Somecity, ST 12344
NMLS ID					
ST License ID			Z765416	Z61456	Z61616
Contact	Joe Smith		Samuel Green	Joseph Cain	Sarah Arnold
Contact NMLS ID	12345				
Contact ST License ID			P16415	P51461	PT1234
Email	joesmith@ficusbank.com		sam@omegare.biz	joe@alphare.biz	sarah@epsilontitle.com
Phone	123-456-7890		123-555-1717	321-555-7171	987-555-4321

Confirm Receipt

By signing, you are only confirming that you have received this form. You do not have to accept this loan because you have signed or received this form.

Applicant Signature Date Co-Applicant Signature Date

CLOSING DISCLOSURE PAGE 5 OF 5 • LOAN ID # 123456789

Reporting Requirements

Who must report

The Tax Reform Act of 1986 requires that persons designated by the act as "real estate brokers" must report a closed real estate transaction to the Internal Revenue Service and provide the information contained in the report to each party to the transaction. The act defines "real estate broker" as any of the following:

- the seller's broker
- the buyer's broker
- the settlement agent, escrow agent, attorney, title company or other party responsible for closing the transaction
- the mortgage lender
- anyone so designated by the Internal Revenue Service

What must be filed

The person reporting files a Form 1099-S information return with the Internal Revenue Service. This form includes the names and addresses of the parties to the transaction and information about the sale proceeds.

The reporting person also provides each party to the transaction with a written statement showing the name and address of the reporting party as well as the information reported in the 1099.

If the transaction involves a non-resident alien, the reporting person may also have tax reporting and withholding responsibilities under the Foreign Investment and Real Property Tax Act of 1980 (FIRPTA), the Deficit Reduction Act of 1984 (DEFRA), and/or the Branch Profits Tax and Technical and Miscellaneous Revenue Act of 1988 (TAMRA).

VI. Types of Financing

Types of Real Estate Loans

Conventional loans

A **conventional mortgage** loan is a permanent long-term loan that is not FHA-insured or VA-guaranteed. Market rates usually determine the interest rate on the loan. Because of the lack of insurance or guarantee by a government agency, the risk to a lender is greater for a conventional loan than for a non-conventional loan. This risk is usually reflected in higher interest rates and stricter requirements for the down payment and the borrower's income qualification. At the same time, conventional loans allow greater flexibility in fees, rates, and terms than do insured and guaranteed loans.

The primary sources of conventional loans are banks and savings and loan associations. Other conventional lenders include credit unions, life insurance companies, pension funds, mortgage bankers, and private individuals. Various types of lenders specialize in mortgage lending for specific purposes and type of borrower, such as commercial, construction, or single-family residential loans.

FHA-insured loans

The Federal Housing Administration (FHA) is an agency of the Department of Housing and Urban Development (HUD). It does not lend money, but *insures* permanent long-term loans made by others. The lender must be approved by the FHA, and the borrower must meet certain FHA qualifications. In addition, the property used to secure the loan must meet FHA standards. The FHA insures that the lender will not suffer significant loss in the case of borrower default. To provide this security, FHA provides insurance and charges the borrower an insurance premium. FHA loans typically have a higher loan-to-value ratio than conventional loans, enabling a borrower to make a smaller down payment.

The basic FHA-insured loan program is the **Title II, Section 203(b)** program for loans on one- to four-family residential properties. Among the features of this program are the following.

FHA mortgage insurance. The FHA determines how much mortgage insurance must be provided and charges the borrower an appropriate mortgage insurance premium (MIP). The initial premium is payable at closing or is added to the borrower's loan balance and financed. Further annual premiums are charged monthly. The amount of the premium varies according to the loan term and the applicable loan-to-value ratio.

Borrower default. The FHA reimburses the lender for losses due to default by the borrower, including costs of foreclosure.

Appraisal. The property must be appraised by an FHA-approved appraiser. The property must also meet the FHA's standards for type and quality of construction, neighborhood quality, and other features.

Maximum loan amount. The FHA has set maximum loan amounts for over 80 regions. Borrowers within a region are limited to the loan ceiling amount in effect for the region. In addition, the maximum loan amount is restricted by the loan-to-value ratios in effect. The maximum FHA-backed loan a borrower can obtain will be the lesser of the regional ceiling amount or the amount dictated by the loan-to-value standard. Calculations are based on the lesser of sale price or appraised value.

Down payment requirement. The minimum down payment for an FHA-backed loan is based on the lower of the appraised value or the sales price. The present requirement for single-family residential loans is 3.5%.

Maximum loan term. Thirty years is the maximum length of the repayment period.
Prepayment privilege. The borrower has the right to pay off the loan at any time without penalty, provided the lender is given prior notice. The lender may charge up to 30 days' interest if the borrower provides less than 30 days' notice.

Assumability. FHA-backed loans on owner-occupied properties are assumable if the buyer is qualified. Lenders and borrowers should check with FHA for current requirements.

Interest rate. The lender and borrower negotiate the interest rate on an FHA- backed loan without any involvement by FHA.

Points, fees and costs. The lender may charge discount points, a loan origination fee, and other such charges. These may be paid by buyer or seller. However, if the seller pays more than a specified percentage of the costs normally paid by a buyer, the FHA may regard these as sales concessions and lower the sales price on which the loan insurance amount is based.
In addition to Section 203(b) loan programs, FHA offers insurance coverage for other loan products. These include:

- home improvement loans
- subsidized loans for low- and middle-income families
- loans for condominiums
- loans for multi-family projects
- graduated-payment loans
- adjustable-rate loans

VA-guaranteed loans

The Department of Veterans Affairs (formerly Veterans Administration) offers *loan guarantees to qualified veterans*. The VA, like the FHA, does not lend money except in certain areas where other financing is not generally available. Instead, the VA partially guarantees permanent long-term loans originated by VA-approved lenders on properties that meet VA standards. The VA's guarantee enables lenders to issue loans with higher loan-to-value ratios than would otherwise be possible. The interest rate on a VA-guaranteed loan is usually lower than one on a conventional loan. The borrower does not pay any premium for the loan guarantee, but does pay a VA funding fee at closing.

Borrower default. The VA reimburses the lender for losses up to the guaranteed amount if foreclosure sale proceeds fail to cover the loan balance.

Appraisal. The property must be appraised by a VA-approved appraiser. The VA issues a *Certificate of Reasonable Value* which creates a maximum value on which the VA-guaranteed portion of the loan will be based. The property must meet certain VA specifications.

Down payment requirement. The VA usually requires no down payment, although the lender may require one.

Maximum loan amount. The VA does not cap the loan amount, but it does limit the liability it can assume, which usually influences the amount an institution will lend. The amount a qualified veteran with full entitlement can borrow without making a downpayment determines the practical loan limits. This amount varies by county. The basic entitlement available to each eligible veteran is $36,000. Lenders will generally lend a maximum of 4 times that amount without a down payment if the veteran is fully qualified and the property appraises for the asking price.

A veteran must apply for a *Certificate of Eligibility* to find out how much the VA will guarantee in a particular situation.

Maximum loan term. The maximum loan term for one- to four-family residences is 30 years. For loans secured by farms, the maximum loan term is 40 years.

Prepayment privilege. The loan may be paid off early without penalty.

Assumability. VA loans are assumable with lender approval. Usually, the person assuming the loan must have VA eligibility, and the assumption may have to be approved by the VA.

Interest rate. Lender and borrower negotiate the interest rate for all VA-insured loans.

Points, fees and costs. The lender may charge discount points, origination fees, and other reasonable costs. These may be paid by seller (with some limits) or buyer, but may not be financed. The VA funding fee, however, may be included in the loan amount. The funding fee is a percentage of the loan amount which varies based on the type of loan, military category, whether the loan is a first-time loan, and whether there is a down payment.

Other VA programs. In addition to insuring loans to veterans, the VA may insure loans for lenders who set up a special account with the VA. The VA may also actually lend money directly when an eligible veteran cannot find other mortgage money locally.

Common loan structures

Variations in the structure of interest rate, term, payments, and principal payback produce a number of commonly recognized loan types. Among these are the following.

Amortizing loan. Amortization provides for gradual repayment of principal and payment of interest over the term of the loan. The borrower's periodic payments to the lender include a portion for interest and a portion for principal. In a fully amortizing mortgage, the principal balance is zero at the end of the term. In a partially amortizing loan, the payments are not sufficient to retire the debt. At the end of the loan term, there is still a principal balance to be paid off.

Negatively amortized loan. Negative amortization causes the loan balance to increase over the term. This occurs if the borrower's periodic payment is insufficient to cover the interest owed for the period. The lender adds the amount of unpaid interest to the borrower's loan balance. Temporary negative amortization occurs on graduated payment loans, and may occur on an adjustable rate mortgage.

Adjustable and fixed rate loans. Loans may have fixed or variable rates of interest over the loan term. Adjustable rate mortgages (ARMs) allow the lender to change the interest rate at specified intervals and by a specified amount. Federal regulations place limits, called rate caps, on incremental interest rate increases and on the total amount by which the rate may be increased over the loan term.

Senior and junior loans. When there are multiple loans on a single property, there is an order of priority in the liens which the mortgages create. The first, or senior, loan generally has priority over any subsequent loans. Second loans are riskier than first loans because the senior lender will be satisfied first in case of default. Therefore, interest rates on second mortgages are generally higher than on first mortgages.

Fixed and graduated payment loans. Loans may have variable payment amounts over the term of the loan, or a single fixed payment amount. With a graduated payment mortgage, the payments at the beginning of the loan term are not sufficient to amortize the loan fully, and unpaid interest is added to the principal balance. Payments are later adjusted to a level that will fully amortize the loan's increased balance over the remaining loan term.

Interest-only loan. In an interest-only loan, periodic payments over the loan term apply only to interest owed, not to principal. At the end of the term, the full balance must be paid off in a lump-sum, "balloon" payment. Since these loans have no periodic principal payback, their monthly payments are smaller than amortizing loans for the same amount at the same rate of interest.

Buydown loan. A buydown loan entails a prepayment of interest on a loan. The prepayment effectively lowers the interest rate and the periodic payments for the borrower. Buydowns typically occur in a circumstance where a builder wants to market a new development to a buyer who cannot quite qualify for the necessary loan at market rates. By "buying down" a borrower's mortgage, a builder enables the borrower to obtain the loan. The builder may then pass the costs of the buydown through to the buyer in the form of a higher purchase price.

Seller financing

The seller may provide some or all of the financing for the buyer's purchase. Some of the most common methods of seller financing are purchase money mortgages, including the wraparound, and the contract for deed.

Purchase money mortgage. With a purchase money mortgage, the borrower gives a mortgage and note to the seller to finance some or all of the purchase price of the property. The seller in this case is said to "take back" a note, or to "carry paper," on the property. Purchase money mortgages may be either senior or junior liens.

Wraparound. In a wraparound loan arrangement, the seller receives a junior mortgage from the buyer, and uses the buyer's payments to make the payments on the original first mortgage. A wraparound enables the buyer to obtain financing
with a minimum cash investment. It also potentially enables the seller to profit from any difference between a lower interest rate on the senior loan and a higher rate on the wraparound loan. A wraparound is possible only if the senior mortgagee allows it.

Contract for deed. Under a contract for deed arrangement, the seller retains title and the buyer receives possession and equitable title while making payments under the terms of the contract. The seller conveys title when the contract has been fully performed.

Special-purpose loans

Home equity loan. The ostensible purpose of this type of loan is to obtain funds for home improvement. Structurally, the home equity loan is a junior mortgage secured by the homeowner's equity, **equity** in general being the portion of the property's value actually owned by the homeowner, expressed as the difference between the property's market value and all loan balances outstanding on the property.

For some lenders, the maximum home equity loan amount is based on the difference between the property's appraised value and the maximum loan-to-value ratio the lender allows on the property, inclusive of all existing mortgage loans. Thus if a home is appraised at $500,000 and the lender's maximum LTV is 80%, the lender will lend a total of $400,000. If the owner's existing mortgage balance is $325,000, the owner would qualify for a $75,000 home equity loan.

Package loan. A package loan finances the purchase of real estate and personal property. For example, a package loan might finance a furnished condominium, complete with all fixtures and decor.

Construction loan. A construction loan finances construction of improvements. This type of loan is paid out by the lender in installments linked to stages of the construction process. The loan is usually interest-only, and the borrower makes periodic payments based on the amount disbursed so far. As short-term, high-risk financing, the interest rates are usually higher than those for long-term financing. The borrower is expected to find permanent ("take out") financing elsewhere to pay off the temporary loan when construction is complete.

Bridge loan. A bridge, or gap, loan is used to cover a gap in financing between short-term construction financing and long-term permanent financing. For instance, a developer may have difficulty finding a long-term lender to take out the construction lender. However, as the construction loan is expensive and must be paid off as soon as possible, the developer may find an interim lender who will pay off the construction loan but not agree to a long-term loan.

Participation loan. In a participation loan, the lender participates in the income and/or equity of the property, in return for giving the borrower more favorable loan terms than would otherwise be justified. For instance, the borrower makes smaller periodic payments than the interest rate and loan amount require, and the lender makes up the difference by receiving some of the property's income. This type of loan usually involves an income property.

Permanent (take-out) loan. A permanent loan is a long-term loan that "takes out" a construction or short-term lender. The long-term lender pays off the balance on the construction loan when the project is completed, leaving the borrower with a long-term loan under more favorable terms than the construction loan offered.

Reverse annuity. In a reverse annuity mortgage, a homeowner pledges the equity in the home as security for a loan which is paid out in regular monthly amounts over the term of the loan. The homeowner, in effect, is able to convert the equity to cash without losing ownership and possession.

Blanket. A blanket mortgage is secured by more than one property, such as multiple parcels of real estate in a development.

MODULE 4 SNAPSHOT REVIEW: COMPLETING THE TRANSACTIONS

I: The Contract for Sale

Legal Characteristics and Enforceability

- A real estate sale contract is a binding agreement in which the vendee agrees to buy and the vendor agrees to sell an identified parcel under specified terms and conditions.
- A sale contract is executory — the parties have yet to perform; it terminates upon successful closing.
- To be enforceable, the contract must be in writing, identify all parties and the property, contain a purchase price, and be signed by the principal parties.
- Both spouses should sign if the sellers are married to release homestead, dower, and curtesy rights and avoid title encumbrances.
- Either party may assign a sale contract unless the agreement prohibits it; listing agreements, however, are not assignable.
- Brokers may assist with contracts using standard promulgated forms but may not draft new contract language, as doing so constitutes unauthorized practice of law.

Contract Contingencies and Default

- A contingency is a condition that must be met before the contract becomes enforceable; the most common is a financing contingency.
- Contingencies must be explicit, include an expiration date, and require diligence to fulfill; vague or open-ended contingencies can invalidate the contract.
- Failure to meet a contingency does not constitute default — it entitles the parties to cancel and return to their original positions.
- If a buyer defaults, the seller may seek liquidated damages, typically the earnest money deposit, provided it is not grossly excessive.
- If a seller defaults, the buyer may sue for specific performance, damages, or cancellation.

II: Offer and Acceptance

- A contract is formed when the offeree gives the offeror unequivocal notice of acceptance of all terms without any changes.
- Any change to the terms of an offer creates a counteroffer and voids the original offer; the original offeree becomes the new offeror.
- An offeror may revoke an offer at any time before the offeree has communicated acceptance.
- An offer may terminate by acceptance, rejection, revocation, lapse of time, counteroffer, or the death or insanity of either party.
- If the offeree pays consideration to keep an offer open and the offeror accepts, an option is created, removing the offeror's right to revoke.
- If acceptance is communicated by mail, the offer is considered accepted as soon as it is placed in the mail.

III: Borrower Qualification

Assets, Liabilities, and Income

- Lenders evaluate liquid assets, which are readily convertible to cash, and fixed assets, which are not; funds must typically be seasoned for at least 60 days.
- Common liabilities include existing mortgages, installment loans, revolving credit, alimony, and child support; contingent liabilities on co-signed loans may be excluded if documented.
- Income must generally be verifiable for at least two years; variable income such as commissions uses a two-year average.
- Income with a defined expiration, such as child support or alimony, must be expected to continue for at least three years after closing.
- Non-taxable income may be grossed up by 115% to 125% to reflect its tax-free nature.

Qualifying Ratios and Federal Requirements

- The Housing Ratio (front-end) compares PITI to gross monthly income and generally should not exceed 28% to 31%.
- The DTI Ratio (back-end) compares all recurring monthly debts to gross monthly income and generally should not exceed 33% to 43%.
- The LTV Ratio compares the loan amount to the lower of the appraised value or purchase price; an LTV over 80% on a conventional loan usually requires private mortgage insurance (PMI).
- The Dodd-Frank Act requires lenders to evaluate a borrower's ability to repay (ATR); Qualified Mortgages (QM) meeting ATR standards receive Safe Harbor legal protection.
- ATR rules prohibit balloon payments, negative amortization, no-documentation loans, and interest-only periods beyond five years.
- Loan flipping or churning — repeated refinancing without a tangible net benefit to the borrower — constitutes loan fraud.

IV: Earnest Money

- The designated broker and branch manager are responsible for managing all trust and escrow accounts and ensuring compliance with Missouri regulations.
- Licensees must promptly deliver trust funds to the broker; the broker must deposit funds within ten banking days of all parties signing and initialing the contract.
- Brokerage firms may not commingle personal or operating funds with trust funds, and may not convert trust funds for personal use.
- If an earnest money dispute arises after a transaction terminates, the broker retains the deposit until all parties sign a written release or a civil action is filed.
- If no written release or civil action is received within 60 days of the dispute, the broker may disburse funds after giving all parties 15 days written notice.
- Licensees may not accept non-cash earnest money such as promissory notes without the seller's written permission.

V: Closing Costs and Settlement

The Closing Event and RESPA

- The closing is the culmination of the transaction; the buyer receives title, the seller receives the purchase price, and all taxes, fees, and charges are settled.

- RESPA is a federal consumer protection law that applies to residential transactions financed by federally-related mortgage loans; it prohibits kickbacks and referral fees when no services are rendered.
- Under TRID, the Loan Estimate must be delivered within three business days of application; the Closing Disclosure must be provided at least three business days before consummation.
- The seller must provide evidence of marketable title, clear any liens, and execute an affidavit of title if required; the buyer should conduct a final walk-through before closing.

Debits, Credits, and Prorations

- A debit is an amount a party must pay; a credit is an amount a party receives; the excess of buyer debits over credits equals the cash the buyer must bring to closing.
- Non-prorated items are paid by one party only; buyers typically pay mortgage recording fees, loan origination fees, and impound reserves, while sellers typically pay the brokerage commission and transfer taxes.
- Prorated items are shared between buyer and seller; common examples include real estate taxes (paid in arrears) and prepaid utilities or rent received in advance.
- The 12-month/30-day method uses a 360-day year and 30-day month; the 365-day method uses actual calendar days; either may apply depending on the item and local custom.
- By custom, the seller owns the property through the day of closing, so the closing day is charged to the seller in proration calculations.

VI: Types of Real Estate Financing

Government-Backed and Conventional Loans

- Conventional loans are not government-insured or guaranteed; they carry greater lender risk and typically require stricter income and down payment standards.
- FHA loans are insured by the Federal Housing Administration; they require a minimum 3.5% down payment and mortgage insurance premiums, and are assumable with lender approval.
- VA-guaranteed loans are available to qualified veterans; they typically require no down payment, carry lower interest rates, and require a VA funding fee rather than mortgage insurance.
- Both FHA and VA loans require properties to be appraised by agency-approved appraisers and to meet specific property standards.

Common Loan Structures and Special-Purpose Loans

- Fully amortizing loans retire the principal balance entirely by the end of the term; partially amortizing loans leave a remaining balance.
- Adjustable rate mortgages (ARMs) allow the lender to change the interest rate at specified intervals, subject to federal rate caps.
- Interest-only loans apply payments exclusively to interest; the full principal balance is due as a balloon payment at the end of the term.
- Seller financing options include purchase money mortgages, wraparound loans, and contracts for deed, in which the seller retains title until the contract is fully performed.
- Special-purpose loans include home equity loans, construction loans, bridge loans, participation loans, reverse annuity mortgages, and blanket mortgages, each designed for a specific financing need.
- A buydown loan involves a prepayment of interest to lower the rate and payment; builders often use buydowns to help buyers qualify for financing at market rates.

MODULE 4 QUIZ: COMPLETING THE TRANSACTION

1. What is the correct term for a buyer in a real estate sale contract?

a. Vendee
b. Vendor
c. Optionee
d. Mortgagor

2. A real estate sale contract is described as executory because:

a. It has been fully performed by both parties at the time of signing
b. Only the seller is required to perform any remaining obligations
c. It must be executed in front of a notary to be enforceable
d. The parties have yet to fulfill their respective obligations and promises

3. When a married couple sells their home, both spouses should sign the sale contract primarily to ensure that:

a. Both spouses release homestead, dower, and curtesy rights to the buyer at closing
b. The contract satisfies the consideration requirement under Missouri law
c. The contract is exempt from the Statute of Frauds
d. The earnest money deposit is held jointly in both spouses' names

4. A well-written contract contingency should include all of the following EXCEPT:

a. An expiration date
b. A requirement that the party diligently try to fulfill the condition
c. Explicit and clear language describing the condition
d. A clause allowing either party to cancel for any reason at any time

5. If a seller defaults under a sale contract, the buyer's available remedies include:

a. Specific performance, damages, or cancellation
b. Forfeiture of the seller's earnest money deposit only
c. Forfeiture of the buyer's deposit as liquidated damages
d. Filing a complaint with the Missouri Real Estate Commission only

6. Under what circumstance does an offer legally become a binding contract?

a. When the offeror delivers the written offer to the offeree
b. When the offeree signs the offer document regardless of whether any changes are made
c. When the earnest money deposit is received by the escrow holder
d. When the offeree communicates unconditional acceptance of all terms to the offeror

7. A buyer mails an acceptance of a seller's counteroffer on Monday afternoon. When is the acceptance legally communicated?

a. When the seller receives the envelope in the mail
b. When the seller opens and reads the letter
c. When both parties' brokers confirm the acceptance in writing
d. When the buyer places the acceptance in the mail

8. A seller receives a buyer's offer, strikes out the closing date, writes in a new one, initials the change, and sends it back. The legal effect of this action is:

a. The seller's change creates a counteroffer and voids the original offer
b. The buyer's original offer becomes binding with the amended closing date
c. Both parties are bound to the contract but may negotiate the closing date separately
d. The change is invalid and the original closing date controls

9. Which of the following correctly describes an option in a real estate transaction?

a. An agreement created when the offeree pays consideration to keep an offer open for a stated period
b. A contingency that allows the buyer to withdraw at any time without penalty
c. A broker's right to extend the listing agreement without the seller's consent
d. A lender's right to call the loan due upon transfer of the property

10. A licensee who drafts original contract language for a client rather than using an approved standard form risks:

a. Violating the NAR Code of Ethics by providing legal advice
b. Violating RESPA's prohibition against referral fees
c. Exceeding the scope of a buyer's agency agreement
d. Engaging in the unauthorized practice of law and exposing themselves to client lawsuits

11. Which income source is generally NOT acceptable for mortgage qualification?

a. Rental income from an investment property, properly documented
b. Social Security disability benefits
c. Unemployment benefits received after a layoff or termination
d. Self-employment income documented with two years of tax returns

12. When a lender grosses up a borrower's non-taxable income by 115% to 125%, the purpose is to:

a. Penalize the borrower for having non-traditional income sources
b. Meet the Qualified Mortgage requirement for income documentation
c. Reduce the borrower's DTI ratio below the lender's threshold
d. Reflect the income's tax-free nature so it can be compared fairly to taxable income

13. A borrower earns $7,000 per month in gross income. Monthly PITI is $1,890. What is the borrower's Housing Ratio?

a. 27%
b. 24%
c. 31%
d. 33%

14. The DTI ratio calculation excludes which of the following monthly expenses?

a. Student loan payments
b. Court-ordered child support
c. Monthly grocery and utility bills
d. Credit card minimum payments

15. The practice of repeatedly refinancing a borrower's loan without providing a tangible net benefit is known as:

a. Negative amortization
b. Loan churning or loan flipping
c. Predatory overfinancing
d. Yield spread premium abuse

16. A licensee receives an earnest money check before any contract has been written or signed. Under Missouri regulations, the broker may deposit these funds only if:

a. The funds are returned to the buyer until the contract is fully executed
b. Written permission is obtained from the person providing the funds
c. The funds are held in the licensee's personal account until contract execution
d. The seller has also signed a written consent form authorizing the deposit

17. After a transaction terminates in dispute and 60 days pass without a written release or civil action, the broker may disburse the earnest money only after:

a. Consulting with the Missouri Real Estate Commission for disbursement instructions
b. Returning the full amount to the buyer as the non-performing party
c. Making a good-faith determination of breach and giving all parties 15 days' written notice
d. Obtaining a court order authorizing the disbursement

18. Interest earned on a brokerage escrow account must be disbursed no later than:

a. Five banking days after the close of the transaction
b. Ten banking days after receiving the next bank statement
c. Thirty days after the end of the calendar quarter
d. The next scheduled closing involving that client

19. RESPA's prohibition on referral fees and kickbacks is best illustrated by which of the following?

a. A commission split between cooperating brokers for services actually rendered
b. A fee paid to a title company for a referral when no actual title service is performed
c. An origination fee disclosed on the Loan Estimate
d. An attorney's fee for representing a client at the closing table

20. Under the TRID rule, the Closing Disclosure must be received by the consumer at least how many business days before loan consummation?

a. One business day
b. Two business days
c. Three business days
d. Five business days

21. On a closing statement, which item is typically a debit to the seller?

a. The purchase price of the property
b. The buyer's earnest money deposit already paid
c. The brokerage commission owed at closing
d. The new mortgage loan proceeds

22. Using the 12-month/30-day proration method, a property closes on June 10. Annual real estate taxes paid in arrears are $2,160. What is the seller's prorated share?

a. $970.00
b. $984.00
c. $1,020.00
d. $1,080.00

23. Which statement about VA-guaranteed loans is correct?

a. The VA lends money directly to all qualified veterans in every market
b. The borrower pays a mortgage insurance premium instead of a funding fee
c. The VA usually requires no down payment, though the lender may require one
d. The VA sets the interest rate on all VA-guaranteed loans

24. A home equity loan is best described as:

a. A first mortgage used to purchase a primary residence with a low down payment
b. A junior mortgage secured by the homeowner's equity in the property
c. A government-backed loan program for home improvement projects only
d. An interest-only construction loan paid out in stages during renovation

25. In a wraparound loan arrangement, the seller:

a. Pays off the original first mortgage and replaces it with a new senior lien
b. Receives a junior mortgage from the buyer and uses those payments to service the original first mortgage
c. Transfers legal title to the buyer immediately while retaining equitable title as security
d. Assigns the original mortgage to the buyer with full lender approval required

MODULE 4 CASE STUDY:

Completing the Transaction

The Hadley Transaction

Scenario

Marcus and Elena Hadley have accepted an offer on their home listed at $315,000. The buyers, Jerome and Tanya Osgood, submitted an offer of $308,000 with a $6,000 earnest money deposit. Their agent, Rosa, collected the earnest money check on a Friday afternoon after the sellers signed the contract. Rosa planned to deliver the check to her broker on Monday morning. The contract included a financing contingency requiring the buyers to secure loan approval within 21 days.

During the loan application process, the underwriter discovered that Jerome had a co-signed auto loan that he had not disclosed on his mortgage application. His stated DTI was 38%, but with the co-signed debt included it rises to 46%. The lender also noted that a $12,000 deposit appeared in Jerome's checking account just nine days before the application date.

On Day 19 of the contingency period, the buyers notified their agent that they could not obtain financing on the terms specified. The sellers, believing the buyers simply changed their minds, refused to release the earnest money. The dispute has now been unresolved for 45 days.

Discussion Questions

1. Rosa collected the earnest money on a Friday and planned to deliver it to her broker the following Monday. Did Rosa handle the trust funds correctly under Missouri regulations? What specific rule applies, and what obligation does the broker have once the funds are received?

____

____

____

____

2. The underwriter found an undisclosed co-signed auto loan that pushed Jerome's DTI from 38% to 46%. What obligation does the loan originator have when undisclosed debt is discovered? How does the concept of a Qualified Mortgage and the Safe Harbor provision factor into this situation?

____

____

____

____

3. The $12,000 deposit that appeared in Jerome's account nine days before application is likely to be flagged by the lender. What concept applies here, and how does it affect the borrower's ability to use those funds toward the purchase?

____
____
____
____

4. The buyers gave timely notice of their inability to obtain financing within the contingency period, but the sellers are refusing to release the earnest money after 45 days of dispute. Under Missouri regulations, what options are now available to the broker? What steps must the broker take before disbursing the funds unilaterally?

____
____
____
____

Module 5: ETHICS AND STANDARDS OF CONDUCT

I. NAR Code of Ethics
II. Cooperating with Other Licensees
III. Compensation

Module 5 Learning Objectives

NAR Code of Ethics

1. Explain the duties a REALTOR® owes to other REALTORS®.
2. Define and differentiate between mediation, arbitration, and the Ombudsman program.
3. Understand the Code of Ethics.
4. Identify the penalties for violating the Code of Ethics.
5. Summarize the overriding thesis of the Pathway to Professionalism.

Cooperating with Other Licensees

1. Explain the Missouri licensee's obligation to cooperate with other brokers under NAR Code of Ethics Article 3, including the distinction between cooperation and compensation, and the specific duties that arise when working on cooperative transactions.

Compensation

1. Explain how broker compensation is structured and negotiated in Missouri real estate transactions.
2. Identify Missouri license law restrictions on compensation practices.

I. NAR Code of Ethics

REALTORS® Code of Ethics

A set of rules and conduct members must practice in their dealings with others. These standards lay out the values of an organization.

Definitions

Business ethics. The standards used by a business or company to make decisions and how they treat their Clients, Customers, Vendors, and Employees.

Client. An individual in which we have a fiduciary relationship, such as a Single Agency Relationship.

Code of Ethics. A set of rules and conduct members must practice in their dealings with others. These standards lay out the values of an organization.

Customer. An individual with whom we do not have a fiduciary relationship and owe limited disclosure, such as a Transaction Brokerage Relationship.

Ethics. A system of moral principles, rules, an individual or business uses to determine how they deal with others.

Morals. A person's individual belief of what is right and wrong; religion, culture, and many other factors influence a person's morals.

Preamble. The opening statement of a document reflecting the values or vision of the organization.

Situational Ethics. A person changing their ethical views to fit a specific situation or changing how they react due to a change in circumstance.

Demographic information. Information gathered on customers or clients. May include information such as age, sex, race, color, or national origin. This information is collected only to assist in operating the brokerage and identifying advertising avenues, not discriminating against anyone in a protected class.

Professional services. The eight professional services a REALTOR® may perform are advertising, buying, auctioning, renting, selling, appraising, leasing, and exchanging.

NAR's protected classes. The NAR Code of Ethics' protected classes include race, color, religion, sex, disability, familial status, national origin, sexual orientation, and gender identity.

Duties to the public. The third section of NAR's Code of Ethics covers how REALTORS® should behave when interacting with the public. Articles 10 to 14 and their Standards of Practices identify specific behavior and guidelines for dealing with the public. This section restates many of the same ideas expressed in Articles 1 through 9; however, it explicitly identifies the duties owed to members of the public.

Arbitration. A voluntary process where an independent third party listens to the individuals involved in the dispute and makes a binding decision on who is the winner.

Mediation. A voluntary process where an independent third person helps the parties agree to resolve their dispute. Mediation is considered a win-win option; the idea is that both sides will walk out feeling they got something from the mediation. In 90 days, if no resolution is met, the parties must move on to another dispute resolution method, preferably arbitration.

Ombudsman. A voluntary process where an individual appointed by a local Board of REALTORS® receives assistance to resolve disputes through constructive communication and advocating for consensus and understanding.

Procuring cause. The agent who starts the uninterrupted chain of events leading to the sale or rental of a listing.

Public trust. Public trust refers to misappropriation of client or customer funds or property, discrimination against the protected classes under the Code of Ethics, or fraud.

Duties to REALTORS® The fourth section of NAR's Code of Ethics covers how REALTORS® should behave when interacting with other REALTORS®· Articles 15 to 17 and their Standards of Practice identify specific behavior and guidelines for dealing with other REALTORS®· This section restates many of the same ideas expressed in Articles 1 through 14; however, it explicitly identifies the duties owed to NAR members.

National Association of REALTORS® Code of Ethics

Historical abstract

In the early 1900s, real estate agents were given licenses by county judges, and often they were "peddlers" licenses. The 1900s was a time of land scams and speculation. In 1908, the National Association of REALTORS® (NAR) formed to eliminate the notion of "Caveat emptor" or let the buyer beware. Their goal was to protect the public and promote homeownership in the United States.

In 1913, NAR introduced the Code of Ethics for REALTORS®® to follow in their dealings with their clients, the public, and other REALTORS®· This document has been fluid and ever-changing over the years. Today, REALTORS® have one of the strongest professional Code of Ethics in the United States.

The Code of Ethics also provides standard practices and procedures setting forth how REALTORS® should react in their dealings with specific individuals and others in their field. The Code of Ethics, however, is not law. Rather, the Code of Ethics enhances local, state, or federal laws.

A quote in the Code of Ethics and Arbitration Manual reads, "Because the Code is a living document and real estate is a dynamic business and profession, the law need never be its substitute. So long as the aspiration to better serve the public remails the underlying concept of the code, it must evolve and grow in significance and importance consonant with but independent of the law."

Structure of the Code of Ethics. The Code of Ethics has four parts:

- The Preamble
- Duties to Clients and Customers (Articles 1 – 9)
- Duties to the Public (Articles 10 – 14)
- Duties to REALTORS® (Articles 15 – 17)

The Articles within the Code of Ethics define the broad statements about the licensee's behavior and duties. The **Standards of Practice**, within each Article, give more specific guidance to the licensee. The Standards of Practice support and interpret the Articles.

In resolving ethics complaints, complainants are to cite only the Article(s) violated and not the Standard of Practice. It will be up to the Professional Standards Committee to give the specific Standard of Practice violated in their final report.

It must be noted that the Code of Ethics contains obligations that may exceed those mandated by law. Should a situation arise where the law and Code of Ethics conflict, the obligations of law must always take precedence.

When reading the Preamble and the Code, the word REALTORS® must be read to also include REALTOR-ASSOCIATE®s.

Preamble

"Under all is the land."

This statement is a powerful start to NAR's Code of Ethics. It means that everything we do, are, or aspire to become begins with the land beneath our feet. The quote shows the importance of the role each REALTOR® holds in our society. Real estate impacts everything.

The Preamble of the Code of Ethics serves as a vision statement on how licensees should conduct themselves and represent their profession to the public. The Preamble calls for REALTORS® to "maintain and improve the standards of their calling." It also states that it is the REALTOR®'s responsibility to "act with integrity and honesty."

The NAR Board of Directors later added that licensees should not dishonor the profession or do anything that will hurt the organization's public trust. The altered Preamble reflects the changes in Article 10 of the Code of Ethics.

Article 1

"When representing a buyer, seller, landlord, tenant, or other client as an agent, REALTORS® pledge themselves to protect and promote the interests of their client. This obligation to the client is primary, but it does not relieve REALTORS® of their obligation to treat all parties honestly. When serving a buyer, seller, landlord, tenant or other party in a non-agency capacity, REALTORS® remain obligated to treat all parties honestly."

Central themes

Article 1 of the Code of Ethics promotes honesty as a critical virtue of any licensee. The 16 Standards of Practice within Article 1 describe the different duties a licensee may have and how they must act in specific situations. The basis of the Standards of Practice is the duties owed to customers and clients based on agency law. Amendments to SP 1-12 and 1-13, effective June 2025, emphasize that broker compensation is fully negotiable.

Article 1 Standards of Practice

The central thrust of Article 1 is reflected in its Standards of Practice 1.1 through 1.16. These are as follows:

SP 1.1 – Be careful to abide by the Code when you are representing yourself in a transaction.
SP 1.2 – The Code of Ethics applies to all transactions.
SP 1.3 – Do not mislead the owner as to the real market value of a piece of property.
SP 1.4 – Do not mislead the savings or benefits of utilizing the services of a REALTOR®.
SP 1.5 – No dual agency. An agent cannot have a fiduciary relationship with both parties in a transaction.
SP 1.6 – Submit all offers and counteroffers promptly.
SP 1.7 – When working as the listing agent, present all offers until closing, unless waived in writing.
SP 1.8 – When working as the buyer's agent, present all offers until contract acceptance, unless waived in writing.
SP 1.9 – Maintain confidentiality even after termination of a relationship.
SP 1.10 – In property management, the licensee must comply with the management agreement and ensure their tenants' rights, safety, and health.
SP 1.11 – Use skill, care, and diligence in all transactions.
SP 1.12 – Listing agreements: Advise sellers and landlords of company's cooperation policy and that broker compensation is fully negotiable and not set by law.
SP 1.13 – Buer-agent agreements: Advise potential clients of company's cooperation policy and that broker compensation is fully negotiable and not set by law.
SP 1.14 – Appraisal fees must not be based on the market value of the property.
SP 1.15 – Disclose any other offers already presented or any expected offers.
SP 1.16 –Listing brokers and property managers may not enter the under any terms and conditions not established by the owner.

Article 1 illustration

A broker was preparing a CMA for a listing appointment. The broker knew the seller was interviewing several other brokers. He decided to increase the property's market value to show the seller how much more money they could earn from hiring him. The violation in this example is of Article 1, Standard Practice 1.3 and 1.4.

Article 2

"REALTORS® shall avoid exaggeration, misrepresentation, or concealment of pertinent facts relating to the property or the transaction. REALTORS® shall not, however, be obligated to discover latent defects in the property, to advise on matters outside the scope of their real estate license, or to disclose facts which are confidential under the scope of agency or non-agency relationships as defined by state law."

Central theme

Article 2 of the Code of Ethics discusses the need for transparency in all transactions. While a licensee is not required to seek out defects in the property, they must disclose any defects they know exists. This duty is necessary no matter the type of agency relationship the broker has established.

Article 2 Standards of Practice

Article 2 has five Standards of Practice:

SP 2.1 – A REALTOR® must disclose any latent defects they know about or that are readily observable to a lay-person. They are not required to be experts in fields other than their own.
SP 2.2 – Moved to Standard of Practice 1.12
SP 2.3 – Moved to Standard of Practice 1.13
SP 2.4 – A REALTOR® must not participate in doctoring the numbers on any contract.
SP 2.5 – REALTORS® must not disclose non-material items not pertinent to the transaction.

Article 2 illustration

Susie is showing a potential buyer a house. The MLS stated that the roof was 25 years old and had a few leaks. During the showing, Susie's customer asked about the condition of the roof. Susie stated she was not aware of any problems. Susie has violated Article 2, Standard 2.1.

Article 3

"REALTORS® shall cooperate with other brokers except when cooperation is not in the client's best interest. The obligation to cooperate does not include the obligation to share commissions, fees, or to otherwise compensate another broker."

Central theme

Article 3 promotes cooperation among brokers unless it is not in their client's best interest. It also addresses compensation negotiation.

Article 3 Standards of Practice

Article 3 has eleven Standards of Practice as follows:

SP 3.1 – REALTORS® must establish terms of cooperation in conjunction with sellers and landlords, including whether compensation is paid or not.
SP 3.2 – Negotiating compensation must not delay or withhold delivery of offers. REALTORS® who change the compensation in a transaction must communicate it to other licensees. Compensation may not unilaterally be changed after an offer has been presented.
SP 3.3 – REALTORS® may change the cooperative compensation.
SP 3.4 – REALTORS® must disclose variable rate commissions.
SP 3.5 – REALTORS® must disclose all pertinent facts before and after the sale.
SP 3.6 - REALTORS® should disclose any current accepted offers.
SP 3.7 – REALTORS® must disclose their status when calling other REALTORS® about a listed property.
SP 3.8 – REALTORS® must not give false information about the availability of property to be shown.
SP 3.9 – Cooperating brokers (and anyone else who is not a listing broker or property manager) must not access or use a listed property in any way other than what is agreed upon by the seller.
SP 3.10 – REALTOR® should share information on listed property and make the property available to other brokers.

SP 3.11 – REALTORS® may not violate Fair Housing laws and refuse to show a piece of property to someone in a protected class.

Article 3 illustration

Janet's seller told her that they did not want to sell their home to anyone who was not white. Janet told potential buyers who were not white that the house was no longer available or was not available to be shown. The violation in this example is of Article 3, Standards of Practice 3.8 and 3.11.

Article 4

"REALTORS® who have a present ownership interest in property for sale or lease, or contemplated interested to purchase or lease property, must disclose in writing the existence of such interest to all parties to the transaction prior to a party signing any agreement."

Central theme.

Article 4 requires REALTORS® to disclose that they have a real estate license when buying or selling property for themselves. If they do not disclose this fact, then they have an unfair advantage over the average consumer. By telling them, the REALTOR® is giving them a chance to obtain representation in the transaction. Thus, keeping it an arm's length transaction.

Article 4 Standards of Practice

Article 4 has two Standards of Practice as follows:

SP 4.1 – REALTORS® must reveal their own ownership interest, as well as ownership of a family member, their own brokerage firm, or an entity in which they have an interest.

SP 4.2 – REALTORS® must only disclose that they have an interest in a property, but not what that interest is.

Article 5

"REALTORS® shall not undertake to provide professional services concerning a property or its value where they have a present or contemplated interest unless such interest is specifically disclosed to all affected parties."

Central theme

Article 5 requires REALTORS® to disclose any conflict of interest before providing any professional services. The only time this would be allowed is with the written permission of all parties involved in providing the service.

Article 5 illustration

ABC Realty shares office space with a lender and a title company. They recommend that all their buyers use these companies since they are in the same location, and it allows them to communicate with the lender and title company to ensure the closing goes smoothly. What the

REALTOR® did not disclose to their customers is the fact that family members own these companies.

Article 6

"REALTORS® shall not accept any commission, rebate, or profit on expenditures made for their client, without the client's knowledge and consent.

When recommending real estate products or services (e.g., homeowner's insurance, warranty programs, mortgage financing, title insurance, etc.), REALTORS® shall disclose to the client or customer to whom the recommendation is made any financial benefits or fees, other than real estate referral fees, the REALTOR® or REALTOR®'s firm may receive as a direct result of such recommendation."

Central theme

Article 6 states a REALTOR® may not accept any compensation in the form of a commission, rebate, kickback, etc., without the client's written consent. This requirement includes gifts from home inspectors, appliance companies, plumbers, etc.

Article 6 illustrated

A REALTOR® hired Ace Home Inspection to inspect a home for a buyer. The REALTOR® did not tell the buyer that he received a $50 gift card for the referral. The REALTOR® violates Article 6 of the Code of Ethics.

Article 7

"In a transaction, REALTORS® shall not accept compensation from more than one party, even if permitted by law, without disclosure to all parties and the informed consent of the REALTOR®'s client or clients."

Central theme

Article 7 states that a REALTOR® cannot accept compensation from more than one person without disclosing the fact to all parties. The REALTOR® should also have that consent in writing.

Article 7 illustrated

A broker has a Buyer's Broker Agreement with a buyer. The agreement states that the broker will get a 3% commission on a home valued at $350,000. The broker finds a home for $300,000 that the buyer likes, and they enter a contract. The broker is getting 3% from the listing broker and then asks the buyer to pay him a 3% commission. The broker tells the buyer he is not getting any commission from the seller's side. This type of action would be a violation of Article 7 of the Code of Conduct. The broker may not receive compensation from more than one party in a transaction unless he has written all the parties' written consent.

Article 8

"REALTORS® shall keep in a special account in an appropriate financial institution, separated from their own funds, monies coming into their possession in trust for other persons, such as escrows, trust funds, clients' monies, and other like items."

Article 8 central themes

Article 8 addresses escrow funds and how to handle other people's money. A Broker must be careful not to commingle funds. Commingle is mixing their personal money with money held in trust for others. The only time commingling is legal is when a Broker puts up to $1,000 of personal funds for a Sales Escrow Account or $5,000 in a Tenant Escrow Account to stop the possibility of conversion.

Article 9

"REALTORS® for the protection of all parties, shall assure whenever possible that all agreements related to real estate transactions including, but not limited to, listing and representation agreements, purchase contracts, and leases are in writing in clear and understandable language expressing the specific terms, conditions, obligations, and commitments of the parties. A copy of each agreement shall be furnished to each party to such agreements upon their signing or initialing."

Central themes

Article 9 states Brokers must ensure all documents related to a real estate transaction be in clear, concise language. The contracts must also clearly represent the terms and conditions of the agreement between the parties.

Article 9 Standards of Practice.

Article 9 has 2 Standards of Practice as follows:

SP 9.1 – REALTORS® should use reasonable care to ensure extensions and amendments.

SP 9.2 – REALTORS® should make a reasonable effort to explain and disclose the different parts of a contract and contract relationships to clients whether this is done in person, electronically, or otherwise.

Article 9 illustrated

Broker Jane is working with a buyer in another state. She sends them an electronic contract and indicates where the buyer needs to sign. Jane does not review the Sales and Purchase Agreement with them or go over any of the disclosures. Upon return of the contract, Jane does not send a copy to the buyer. Broker Jane violates Article 9 of the Code of Articles, which requires brokers to explain contracts to clients when done in person, electronically, or otherwise.

Article 10

"REALTORS® shall not deny equal professional services to any person for reasons of race, color, religion, sex, handicap, familial status, national origin, sexual orientation, or gender identity. REALTORS® shall not be parties to any plan or agreement to discriminate against a person or persons on the basis of race, color, religion, sex, disability, familial status, national origin, sexual orientation, or gender identity."

"REALTORS® in their real estate employment practices, shall not discriminate against any person or persons on the basis of race, color, religion, sex, disability, familial status, national origin, sexual orientation, or gender identity."

Central theme

Article 10 of the Code of Ethics prohibits REALTORS® from discrimination against the protected classes identified in the Code of Ethics.

Article 10 Standards of Practice

Article 10 has 5 Standards of Practice as follows:

SP 10.1 – REALTORS® may provide necessary demographic information of a neighborhood; however, they cannot provide information about the neighborhood's racial, religious, or ethnic composition. This SP specifically emphasizes a prohibition on steering.

SP 10.2 – REALTORS® may gather demographic information; however, they must be careful how the information is used and distributed.

SP 10.3 – REALTORS® should be cautious with any advertisement that indicates a neighborhood's racial or ethnic makeup or targets one of the protected classes.

SP 10.4 –REALTORS® must follow fair employment practices of employees or independent contractors.

SP 10.5 – REALTORS® may not harass someone in one of the protected classes. Harassment refers to any behavior intended to create a hostile, abusive, or intimidating environment.

Amendments to SP 10.5

After extensive research, the Professional Standards Committee recommended changes that effectively broadened the context of Practice 10.5. In the past, the Code of Ethics only covered REALTORS® activities during a real estate transaction. The applicability of the new Standard of Practice 10.5 covers all activities of a REALTOR®.

Under the changes a REALTOR® can be found guilty of a Code of Ethics violation whether the infraction related to a transaction, or other membership-related context. Presently, any potential breach of Article 10 will be looked at individually to see if it is a violation or if it is someone expressing their First Amendment rights.

The new wording of Article 10, SP 10.5 became:

> "REALTORS® must not use harassing speech, hate speech, epithets, or slurs" based upon an individual or group that falls under one of the protected classes."

Further changes were made after a series of meetings in 2025 that considered a more specific definition of "harassment." These came into effect on June 5, 2025, and read as follows:

> *"REALTORS®, in their capacity as real estate professionals, in association with their real estate businesses, or in their real estate-related activities, shall not harass any person or persons based on race, color, religion, sex, disability, familial status, national origin, sexual orientation, or gender identity."*
>
> *"As used in this Code of Ethics, harassment is unwelcome behavior directed at an individual or group based on one or more of the above protected characteristics where the purpose or effect of the behavior is to create a hostile, abusive, or intimidating environment which adversely affects their ability to access equal professional services or employment opportunity."*

Article 10 illustration

A REALTOR® created an advertisement using models and demographic information about a neighborhood's racial makeup. The purpose was primarily to steer specific individuals to a particular community. This action is a violation of Article 10, Standards of Practice 10.1, 10.2 and 10.3.

Article 11

> *"The services which REALTORS® provide to their clients and customers shall conform to the standards of practice and competence which are reasonably expected in the specific real estate disciplines in which they engage; specifically, residential real estate brokerage, real property management, commercial and industrial real estate brokerage, land brokerage, real estate appraisal, real estate counseling, real estate syndication, real estate auction, and international real estate."*

"REALTORS® shall not undertake to provide specialized professional services concerning a type of property or service that is outside their field of competence unless they engage the assistance of one who is competent on such types of property or service, or unless the facts are fully disclosed to the client. Any persons engaged to provide such assistance shall be so identified to the client, and their contribution to the assignment should be set forth."

Central theme

REALTORS® should only work within real estate areas in which they have sufficient knowledge to protect their customer or client. One agent can't know everything about all areas of specialization within the industry.

Article 11 Standards of Practice

Article 11 has four Standards of Practice as follows:

SP 11.1 – When preparing an opinion of value on a piece of property, they must know that specific area of real estate and provide detailed information to the customer or client.
SP 11.2 – A REALTOR® should perform only in an area that they have reasonable competence.
SP 11.3 – When providing consulting services or advice, they shall objectively present the material. The fee shall be contingent on the level of difficulty and the market value of the real property.
SP 11.4 – Competency required under Article 11 is based on the services agreed to by the customers or clients and follows the Code of Ethics and state law.

Article 11 illustration

A REALTOR® is asked to prepare an appraisal for a bank on a commercial building's short sale. The agent had no experience in doing an appraisal or in commercial real estate. This agent would be guilty of violating Article 11 Standards of Practice 11.1, 11.2, and 11.4.

Article 12

"REALTORS® shall be honest and truthful in their real estate communications and shall present a true picture in their advertising, marketing, and other representations. REALTORS® shall ensure that their status as real estate professionals is readily apparent in their advertising, marketing, and other representations and that the recipients of all real estate communications are, or have been, notified that those communications are from a real estate professional."

Central theme

REALTORS® should be honest in all their advertising and marketing.

Article 12 Standards of Practice

Article 12 has 13 Standards of Practice:

SP 12.1 – REALTORS® who advertise something as free must disclose if they will receive any compensation and from whom they are going to receive the payment.
SP 12.2 – Deleted in January 2020.
SP 12.3 – REALTORS® should use care if offering a prize or other compensation for real estate services. They must fully disclose the requirement to receive the compensation.
SP 12.4 – REALTORS® should not advertise a property they are not authorized to market.
SP 12.5 – REALTORS® must be careful not to practice Blind Advertising. The brokerage name must always appear in all advertising.
SP 12.6 – When selling their own property, a REALTOR® must disclose their license status.
SP 12.7 – Only the brokers directly involved in a transaction may advertise that they sold or have a contract on the property with permission from the owner.
SP 12.8 – A REALTORS® website should present current, accurate information, and they should keep the information current.
SP 12.9 – A REALTORS® website shall disclose the brokerage's name and licensure state in a readily apparent manner.
SP 12.10 – REALTORS® must advertise truthfully and give correct information and not deceptive the public in their URLs, websites, or the images they use.
SP 12.11 – REALTORS® who intend to sell consumer information should disclose this wherever they gather the data.
SP 12.12 – REALTORS® shall not use URL or domain names that may mislead the public.
SP 12.13 - REALTORS® are only allowed to use designations, certifications, and other credentials they have earned and have maintained membership.

Article 12 illustration

A REALTOR® developed a website in which he promoted himself as the top producing agent in his area. He also stated that he had the following designations, Certified International Property Specialist (CIPS) and Graduate Realtor Institute (GRI). He had earned these designations; however, he did not keep up the designations' annual renewal. He also did not put the name of the brokerage on his website. The REALTOR® has violated Article 12 and Standards of Practice 12.5, 12.9, and 12.13.

Article 13

"REALTORS® shall not engage in activities that constitute the unauthorized practice of law and shall recommend that legal counsel be obtained when the interest of any party to the transaction requires it."

Central theme

REALTORS® must not represent themselves as attorneys nor give legal advice.

Article 13 illustration

While filling out an offer to buy a piece of real property, REALTOR® John was asked by his customer how they should take title to the property. John asked the question without telling his customer that they should seek legal advice. John was practicing law by answering the question and thus in violation of Article 13.

Article 14

"If charged with unethical practice or asked to present evidence or to cooperate in any other way, in any professional standards proceeding or investigation, REALTORS® shall place all pertinent facts before the proper tribunals of the Member Board or affiliated institute, society, or council in which membership is held and shall take no action to disrupt or obstruct such processes."

Central theme

REALTORS® must assist the Professional Standards Committee in any investigation or hearing. They must always present the truth and not interfere with the process.

Article 14 Standards of Practice

Article 14 has four Standards of Practice:

SP 14.1 – Only one board may hear any case of alleged violations of the Code of Ethics.
SP 14.2 – A REALTOR® should not disclose any information they learned at an ethics hearing.
SP 14.3 – A REALTOR® should not threaten or intimidate a witness or respondent in an ethics case.
SP 14.4 – A REALTOR® should not mislead the investigation into an Ethics case, nor can they file multiple charges based on the same transaction.

Article 14 illustration

Broker Alicia was named in a Code of Ethics violation. She denies the allegations. Trying to get the case canceled, Alicia threatens the person who filed the charges against her and refuses to turn over information to the Professional Standards Committee. Alicia violates Article 14 Standards of Practice 14.3 and 14.4.

Article 15

" REALTORS® shall not knowingly or recklessly make false or misleading statements about other real estate professionals, their businesses, or their business practices."

Central theme.

Article 15 of the Code of Ethics prohibits REALTORS® from making a false or misleading statement about other real estate professionals, their own business, or their business practices.

Article 15 Standards of Practices: Article 15 three Standards of Practice as follows:

SP 15.1 – REALTORS® may not file false or misleading statements about their business.
SP 15.2 – REALTORS® may not make a false or misleading statement about other REALTOR®. This Standard covers the false statements no matter what medium they are presented, i.e., digital, written, in person, etc.
SP 15.3 – REALTORS® publish clarification if they discover a previous statement is false or misleading.

Article 15 Illustration

A REALTOR® told everyone at her office that a competitive brokerage broker was not doing well financially. She even posted these statements on her Facebook page. She was trying to get agents from the other brokerage to join her company. She then boasted about how great her business was doing when in fact, it was struggling. This violation is of Article 15, Standard of Practices 15.1 and 15.2.

Article 16

" REALTORS® shall not engage in any practice or take any action inconsistent with exclusive representation or exclusive brokerage relationship agreements that other REALTORS® have with clients."

Central theme

REALTORS® must not try to steal away another broker's client. If they know someone is already working with a REALTOR® they must not try and get that client to come to them.

Article 16 Standards of Practice

Article 16 has 20 Standards of Practice as follows:

SP 16.1 – This Standard of Practice serves to set boundaries a REALTOR® should not cross with respect to other practitioners. It is not trying to eliminate aggressive or innovative business practices.

SP 16.2 – A REALTOR® may make general statements about their business and participate in marketing campaigns without infringing on other licensees' client relationships. Standard of Practice 16.2, however, outlines two unethical types of solicitation:

1.) Telephone or personal solicitation of sellers identified by yard signs or through MLS information; and,
2.) Mail or other written solicitation sent to customers or clients of other REALTORS® that are not part of a mass marketing campaign.

SP 16.3 – A REALTOR® may contact a client or customer of another REALTOR® to offer different services than those the client is already under contract. REALTORS® cannot use MLS information to target potential customers.

SP 16.4 & 16.5 – A REALTOR® should not try to steal listings or represented buyers from another agent. The only time a REALTOR® may contact another REALTORS® client is to get specific information not available by the other agent or not listed in the MLS.

SP16.6 – If someone under contract with another REALTOR® contacts a REALTOR® the REALTOR® may discuss how they would work with the customer once their contract is up with the other real estate agent.

SP16.7 – The fact that a customer has worked with a specific REALTOR® in the past does not prohibit another REALTOR® from trying to get hired once any existing contract has expired. People do not have to return to the same REALTOR® for every transaction they complete.

SP 16.8 – The fact that an exclusive agreement existed in the past does not prohibit another REALTOR® from entering into a similar agreement once the first contact expires.

SP 16.9 – Before entering into an agreement with a client, a REALTOR® must ensure that the client is not already in another contract with a different REALTOR®.

SP 16.10 – A buyer's agent should disclose that the agreement exists between them when they begin to negotiate a contract.

SP 16.11 – For unlisted property, REALTORS® must disclose any relationship between themselves and other customers. They should also request and negotiate any desired compensation at the first meeting.

SP 16.12 – All contractual relationships should be disclosed before entering into a Purchase agreement.

SP 16.13 – REALTORS® should communicate to the co-broking REALTOR® and not the customer or client.

SP 16.14 – A REALTOR® may enter into any representation but may not require them to pay compensation if the other party is contracted to pay compensation.

SP 16.15 – All monies and compensation must be paid broker to broker.

SP 16.16 –SP deleted and incorporated into SP 3-2.

SP16.17 – REALTORS® shall not attempt to extend a listing broker's offer of cooperation without the listing broker's consent.

SP 16.18 – A REALTOR® shall not use information obtained from another agent or the MLS to negotiate the client away from the firm.

SP 16.19 – REALTORS® must have the owner's permission before placing signs on the property.
SP 16.20 – When a REALTOR® leaves a brokerage, their listing stays with the brokerage. Agents are not allowed to entice customers to follow them to another agency.

Article 16 Illustration

A REALTOR® is holding an open house. A couple comes in and begins looking around. They start asking the REALTOR® questions and state they want to put an offer in on the house. The agent writes up an offer and presents it to the seller, who accepts it. Only after the offer is accepted does it come out that the buyers have a Buyer's Broker Agreement with another REALTOR®.

The REALTOR® holding the open house should have asked if they were under contract with another REALTOR®. This is a violation of Article 16 under the Code of Ethics.

Article 17

"In the event of contractual disputes or specific non-contractual disputes as defined in Standard of Practice 17-4 between REALTORS® (principals) associated with different firms, arising out of their relationship as REALTORS®, the REALTORS® shall mediate the dispute if the Board requires its members to mediate. If the dispute is not resolved through mediation, or if mediation is not required, REALTORS® shall submit the dispute to arbitration in accordance with the policies of the Board rather than litigate the matter.

In the event clients of REALTORS® wish to mediate or arbitrate contractual disputes arising out of real estate transactions, REALTORS® shall mediate or arbitrate those disputes in accordance with the policies of the Board, provided the clients agree to be bound by any resulting agreement or award.

The obligation to participate in mediation and arbitration contemplated by this Article includes the obligation of REALTORS® (principals) to cause their firms to mediate and arbitrate and be bound by any resulting agreement or award."

Central theme

REALTORS® should first commit to mediation if there are unsettled disputes. If mediation does not settle the conflicts, then the agents will move to binding arbitration.

Article 17 Standards of Practice

Article 17 has five Standards of Practice:

SP 17.1 – REALTORS® who file litigation and refuse to withdraw in an arbitrable issue will constitute a refusal to arbitrate.
SP 17.2 – Parties to a dispute are not required to commit to mediation, but they are not relieved of the duty to arbitrate by not entering mediation.
SP 17.3 – REALTORS® when acting solely as principals, are not obligated to arbitrate disputes with other REALTORS®.
SP 17.4 – This Standard of Practice lays out specific times when non-contractual disputes are subject to arbitration. Procuring cause disputes fall under this category.
SP 17.5 – The requirement to arbitrate includes disputes between REALTORS® from different states. It also states which association will have jurisdiction over the disputes.

Article 17 illustration

Whenever there is a dispute among REALTORS® or the parties to a real estate transaction, the parties, per our contract, should first go to mediation and then to binding arbitration. REALTORS® should work to keep disputes out of the legal system whenever they are able.

NAR Dispute Resolution

Processing complaints

Anyone can file a complaint. It can be REALTOR® vs. REALTOR® or client/customer against REALTOR®. Once filed with a local association of REALTORS®, the complaint is then forwarded to the Grievance Committee to determine if there is a violation of the code of ethics and an arbitrational issue. If the Grievance Committee believes there is sufficient evidence of an Ethics violation, a hearing will be scheduled with the Professional Standards Committee to hear the case and recommend the Board of Directors on outcome and punishment.

If there is a monetary issue, then the matter will be sent to the local Board's Ombudsman program to help the parties decide. If the Ombudsman does not settle the dispute, the parties will be offered the opportunity to enter mediation and then go on to arbitration to resolve the dispute.

Penalties

Possible penalties for violation of the Code of Ethics include:

- Letter of warning;
- Letter of reprimand;
- Education courses;

- Fines not to exceed $15,000;
- Probation for not less than 30 days or more than one year;
- Membership suspension for not less than 30 days or more than one year;
- Expulsion from membership for one to three years; and/or,
- Suspension or termination of MLS rights and privileges.

Pathways to Professionalism

While the Code of Ethics establishes enforceable standards that REALTORS® must follow, it does not set out standards of common courtesy or etiquette that a REALTORS® should use in their dealings with other REALTORS® or the public. This is accomplished with NAR's set of professional courtesy standards called the Pathways to Professionalism.

There are three sections to the Pathways to Professionalism:

1. Respect for the Public
2. Respect for Property
3. Respect for Peers

These Professional courtesies are intended to be used by REALTORS® voluntarily. They cannot form the basis for a professional standards complaint.

Pathways to Professionalism

Respect for the Public

1. Follow the "Golden Rule": Do unto other as you would have them do unto you.
2. Respond promptly to inquiries and requests for information.
3. Schedule appointments and showings as far in advance as possible.
4. Communicate promptly if you are delayed or must cancel an appointment or showing. If a prospective buyer decides not to view an occupied home, promptly communicate the situation to the listing broker or the occupant.
5. When entering a property ensure that unexpected situations, such as pets, are handled appropriately.
6. Never criticize property in the presence of the occupant.
7. When showing an occupied home, always ring the doorbell or knock—and announce yourself loudly before entering. Knock and announce yourself loudly before entering any closed room.
8. Present a professional appearance.
9. If occupants are home during showings, ask their permission before using the bathroom.
10. Encourage the clients of other brokers to direct questions to their agent or representative.
11. Communicate clearly; ensure specialized language and real estate terminology is understood.
12. Be aware of and respect cultural differences. Show courtesy and respect to everyone.
13. Be aware of—and meet—all deadlines.
14. Promise only what you can deliver—and keep your promises.
15. Do not tell people what you think—tell them what you know.

Respect for Property

1. When showing a property, be responsible for your clients/customers and keep the group together.
2. Make reasonable and timely accommodations to provide access to listed properties.
3. Make reasonable and timely requests to access listed properties.
4. Leave the property as you found it (lights, heating, cooling, drapes, etc.) If you think something is amiss (e.g. vandalism), contact the listing broker immediately.
5. Be considerate of the seller's property. Do not allow anyone to eat, drink, smoke, dispose of trash, use bathing or sleeping facilities, or bring pets. When instructed or appropriate, remove footwear when entering property.
6. Obtain permission from appropriate parties (e.g., listing broker) before photographing, videographing, or streaming the interiors or exteriors of properties, or allowing others to do so.

Respect for Peers

1. Respond to other real estate professionals' communications promptly and courteously.
2. Contact the listing broker if there appears to be a discrepancy in the listing information.
3. Inform anyone accessing the property about important information, (e.g., pets, security systems, video and audio recording equipment).
4. Inform if sellers or listing agent will be present during the showing.
5. Show courtesy, trust, and respect to other real estate professionals.
6. Avoid the inappropriate use of endearments or other denigrating language.
7. Do not prospect at other REALTORS®' open houses or similar events.
8. Secure property and lockbox and/or return keys promptly.
9. Real estate is a reputation business. What you do today may affect your reputation—and business—for years to come.

The above is from the NAR Code of Ethics and Arbitration Manual, Pathways to Professionalism, which can be accessed at: https://www.nar.realtor/code-of-ethics-and-arbitration-manual/pathways-to-professionalism

Commitment to Excellence (C2EX)

Commitment to Excellence (C2EX) from the National Association of REALTORS® empowers REALTORS® to evaluate, enhance and showcase their highest professional levels. It's not a course, class, or designation—it's an Endorsement that REALTORS® can promote when serving clients and other REALTORS®.

The NAR Board of Directors has requested that all Board of Directors, committee members, and leadership complete the C2EX program. To date, over 50,000 REALTORS® have completed this program.

II. Cooperating with Other Licensees

One of the foundational principles of professional real estate practice in Missouri is the expectation that licensees will cooperate with one another in serving their clients. Cooperation among brokers is not simply a courtesy, it is an ethical obligation for members of the National Association of REALTORS® and a practical necessity in a marketplace where buyers and sellers depend on broad access to available properties.

Article 3 of the NAR Code of Ethics speaks directly to this obligation: "REALTORS® shall cooperate with other brokers except when cooperation is not in the client's best interest." This is an important distinction. Cooperation is the default expectation, but the client's interest always takes priority. A Missouri licensee who declines to cooperate with another broker must be able to demonstrate that doing so genuinely serves their client rather than simply reflecting personal or financial preference.

It is equally important to understand what cooperation does not require. Article 3 makes clear that the obligation to cooperate does not include the obligation to share commissions or otherwise compensate another broker. Compensation and cooperation are separate matters, and Missouri licensees should not confuse the two. The terms under which a cooperating broker may be compensated must be established in conjunction with the seller or landlord, clearly disclosed, and communicated to all relevant parties before any offer is presented.

Missouri licensees should also be aware of several specific duties that flow from the cooperation obligation. A licensee must promptly communicate any changes to cooperative compensation to other brokers involved in a transaction, and that compensation may not be unilaterally altered after an offer has already been presented. Any variable commission arrangements must be disclosed to cooperating brokers in advance. Additionally, a licensee must never misrepresent the availability of a property or refuse to show a property to a prospective buyer on the basis of that buyer's membership in a protected class, conduct that would simultaneously violate both fair housing law and the Code of Ethics.

For Missouri licensees, embracing a spirit of genuine cooperation means keeping the focus where it belongs: on the client's successful outcome. Brokers and agents who work collaboratively, communicate clearly, and deal honestly with one another build the kind of professional reputation that sustains a long career. Real estate in Missouri is a relationship business, and the licensees who treat their fellow professionals with respect and transparency are the ones who earn lasting trust in the marketplace.

III. Compensation

Buyer's and seller's brokerage agreements cover the provisions for the broker's terms of compensation. The listing agreement identifies whether the listing broker may cooperate with and compensate other designated brokers. Any buyer's brokerage agreement should specify whether or not the designated broker is authorized to cooperate with and compensate other designated brokers.

The compensation amount is negotiable between thc parties. It is illegal for firms or licensees to lead consumers to believe that a set compensation rate exists.
Licensees can only receive compensation through their broker. Brokers may pay licensees through the licensee's business instead of the individual licensee if the licensee desires. Licensees cannot compensate any unlicensed individual.

NAR Settlement and Compensation Changes

As of August 17, 2024, significant changes to how buyer agent compensation is handled took effect as a result of the National Association of REALTORS® settlement. Prior to the settlement, it was standard practice for offers of buyer agent compensation to be published in the MLS. That practice is now prohibited. Offers of buyer agent compensation may no longer appear in MLS listings, though sellers may still offer to compensate a buyer's agent through other channels, such as direct broker-to-broker communication, marketing materials, or as a negotiated term within the purchase contract itself.

The settlement also requires that a written buyer representation agreement be in place before a licensee shows a buyer any property. This agreement must clearly state the compensation the buyer's agent is seeking and how it will be paid. Missouri licensees are required to clearly communicate to both buyers and sellers that broker compensation is fully negotiable and is not set by law. This obligation is also reflected in Standards of Practice 1.12 and 1.13 of the NAR Code of Ethics, amended effective June 2025, which explicitly require licensees to advise clients of this fact in both listing and buyer-agent agreements.

Commissions and Commission Splits

Brokers typically calculate commissions as a percentage of the property's final sales price. Internal compensation agreements between the brokerage firm and its affiliated licensees, often called a commission split, dictate the amount of compensation due from the firm to affiliated licensees who work directly with clients to close transactions.

To illustrate, assume a seller agrees to pay a 6% commission on a $200,000 sale, with half of the commission going to the listing broker and half to the cooperating broker. At closing, the seller's brokerage firm receives $12,000 (6% of $200,000). The seller's broker retains $6,000 and pays the remaining $6,000 to the cooperating broker. Each firm will then split the commission earned with the respective listing or selling agent based on the agreed-upon commission split. If the broker and agent have a 60/40 split, the agent receives 60% of the $6,000, or $3,600, and the firm keeps the remaining $2,400.

Compensation and Agency

In a real estate transaction, any party, including the seller, landlord, buyer, tenant, or a third party, may pay all or part of the agreed-upon compensation if all parties agree.

It is essential to understand, however, that the source of compensation does not impact the agency relationship. In other words, compensation does not create a brokerage relationship — the signed brokerage agreement establishes that relationship. For instance, if a seller's parents agree to pay the commission owed on their adult son's or daughter's listing, the agency relationship is still between the seller and the brokerage firm, not the parents and the brokerage firm.

Reasonable Cause Required for Referral Compensation

Missouri license law prohibits licensees from paying or requesting payment from another person unless a reasonable cause or contractual relationship exists. For example, paying a referral fee to another licensee is illegal unless that licensee referred a client before a brokerage relationship was established between the client and the licensee paying the referral.

Altering Another's Brokerage Agreement

As a related restriction, it is illegal to engage in counseling another licensee's client or customer on how to terminate or amend an existing brokerage agreement in order to earn a commission. This violation is also called "sign crossing" or broker interference.

MODULE 5 SNAPSHOT REVIEW: ETHICS AND STANDARDS OF CONDUCT

I. NAR Code of Ethics

REALTORS® Code of Ethics

- Rules members practice in dealings with others

Definitions

- Business ethics-business make decisions; treat Clients, Customers, Vendors, Employees
- Client- individual with fiduciary relationship
- Code of Ethics-lay out the values of an organization
- Customer-individual with no fiduciary relationship; limited disclosure
- Ethics- moral principles, rules to determine how to deal with others
- Morals- person's individuals belief of right/wrong; religion; culture
- Preamble- opening statement of document reflecting values/vision of organization
- Situational Ethics-person changing ethical views to fit situation
- Demographic information-Information gathered on customers/clients; age, sex, race, color, national origin. Assist operating brokerage and advertising avenues
- Professional services- advertising, buying, auctioning, renting, selling, appraising, leasing, exchanging.
- NAR's protected classes-race, color, religion, sex, handicap, familial status, national origin, sexual orientation, gender identity
- Public trust-misappropriation of client or customer funds or property; discrimination against the protected classes under the Code of Ethics, or fraud
- Duties to the public-how REALTORS® behave when interacting with public
- Arbitration-voluntary process where independent third party listens to individuals in dispute
- Mediation-voluntary process where third person helps parties agree to resolve dispute
- Ombudsman-voluntary process where individual appointed by local Board of REALTORS®® receives assistance to resolve disputes through constructive communication
- Procuring cause-agent who starts uninterrupted chain of events leading to sale/rental of listing
- Duties to REALTORS® -how REALTORS® should behave when interacting with other REALTORS®.

NAR'S Code of Ethics

- For REALTORS® to follow in dealings with clients, public, and other REALTORS®

Preamble

- Everything we do, are, or aspire to become, begins with land beneath our feet

Articles 1-17

- Article 1- honesty as critical virtue of any licensee
- Article 2-transparency in all transactions

- Article 3-Cooperation among brokers unless it's not in their client's best interest; emphasizes compensation is negotiable and not set by law
- Article 4- REALTORS® disclose real estate license when buying/selling property for themselves
- Article 5- disclose conflict of interest before providing any professional services
- Article 6- REALTOR® may not accept any compensation in form of commission, rebate, kickback, etc., without client's written consent
- Article 7- REALTOR® cannot accept compensation from more than one person without disclosing to all parties
- Article 8-escrow funds; handling other people's money
- Article 9-brokers ensure documents are written in clear, concise language; all contracts and relationships must be explained fully, whether in person, electronically, or through any other means
- Article 10- prohibits REALTORS® from discrimination against protected classes identified in Code of Ethics
- Article 11-REALTORS® should only work within real estate areas in which they have sufficient knowledge to protect customer/client
- Article 12-honesty in advertising/marketing
- Article 13-REALTORS® must not represent themselves as attorneys nor give legal advice
- Article 14- REALTORS® must assist Professional Standards Committee in investigations
- Article 15-prohibits REALTORS® from false statements about real estate professionals, their own business, business practices
- Article 16- REALTORS® must not steal another broker's client
- Article 17- REALTORS® should commit to mediation if unsettled disputes

NAR Dispute Resolution

- Complaint with local association of REALTORS® >Grievance Committee reviews for violation> hearing scheduled with Professional Standards Committee>Ombudsman settles dispute or parties can enter mediation then arbitration

Pathways to Professionalism

- NAR's set of professional courtesy standards
- Respect for the Public; respect for Property; respect for Peers

Commitment to Excellence (C2EX)

- Empowers REALTORS® to evaluate, enhance, showcase highest professional levels

II. Cooperating with Other Licensees

- Cooperation among brokers is an ethical obligation under NAR Code of Ethics Article 3, not merely a professional courtesy.
- The default rule is to cooperate; a licensee who declines must demonstrate that doing so genuinely serves the client's best interest, not personal or financial preference.
- Cooperation does not require sharing commissions. Compensation and cooperation are entirely separate obligations.
- Compensation terms for a cooperating broker must be established with the seller or landlord, clearly disclosed, and communicated to all parties before any offer is presented.

- Cooperative compensation may not be unilaterally altered after an offer has been presented; any changes must be communicated promptly.
- Variable commission arrangements must be disclosed to cooperating brokers in advance.
- A licensee may never misrepresent the availability of a property or refuse to show a property based on a buyer's membership in a protected class — a violation of both the Code of Ethics and fair housing law.

III. Compensation

- Listing agreements and buyer representation agreements must specify whether the broker is authorized to cooperate with and compensate other designated brokers.
- Compensation is fully negotiable. It is illegal to suggest to consumers that a standard or set rate exists.
- Licensees may only receive compensation through their broker. Licensees may not compensate any unlicensed individual.

NAR Settlement — Effective August 17, 2024

- Offers of buyer agent compensation are prohibited from appearing in MLS listings.
- Sellers may still offer buyer agent compensation through broker-to-broker communication, marketing materials, or as a negotiated term in the purchase contract.
- A written buyer representation agreement disclosing the agent's compensation must be in place before showing any property.
- Missouri licensees must clearly communicate to both buyers and sellers that compensation is fully negotiable and not set by law, as required by NAR Standards of Practice 1.12 and 1.13 (amended June 2025).

Commission Splits, Agency, and Referral Restrictions

- Commissions are typically calculated as a percentage of the final sales price and split between the listing broker and cooperating broker per the agreed terms.
- The source of compensation does not determine the agency relationship. The signed brokerage agreement establishes the relationship, not who pays the commission.
- Any party — seller, buyer, or third party — may pay all or part of a commission if all parties agree.
- Missouri license law requires reasonable cause or a contractual relationship before a referral fee may be paid; paying a fee without a prior referral is prohibited.
- It is illegal to counsel another licensee's client on how to terminate or amend an existing brokerage agreement in order to earn a commission. This is known as sign crossing or broker interference.

MODULE 5 QUIZ– ETHICS AND STANDARDS OF CONDUCT

1. The four parts of the Code of Ethics include the Preamble, duties to Clients and Customers, duties to the Public, and ___________.

    a. duties to REALTORS®.
    b. duties to Mortgage Lenders.
    c. duties to Title Agents.
    d. the Conclusion.

2. Article 2 of the Code of Ethics discusses latent defects in a client's property. Which of the following best reflects Article 2's provisions?

    a. REALTORS® are obligated to conduct detailed inspections of both latent and manifest defects.
    b. REALTORS® are not obligated to discover latent defects.
    c. REALTORS® must not disclose defects that violate client confidentiality.
    d. REALTORS® must advise clients on legal matters if they are familiar with such matters.

3. The three sections of Pathways to Professionalism are respect for the Public, respect for Peers, and respect for _________.

    a. REALTORS®
    b. Brokers
    c. Property
    d. Mayors

4. Which of the following is an endorsement that REALTORS® can promote to showcase the highest professional level?

    a. Commitment to Excellence
    b. NAR Ethics Standard
    c. Code of Ethics Achievement
    d. Platinum Service Commitment

5. Article 14 of the Code of Ethics requires REALTORS® to assist the Professional Standards Committee in any investigation or hearing. Which of the following is additionally true as provided by Article 14?

    a. REALTORS® must not practice law without a license
    b. REALTORS® must not misrepresent the condition of a listed property.
    c. REALTORS® may appeal an alleged violation to another board.
    d. REALTORS® must not disclose information ascertained from a hearing.

6. Why was NAR formed in 1908?

   a. To protect the public and promote homeownership
   b. To earn money off of REALTORS®
   c. To promote the notion of "Caveat emptor"
   d. To encourage agents to be professional

7. The agent who starts the uninterrupted chain of events leading to the sale of a listing has _____________.

   a. public trust.
   b. procuring cause.
   c. arbitration.
   d. mediation.

8. According to Article 17 of the Code of Ethics, REALTORS® should first commit to ______ if there are unsettled disputes.

   a. arbitration
   b. jury trial
   c. mediation
   d. a NAR panel discussion

9. A REALTOR® posted a blog post about a competing broker who was not doing well financially. What does this violate?

   a. The Preamble of the Code of Ethics
   b. Article 15 of the Code of Ethics
   c. The NAR handbook
   d. The Virginia Real Estate Licensee Act

10. Which portion of the Code of Ethics serves as a vision statement on how licensees should conduct themselves?

   a. Article 1
   b. The Conclusion
   c. Article 18
   d. The Preamble

11. Without the client's knowledge, Charles refers his client to a roofer in order to receive a $150 gift card. Which specific ethical practice of the Code of Ethics does Charles violate?

   a. The prohibition against paid referrals
   b. The prohibition against receiving gift cards, specifically
   c. The prohibition against undisclosed compensation
   d. No violation has been committed.

12. Who can file a complaint to NAR?

a. Anyone
b. Only clients
c. Only customers
d. Only REALTORs®

13. What is the maximum fine for a Code of Ethics violation?

a. $1,000
b. $15,000
c. $25,000
d. $50,000

14. Which of the following is a possible penalty for a Code of Ethics violation?

a. Membership suspension for five days
b. A $20,000 fine
c. Membership probation for seven years
d. Expulsion from membership for one to three years

15. What is the name of a voluntary process where an individual appointed by a local Board of REALTORS® provides assistance to resolve disputes through constructive communication?

a. Arbitration
b. Mediation
c. Ombudsman
d. Situational ethics

16. Under NAR Code of Ethics Article 3, a Missouri REALTOR® who declines to cooperate with another broker must be able to demonstrate that:

a. The cooperating broker has a history of unprofessional conduct
b. Declining to cooperate genuinely serves the client's best interest rather than the licensee's personal or financial preference
c. The property is already under contract with another buyer
d. The cooperating broker has not yet presented a written buyer representation agreement

17. Which of the following statements best describes the relationship between cooperation and compensation under the NAR Code of Ethics?

a. The obligation to cooperate automatically includes the obligation to share commissions with a cooperating broker
b. Compensation and cooperation are separate matters; cooperation does not require sharing commissions or compensating another broker
c. A cooperating broker is always entitled to a minimum of 50% of the commission earned on the transaction
d. Compensation terms may be established by the listing broker at any point before the closing date

18. As a result of the August 17, 2024 NAR settlement, which of the following practices is now prohibited?

a. Sellers offering to compensate a buyer's agent through a negotiated term in the purchase contract
b. Brokers communicating compensation offers directly to one another outside of the MLS
c. Publishing offers of buyer agent compensation in MLS listings
d. Requiring a written buyer representation agreement before showing a property

19. A seller's parents agree to pay the brokerage commission on their adult child's home sale. Which of the following is true regarding the agency relationship in this transaction?

a. The agency relationship is now between the parents and the brokerage firm since they are paying the commission
b. No valid agency relationship exists because the seller did not personally pay the commission
c. The agency relationship remains between the seller and the brokerage firm, because the signed brokerage agreement establishes the relationship, not the source of compensation
d. The brokerage firm must obtain a separate written agreement from the parents before accepting their payment

20. A seller agrees to pay a 6% commission on a $250,000 sale, with the commission split equally between the listing broker and the cooperating broker. The cooperating broker and her agent have a 60/40 split in favor of the agent. How much does the cooperating agent receive?

a. $6,000
b. $7,500
c. $9,000
d. $4,500

21. A Missouri licensee contacts a buyer who is already represented by another broker and advises the buyer on how to terminate that existing brokerage agreement so the licensee can earn the commission. This conduct is best described as:

a. A permissible competitive business practice as long as no money is exchanged
b. Acceptable provided the licensee discloses the intent to the Missouri Real Estate Commission in advance
c. A violation only if the original brokerage agreement has not yet expired
d. Sign crossing or broker interference, which is prohibited under Missouri license law

MODULE 5 CASE STUDY:

Ethics and Standards of Conduct

CASE STUDY #1:

Agent John showed Broker Eric's listing to buyer clients, Adam and Eve. The list price in the MLS was $210,000. John contacted Eric to inquire about any offers on the property. Eric told John he had no offers. John then prepared an offer to submit to Eric.

Eric did have an offer for $185,000 cash from Jill and Jack. The seller accepted the offer, not knowing that John's clients submitted a bid for $205,000 with FHA financing and a 5% down payment.

Once John had submitted the offer, he asked Eric for written confirmation that the offer was presented to the seller. Eric never presented the offer, nor were Adam and Eve advised that there was another offer.

When asked, Eric stated that the seller had rejected the offer for a cash deal. Eric decided not to present the offer to the seller because it involved financing and would take longer to close. Eric wanted it to close before the end of the month to win an office selling contest.

DISCUSSION QUESTIONS:

1. How would you have handled the offers if you were Eric?

____

____

____

____

2. What Articles of the Code of Ethics do you feel were violated?

____

____

____

____

3. What specific Standards of Practice do you feel were violated?

____

____

____

____

CASE STUDY #2:

A real estate agent is involved in local politics. During the County Commission meeting, the agent made a racist comment to a Black member of the Commission. After the meeting, she went to her social media accounts and made additional derogatory comments against the Commissioner. She also suggested that the county would be better off if the County Commissioner died. Based on this information, discuss this scenario and answer the questions below.

Discussion Questions:

1. Which Article of the Code of Ethics do you feel was violated in this example?

____

____

____

____

2. What specific Standard of Practice do you feel was violated?

____

____

____

____

3. How could the situation be handled without violating the Code of Ethics?

____

____

____

____

CASE STUDY #3:

Dan, who held an exclusive listing of Joey's property, invited Janet to cooperate with him. Shortly thereafter, Janet received an offer to purchase the property and took it to Dan. Janet asked to be present at the presentation of the offer, and Dan allowed this. Together, they started negotiations with the seller. The next day, Janet called Joey, recommending that Joey accept the offer, which was less than the list price, and Joey agreed. The contract was signed and closed.

Discussion Questions:

1. What Article has is Janet violated?

2. What were Standards of Practice violated?

3. How could the situation be handled without violating the Code of Ethics?

Module 6: RISK MANAGEMENT

I. Avoiding Misrepresentation and Reducing Risk

Module 6 Learning Objectives

Avoiding Misrepresentation and Reducing Risk

1. **Identify numerous ways to capitalize on risk reduction via the adoption of key risk management strategies**
2. **Define and summarize the principal forms of antitrust legislation, including The Sherman Antitrust Act and Clayton Antitrust Act.**
3. **Identify the various insurance options for property owners, managers, and licensees.**
4. **Discuss the potential risks of misrepresenting clients.**

I. Avoiding Misrepresentation and Reducing Risk

Risk Management Strategies

Four well- established strategies for managing risk are:

- Avoidance (elimination)
- Reduction (mitigation, sharing)
- Transference (outsourcing, insuring)
- Retention (acceptance and budgeting)

Not all of these strategies are always possible or available, but a real estate firm or licensee who fails to make a conscious effort to employ one or more of them increases the likelihood of loss from the many potential risks that are always present in the real estate business.

Avoidance

Avoidance includes refraining from an activity that carries risk. One can avoid the risks of being in an automobile accident by not riding in automobiles. Avoiding risks also means missing the opportunity to benefit from the avoided activity. By avoiding automobile travel, one is confined to modes of transportation, such as buses and walking, that do not offer the same high degree of personal freedom and efficiency. Complete avoidance of risk in real estate practice is almost impossible. A broker, for instance, may believe that hiring only experienced affiliates eliminates the risk that affiliates will commit license law violations. However, even experienced practitioners may not know the law, and, sometimes, people break the law deliberately. The risk may be reduced, but it remains.

Reduction

Reduction involves taking steps to reduce the probability or the severity of a potential loss. However, this strategy may result in reducing risk in one area only to increase it in another. A familiar example is a sprinkler system that dispenses water to reduce the risk of fire but at the same time increases the risk of water damage.

In real estate practice, one risk reduction tactic is to share responsibility for making a decision. The agent provides the consumer with expertise, and perhaps some advice, but lets the consumer decide how much to offer. In this way, the agent gets some relief from the risks inherent in the buyer's decision to purchase.

Transference

Transference means passing the risk to another party, by contract or other means. An insurance policy is the common example, but sometimes the wording of a sales or personal services contract can transfer risk without resorting to insurance.

In the real estate business, transference is typically and most successfully accomplished by means of an errors and omissions (E&O) insurance policy, either on the individuals in a firm or on the firm itself. State law may require such insurance.

Retention

Retention of risk means entering into an activity in spite of known risks and taking full responsibility for the consequences. This is, in effect, self-insurance, the only strategy left when risk cannot be reduced or transferred and one has decided not to avoid it because of the desirability of the potential benefits.

Risk Management Procedures

Experience shows that the most practical strategies for risk management in real estate practice are reduction and transference, with procedures focusing on:

- Education
- Disclosure
- Documentation
- Insurance

Education

Education is the first line of defense against risk. When agents are familiar with the forms provided by the office, how and when to complete them and where to send them, the likelihood of errors is reduced. Likewise, agents need to be able to identify and understand common contract elements, complete contract forms developed by attorneys, and evaluate offers received from co-op agents on their listings without committing a license violation or breach of law.

In most states, brokers have a legal obligation to provide training to affiliated licensees. Licensees also have the obligation to seek out appropriate education and training outside the brokerage to ensure that they know how to comply with the law. In addition, licensees must satisfy legal requirements for continuing education, while those who care about personal excellence will seek further education and training to enhance their professional skills.

Disclosure

By ensuring that all parties have the information they are entitled to, proper disclosure reduces the risk that clients and customers will accuse a licensee of misleading or inducing them to make a decision with incomplete information. Further, laws in every state require disclosures of one kind or another.

Disclosure may be made in writing or verbally and may or may not require written acknowledgment from the receiving party.

Required disclosures usually include:

- agency relationships
- property condition
- duties and obligations
- personal interest in the transaction
- personal interest in referrals

Documentation and record keeping

Documentation provides evidence of compliance with laws and regulations. It proves what clients and customers and licensees said and did in a transaction. Some documentation is required by law.

The components of a thoroughly documented paper trail include:

- Policy and procedure manuals
- Standard forms
- Communication records
- Transaction records
- Contracts
- Accounting
- Other important documents

Policy and procedures manual

A written and uniformly enforced company policy lets everyone in the firm know what to expect before problems arise. The policy manual should cover the company's rules in such areas as floor duty privileges, assignment of relocation properties to agents, referrals between agents within the company, and requirements for continuing education, sales meeting participation, and property tours.

The company's procedures manual should spell out how to handle every aspect of the company's business that agents and brokers need to know—from handling consumers' funds and documents, conducting consumer transactions, dealing with MLS-related matters, and placing signage, to all procedures prescribed by state or federal law, especially license, banking and fair housing laws. Adherence to a procedures manual reduces the risk that an individual will inadvertently commit an unlawful act. Whenever changes are made to the policy or procedures manual, each agent should sign the revised manual as evidence that the agent has examined it.

Standard forms

Standard forms save time and protect against the unauthorized practice of law. Since they are most often prepared by lawyers familiar with the market area, they can address contingencies that are common in the area in a manner that reflects the real estate laws of the state. On the other hand, a licensee often needs to adapt a standardized form for a client by assisting with filling in blanks, modifying terms, and attaching addenda. The licensee must always remain aware of the limitations the state has placed on such activities.

Here are a few of the standard forms a brokerage should provide for its agents and affiliates:

- buyer and seller representation agreements, exclusive and nonexclusive
- agreement to show property
- purchase and sale agreement
- agency disclosure form
- property condition disclosure, disclaimer, and exemption form
- lease agreement
- personal interest disclosure form
- referral for service disclosure form
- lead-based paint disclosure form
- special disclosure forms (mold, radon, subsurface sewage system, impact fees/adequate facilities taxes, etc.)
- referral agreement
- independent contractor agreement
- closing checklist

Communication records

Some communications with transaction parties are good and necessary for business. Others are required by law, such as certain disclosures. A transaction checklist is a good tool for managing risk associated with the failure to make required communications to all principals and for keeping track of required communications from co-op agents.

Retaining evidence that information has been communicated is a necessary procedure. Electronic communications should be archived on suitable electronic media. Copies of mailed or faxed communications should be maintained in the transaction folder.

It is always difficult to document telephone or face-to-face conversations, especially with the constant use of cell phones from a variety of locations. It is a good practice to make brief notes at the time and then write them up later for mailing or faxing to the other party. Be sure, however, that you can produce these notes on demand, lest you be accused later of withholding documentation that has been promised.

Maintaining a good record of communications is useful for resolving disagreements where parties dispute what has been said because it allows the agent to produce a dated document that resolves the issue definitively.

Transaction records

State laws require licensees to document transactions. Firms are required to keep written records of all real estate transactions for a number of years (usually three to five) after closing or termination. Required records typically include:

- listing agreements
- offers
- contracts
- closing statements
- agency agreements
- disclosure documents
- correspondence and other communication records
- notes and any other relevant information

Accounting

In addition to other accounting records, there is the requirement to maintain written accounting of escrow funds. For each transaction, property, and principal, escrow records will include:

- depositor
- date of deposit
- date of withdrawal
- payee
- other information deemed pertinent by the real estate commission

Other documents

Additional documents may be required by law or regulation, or should be kept simply as protection in case of disputes and lawsuits. These would include copies of advertising materials, materials used in training agents, records of compliance with continuing education requirements, safety manuals, and anything else that shows how the firm conducts its business and safeguards its staff as well as the rights of consumers.

Insurance

Many forms of insurance are available for property owners and managers. Some of these types are also used to manage certain risks of brokers and licensees.

General Liability

General liability insurance provides coverage for risks incurred by a property owner when the public or a licensee enters the owned property (**public liability**). The insurer pays the covered claim and legal fees, costs, and expenses, including medical expenses, resulting from owner negligence or other causes. This type of insurance does not cover **professional liability,** for which an Errors & Omissions policy is necessary.

Errors and Omissions

Professional liability is of two general types:

1. Unprofessional conduct – a claim that one has failed to carry out fiduciary duties and provide an acceptable standard of care
2. Breach of contract – a claim that one has failed to perform services under the terms of a contract in a timely manner

The primary method for transferring the professional liability risks of brokers, managers, and licensees is Errors & Omissions (E&O) insurance. A standard E&O policy provides coverage for "damages resulting from any negligent act, error or omission arising out of Professional Services." A standard policy does NOT cover:

- violations of law
- fraudulent, dishonest, criminal or malicious acts
- mishandling of escrow moneys, earnest money deposits, or security deposits
- antitrust violations
- sexual harassment
- Fair Housing violations
- agent-owned properties
- environmental violations
- failure to detect or disclose environmental conditions, including mold
- acts committed prior to licensure or after termination of active status
- activities as an appraiser if licensing other than a real estate license is required

E&O insurance, in short, covers "mistakes" but not crimes.

Fire and hazard

The risks of property damage caused by fire, wind, hail, smoke, civil disturbance, and other such causes are covered by fire and hazard insurance.

Flood

The risks of property damage caused by floods, heavy rains, snow, drainage failures, and failed public infrastructures such as dams and levies are covered by a specialized flood policy. Regular hazard policies do not include flood coverage.

Other insurance

Other common types of insurance coverage for income and commercial properties include:

- **casualty**—coverage for specific risks, such as theft, vandalism, burglary, illness and accident, machinery damage
- **workers' compensation**—hospital and medical coverage for employees injured in the course of employment, mandated by state laws
- **contents and personal property**—coverage for building contents and personal property when they are not actually on the building premises
- **consequential loss, use, and occupancy**—coverage for the business losses resulting from a disaster, such as loss of rent and other revenue, when the property cannot be used for business
- **surety bond**—coverage against losses resulting from criminal or negligent acts of an employee

Primary Areas of Risk

Risks for licensees are present every day in business transactions. Many of these risks carry legal implications as well as possible financial and professional consequences.

Agency

The risks of agency will occur in one of two areas:

- thc rcquircment to inform and disclose
- the requirement to carry out an agency duty

Most states require agency relationships to be in writing and to be disclosed to all parties to a transaction. State law may spell out agency duties, or the duties may be a part of general agency law. In states that do not use agency, there is still the obligation to explain and disclose the nature of the relationship.

Disclosure requirements

A licensee may be acting in a transaction as facilitator, agent, subagent, designated agent, single agent, dual agent, non-agent or in some capacity. Regardless of status, the licensee must follow state disclosure requirements. These are, typically, to:

- disclose status ***verbally*** to other licensees on initial contact
- disclose status ***verbally*** to buyer and seller before providing real estate services
- confirm the disclosure ***in writing*** before signing a listing agreement or presenting a purchase offer (to an unrepresented seller) or before preparing a purchase offer (to an unrepresented buyer)
- get a ***signed receipt*** indicating the written disclosure has been made

Carrying out the duties of agency also require disclosures of :

- personal interest the agent has in a transaction (such as owner or buyer)
- personal benefit the agent will derive from a service referral
- required property and market information
- information about customers a client is entitled to have

Duties

A licensee who acts for a principal in a real estate transaction is required by law to assume certain responsibilities toward the parties to the transaction. Whether a state applies the fiduciary duties of agency law or specifies its own duties toward clients and consumers, the basic duties remain:

To all parties

- honesty
- fairness
- reasonable care and skill
- disclosures

To clients

- skill
- care
- diligence
- loyalty
- obedience
- confidentiality
- accounting
- full disclosure

The duty to exercise **skill, care and diligence** means that licensees may not be casual or negligent in their actions. Licensee negligence is actionable when principals are harmed by the licensee's failure.

The duty of **loyalty** requires the agent to *put the client's interests above those of everyone else*, including his or her own.

The duty of **obedience** requires the agent to act on the principal's wishes regarding the transaction as long as they do not result in any illegal action. The duty of obedience never overrides the legal obligation of agents to deal fairly and honestly with all parties.

The duty of **confidentiality** requires the agent to hold in confidence any information that would harm the client's interests or bargaining position or anything else the client wishes to keep secret, unless the law requires disclosure. The duty of confidentiality survives the termination of the listing contract.

The duty of **accounting** applies to all funds involved in a real estate transaction. Accounts must be maintained as required by law, and escrow funds are to be handled strictly in accordance with the law.

The duty of **disclosure** applies to both parties to a transaction, although usually with some differences. Proper disclosure to customers primarily concerns agency, property condition, and environmental hazards. To the client, it generally concerns all known facts regarding the property and the transaction, including information about the other transaction party. State laws prescribe what may, must, and must not be disclosed. Licensees must be vigilant to avoid oversights and conflicts of interest that can lead to a disclosure to the wrong party or disclosure of information that is confidential.

Conflicts of interest

Conflicts of interest arise when an agent forgets to put the best interests of a client ahead of those of everyone else. This can happen in situations involving undisclosed dual agencies, broker-owned listings, licensees buying for their own account, vendor referrals, and property management subcontracting of services, among many others. Even ordinary, everyday transactions carry a built-in risk of conflict of interest. Consider the fact that a licensee usually receives no compensation for a failed transaction. Therefore, it is in the licensee's interest to see the transaction completed, even if it may not be in the client's best interest. A negative result from a home inspection or other test has the potential to cause a buyer to back out of a contract. A licensee who has forgotten whose best interest should be primary might be tempted to recommend inspectors who will overlook problems in exchange for receiving referrals. Licensees must always disclose any self-interest they have in a transaction, and always remember their duties to clients and consumers.

Confidentiality

Licensees have a responsibility to maintain the confidentiality of certain kinds of information they obtain concerning clients and customers. The duty to maintain confidentiality generally survives the termination of a listing agreement into perpetuity. If it seems that revealing confidential information might benefit the client, the licensee should obtain the client's written permission to proceed.

Confidential information generally includes information about a client's motivations in a transaction, financial and personal details, and information specifically designated as confidential by the client. Public information, such as that contained in public records, information that becomes known without the licensee's participation, or that the client reveals to another, is not considered confidential.

State laws often require businesses to provide security for the personal information they obtain about consumers. Security procedures should protect personal information from unauthorized access, destruction, use, modification, or disclosure. Confidential information, when it is not to be retained, must be disposed of in a secure manner.

Penalties

Possible penalties for breach of agency relationships include:

- rescission of transaction
- loss of compensation
- fees and costs
- punitive damages
- ethics discipline
- license discipline

Property Disclosures

Property condition

Most states require the seller of a residential property to deliver to the buyer a written disclosure or disclaimer about the property's condition, including any material defects the owner knows about. The disclosure is usually required before any purchase contract is accepted. A second disclosure may be required at closing. The licensee should always obtain the parties' signatures acknowledging receipt of these disclosures.

Depending on the state, the licensee may have no further duty to disclose property condition after properly informing parties of their rights and obligations. However, the licensee may still be subject to legal action for

- deliberately distorting the facts (intentional misrepresentation)
- cheating any party (fraud)
- concealing or failing to disclose adverse facts which the licensee knew about or should have known about (intentional or unintentional misrepresentation)

Lead-based paint and other disclosures

Federal law requires sellers of houses built before 1978 to make a lead-based paint disclosure before accepting an offer to purchase. The licensee must tell the seller about this requirement, give the seller the proper disclosure form, and make sure that the buyer receives it.

Mold

This is a fungus that grows under moist conditions and causes allergic reaction for some people. The presence of mold in the home must be disclosed as a latent defect. Flooding and water damage must also be disclosed as both of those can lead to mold growth. Inspections do not always find mold because it often grows inside walls and ductwork. Most molds require removal by a professional.

Listing and Selling Process

Nature and accuracy of the listing agreement

In most states including Missouri, a listing agreement is enforceable only if it is in writing. Most states forbid net listings, because they violate the requirement that a valid listing agreement must specify a selling price and the agent's compensation. The licensee, in accordance with the duty of due diligence, must verify the accuracy of the statements in the listing regarding the property, the owner, and the owner's representations. Especially important facts for a broker or agent to verify are:

- the property condition
- ownership status
- the client's authority to act

An agent who does not to act with a reasonable degree of due diligence in these matters may be exposed to liability if it turns out that the property is not as represented or the client cannot perform the contract as promised.

Comparative Market Analysis (CMA)

In preparing a Comparative Market Analysis, licensees should guard against using the terms "appraisal" and "value," which are reserved for the use of certified appraisers. Misuse of these terms could lead to a charge of misrepresenting oneself as an appraiser. In discussing listed properties with clients or customers, real estate licensees should be careful to use guarded terms such as "recommended listing price," "recommended purchase price,' and "recommended listing price range."

Agents should make every effort to help the sellers find a reasonable listing price based on the current market. If the CMA leads the seller to list at a price that is too high, the seller may blame the agent when the transaction fails because of an appraisal that comes in below the selling price. To minimize this risk, it is best to be conservative in the CMA and retain documentation that the seller went above the recommended price in spite of the agent's advice.

Estimate of Closing Costs

In preparing an estimate of closing costs for a seller or buyer, there is the risk of forgetting something, leading to an unpleasant surprise when the consumer suddenly faces unexpected costs or conditions. Licensees should use their broker's form, if there is one, and make it clear to the consumer that it is only an estimate of likely costs, not a statement of actual costs. In some states, brokers and agents do not prepare closing cost estimates, leaving that task to the lender.

Advertising

State and federal laws regulate advertising, including the federal Fair Housing laws as they pertain to discriminatory advertising and providing of services. Advertising includes electronic communication, social media/networking, and internet marketing. Usage must be consistent with company image and legal requirements. The license laws of most states list illegal advertising actions subject to discipline such as:

- making any substantial and intentional misrepresentation
- making any promise that might cause a person to enter into a contract or agreement when the promise is one the licensee cannot or will not abide by
- making continued and blatant misrepresentations or false promises through affiliate brokers, other persons, or any advertising medium
- making misleading or untruthful statements in any advertising, including using the term "REALTOR®" when not authorized to do so and using any other trade name, insignia or membership in a real estate organization when the licensee is not a member.

Committing such acts may result in license suspension or revocation.

Authorizations and permissions.

Licensees should stay within the bounds of the authority granted by the agency agreement or must not do anything requiring permission without first getting that permission in writing. For instance, permission should be obtained before doing any of the following unless the listing agreement specifically grants the authority:

- post a sign on the property
- remove other signs
- show the property
- hand out the property condition disclosure
- distribute marketing materials
- advertise in various media
- use a multiple listing service
- cooperate with other licensees
- divide the commission or negotiate a commission split
- share final sales data with the MLS
- place a lock box on the property
- appoint subagents
- appoint a designated agent
- change agency status

Scope of expertise

Real estate licensees are not, by nature, financial consultants, accountants, appraisers, soil scientists, well diggers, lawyers, decorators, contractors, builders, plumbers, carpenters, inspectors, prognosticators, and a number of other kinds of expert. However, in today's competitive environment, consumers often demand much more from a licensee than the traditional basic services. An agent who fails to live up to prevailing standards may be held liable for negligence, fraud, or violation of state real estate license laws and regulations. At the same time, agents must be particularly careful about the temptation to misrepresent themselves as experts and offer inappropriate expert advice. Disclaimer and referral are always the best risk control procedures to forestall an accusation of misrepresentation from a consumer who claims to have been harmed by reliance on the licensee's non-existent expertise. The exact nature of the services to be provided should be stated as clearly as possible in the listing agreement.

Contracting process

According to the Statute of Frauds, all contacts for real estate must be in writing to be enforceable. Contracts that contain incorrect information or are inadequately prepared can pose a serious liability for a licensee. To avoid such a situation, it is imperative for the contract to reflect the terms that the parties have agreed upon in the most accurate and honest manner. The agent must also be careful to comply with the letter of the real estate law. Violations can jeopardize the enforceability of a listing or sales contract, in addition to resulting in criminal prosecution.

Common risks and errors in the contracting process include:

- using an illegal form
  A licensee may be punished for using any real estate listing agreement form, sales contract form, or offer to purchase form that lacks a ***definite termination date***.
- failing to state inclusions and exclusions
  The parties should identify as included in or excluded from the transfer any ambiguous items. Unwritten agreements between the parties are a source of later dispute and trouble.
- failing to track the progress of contingency satisfaction
  The time period for completing contingencies such as inspections is specific and limited. Failure to meet or waive a condition may terminate the contract. A "time is of the essence" clause in the standard agreement makes the time period for contingencies critical.
- mistakes in entering data in a form
  All data should be checked and verified: dates, times, amounts, warranties, descriptions, names, representations, promises, procedures, authority, etc. One way to reduce risk in the contracting process is to use a checklist that covers all the contract items.

Unauthorized practice of law

The unintentional practice of law without a license is a great risk in the contracting process, as well as in the representation process. It is illegal for real estate professionals who are not attorneys to draw up contracts for transactions they are not involved in or to charge a separate fee for preparing a contract.

Such licensees may fill in blanks or make deletions on a preprinted contract form prepared by a lawyer. While a licensee may make deletions, additions to a form should be drafted by an attorney. The principals themselves can make changes as long as each change is signed or initialed by all signers. Preprinted riders can often be attached as addenda to a contract without an attorney.

It is also illegal for real estate licensees who are not lawyers to give legal advice or interpret contract language. Licensees, however, may express opinions. For instance, if a licensee believes that a party has grasped the meaning of a contract, it is permissible to say something like, "Though I am not an attorney, in my opinion your understanding of this contract is correct." It would be questionable to make a definitive statement like, "That's correct."

Fair Housing

The risk of violating fair housing laws can be minimized through ongoing education that addresses both the content and the intent of the laws. It is especially necessary for paperwork and documentation to be accurate and concise in a situation where a fair housing issue could arise.

Advertising

The Fair Housing Act forbids real estate advertising that mentions race, color, religion, national origin, sex, handicap, or familial status in any way that suggests preference or discrimination. State laws may add other protected categories, such as creed and age.

Risk can be reduced by the use of street names or other non-biased geographical references when stating where the property is located, and by describing the property rather than the type of persons who might live in or around it. Even if a home appears "ideal for a young family," it is best not to advertise it as such. Such advertising would exclude other groups such as singles, the elderly, and older families.

In advertising the sale or rental of housing covered by the Fair Housing Act, HUD recommends using the Fair Housing Logo or phrase "Equal Housing Opportunity."

Answering questions

When faced with questions that might lead to a ***steering*** charge or other violation of fair housing laws, it is best for the licensee to limit the response to features of the home and to the process of selling, buying, and listing properties, and refer the questioner to someone else to answer questions about such matters as the demographic make-up of the neighborhood. It is illegal for the licensee to voice an opinion based on race, religion, color, creed, national origin, sex, handicap, elderliness, or familial status. The agent should explain this fact to the buyer and be wary of any situation where the agent's behavior might be construed as discriminatory.

Listing agreements

Before entering into a listing agreement, a licensee should explain that it is necessary to comply with fair housing laws and obtain the potential client's acknowledgment and agreement. The agent should make it clear that the agent will

- reject the use of terms indicating race, religion, creed, color, national origin, sex, handicap, age or familial status to describe prospective buyers.
- terminate the listing if the seller uses race, religion, creed, color, national origin, sex, handicap, age, or familial status in the consideration of an offer.
- inform the broker if the seller makes any attempt to discriminate illegally.

Offers

A seller cannot refuse to sell a property to an individual based on the individual's belonging to a protected class, and if this is attempted, the real estate professional must not be involved. If the seller asks about the color, religion, creed, national origin, ethnicity, age, or familial status of a buyer, the agent must explain that it is illegal to give out such information. The best risk reduction procedure is to treat all buyers and sellers equally, showing no preference for one over another.

Antitrust

Antitrust laws forbid brokers to band together to set a price on their services in listing and selling property. Even being overheard discussing commission rates or being present at such a conversation can lead to charges of ***price fixing***.

The law recognizes that some cooperative arrangements between firms – such as joint development projects – may help consumers by allowing these firms to compete more effectively against each other. Even so the government does not prosecute all agreements between companies, but only those that will raise prices for the public or deny the public new and better products.

Sherman Antitrust Act

The ***Sherman Antitrust Act*** makes illegal all contracts, agreements, and conspiracies among competitors that would unfairly restrict interstate trade by fixing prices, rigging bids, or other means. An unlawful monopoly is created when one company becomes the only supplier of a product or service by getting rid of competition via secret agreements with other companies.

Clayton Act

The ***Clayton Act*** prohibits mergers or acquisitions that are likely to lessen competition and increase prices to consumers. The Act also prohibits certain other business practices that under certain circumstances may harm competition. Private parties injured by an antitrust violation may sue in federal court for three times their actual damages, plus court costs and attorneys' fees.

Federal Trade Commission Act

The ***Federal Trade Commission Act*** forbids unfair competition in interstate commerce but establishes no criminal penalties.

Enforcement

Federal antitrust laws are enforced in three main ways:

- the Antitrust Division of the Department of Justice (DOJ) brings criminal and civil enforcement actions
- the FTC brings civil enforcement actions
- private parties bring lawsuits claiming damages

To collect evidence, Department of Justice lawyers often work with the Federal Bureau of Investigation (FBI) on court-authorized searches of a business, monitoring phone calls and employing informants equipped with secret listening devices.

State attorneys general may sue under the Clayton Act on behalf of injured consumers in their states, and groups of consumers often bring lawsuits on their own.

Anyone associated with an organization found guilty of an antitrust violation and determined to have had knowledge of that violation may also suffer legal consequences.

Penalties. Penalties for Violation of Antitrust Laws include:

- fines for individuals and corporations, as well as possible imprisonment.
- Under the Clayton Antitrust Act, parties can sue antitrust violators and recover three times the damages they incurred plus court costs and attorneys' fees.

Rules and Regulations

State real estate laws and commissioners' rules and regulations attempt to cover every possible risky situation. Non-compliance poses a direct threat to the legal and financial status of licensee and license in the following general ways:

- license expiration
- license revocation or suspension
- licensee discipline
- suit for damages

License expiration. Licenses expire because licensees neglect to:

- maintain E & O insurance when required
- meet education requirements
- observe correct renewal procedures

License revocation or suspension. Licenses are typically revoked or suspended when a licensee is found guilty of:

- obtaining a license under false pretenses
- committing a "prohibited act"
- neglecting to present every written offer as required
- neglecting to deliver signed copies of accepted offers to transaction parties as required

- failing to make sure that all required terms and conditions are present in a contract to purchase
- handling earnest money and other escrow funds improperly

Licensee discipline

A state real estate commission may assess a civil penalty for violations of a statute, rule, or order. Licensees are disciplined for:

- acting without a license when a license is required
- demanding a referral fee without reasonable cause
- entering into a net listing
- trying to induce another licensee's client to end or change an existing agency contract
- paying a commission to an unlicensed individual or company
- receiving an illegal referral fee, rebate or kickback
- practicing with an expired license

Licensee lawsuits

A licensee may be sued by the Department of Justice, Federal Trade Commission, a state real estate commission, a human rights commission, another licensee or firm, or an individual consumer. Licensees are mainly sued for:

- fair housing violations
- antitrust violations
- license law and other state law violations
- breach of contract
- agency duty violations
- illegal practice of law
- failures to disclose
- customer or client dissatisfaction
- fraud
- theft

Misrepresentation

Misrepresentation may be unintentional or intentional.

Unintentional misrepresentation

This type of misrepresentation occurs when a licensee *unknowingly* conveys inaccurate information to a consumer concerning a property, financing or agency service. False or inaccurate information that the licensee, as a professional, should have known to be false or inaccurate may be included in the definition. Those found guilty generally have to pay fines and may be disciplined by state real estate regulators and professional organizations.

Risky areas for unintentional misrepresentation include:

- making and reporting measurements
- describing property
- offering opinions about future growth and development of a neighborhood or neighboring property
- making declarative statements about the presence or absence of hazardous materials

The risks of unintentional misrepresentation are reduced if an agent

- learns to measure and calculate areas accurately
- relies on measurements reported by others only with extreme caution and specific disclaimers
- refrains from exaggeration
- avoids stating opinions a consumer might take for expertise

Intentional misrepresentation

Also known as fraud, this kind of misrepresentation occurs when a licensee *knowingly* conveys false information about a property, financing or service. Fraud is a criminal act that may result in fines and incarceration, in addition to discipline from state regulators and professional organizations.

Recommending providers

There are several risks attending the recommendation of vendors and service providers to a consumer. First, the consumer may not be satisfied with the performance of the recommended party and blame the licensee. Second, in cases where a recommended provider performs illegal acts, there may be legal consequences for the licensee. Third, if a licensee has a business relationship with a recommended vendor or provider and neglects to disclose the fact, there are license violation consequences.

The major risk management technique is to shift the responsibility for choosing a vendor to the consumer. This can be done by refusing to recommend vendors at all; by presenting a broad range of choices and allowing the consumer to select; or by presenting a short list of thoroughly vetted vendors and allowing the consumer to make the decision, always with the disclaimer that ***to the best of the licensee's knowledge***, the vendors on the list are competent and honest, but that the consumer is responsible for investigating and making his or her own judgment before hiring or buying.

Financing and closing

In the financing and closing phases of a transaction, a consumer may feel that a licensee has been incompetent or misleading. Licensees have an obligation to inform and educate their clients throughout the transaction process. Surprises and accusations of incompetence or misrepresentation are among possible results of failing to keep the party informed.

Discrimination

Of course, it is important to comply with relevant laws. Licensees must be mindful of the requirements of ECOA and refrain from participating in any manner of discriminatory lending. It is illegal to:

- threaten, coerce, intimidate or interfere with a person who is exercising a fair housing right or assisting another other to exercise that right.
- indicate a limitation or preference based on race, color, national origin, religion, sex, familial status, or handicap in any advertisement or communication. Single-family and owner-occupied housing that is otherwise exempt from the Fair Housing Act is subject to this prohibition against discriminatory advertising.

Progress reporting

All inspections and tests must comply with local and state laws and with the purchase contract. Progress reports should be accurate, timely, in writing, and free of speculation. If a consumer has a question about the meaning of something in an inspection report, the licensee should refer the consumer to the person who wrote the report rather than trying to explain it. This method transfers some of the risk inherent in interpreting the report.

Qualifying buyers

Many transactions fail because a buyer has been improperly qualified before the offer is presented. Using a lender to qualify the buyer saves time and protects the agent against leading a seller to believe a purchaser is fully qualified when this may not be the case. Also, lenders and loan agents are better able to look into the buyer's qualifications than a real estate licensee is. If it becomes necessary to show a property to a potential buyer who has not been qualified by a lender, the licensee can gain some protection by performing an informal qualification and documenting the fact that it was based on the information provided by the buyer. The buyer's signature on this documentation indicates the buyer's acceptance of at least partial responsibility for the qualification.

Lending fees disclosure

The licensee should explain loan fees, charges, amounts, timing, and responsibilities. Agents can assist in the loan decision by explaining how to compare loans with differing charges and interest rates. The fact that a high origination fee and points may make a loan with a low interest rate unattractive to a borrower is important information for the agent to provide, and providing it may protect the agent against a later complaint that the buyer suffered a loss because of the agent's failure to inform.

Appraisal problems

Delays and appraised value are the typical problem areas. Failure to inform parties about delays can compromise the transaction. An under-appraisal will require the buyer to make a larger down payment or the seller to lower the price. If the property appraises for more than the purchase price, the seller may blame the agent for suggesting the lower price. In such a case, the seller's agent's defense is that the seller agreed to the listing price and that the price was a factor in attracting the buyer to the property.

RESPA Violations

The **Real Estate Settlement Procedures Act (RESPA)** stipulates that the parties to certain purchase transactions must be given accurate information reflecting their closing costs. It also prohibits certain business practices that are not considered to be in the consumer's best interest.

The licensee's risks regarding RESPA primarily relate to

- failing to ensure that the consumer is informed about his or her rights under the law
- giving or receiving an illegal kickback.

RESPA currently requires lenders to:

- give a copy of a Consumer Financial Protection Bureau loan information booklet to the applicant. The booklet explains RESPA provisions, general settlement costs, and the required **Closing Disclosure** form. The lender must provide the estimate of closing costs within three business days following the borrower's application.
- give the applicant a Loan Estimate (Form H-24) of expected closing costs within three business days of receiving the application. Actual closing costs may not vary from the estimate beyond certain limits.
- give the buyer the Closing Disclosure (Form H-25) specifying costs to be paid by buyer and seller at closing three business days before consummation.
- give the ***buyer*** the opportunity to review the final settlement statement *one business day prior to closing.*

RESPA specifically ***prohibits*** any fee or kickback paid to a party for a service when the party has not actually rendered the service. For example, it is prohibited for an insurance company to pay a real estate agent or a lender for referring a client.

Fees for referring clients to the following services are strictly forbidden:

- title services (search, insurance)

- appraisals
- inspections
- surveys
- loan issue
- credit report
- attorney services

The sharing of commissions and the payment of referral fees among cooperating brokers and multiple-listing services are not RESPA violations.

Trust fund handling

State laws prescribe how licensees must handle any escrow or earnest money deposits they receive. Those laws usually state that a broker must hold money received in connection with the purchase or lease of real property in a trust fund account. The type of account and financial depository are specified. The broker must record receipt of the money and place that money in the trust account within a specified time period. Usually, the law allows the broker to hold an earnest money check uncashed until the offer is accepted, provided the buyer gives written permission and the seller is informed.

Typical trust fund handling requirements include:

- the broker named as trustee of the account
- a federally-insured bank or recognized depository located in the state
- an account that is not interest-bearing if the financial institution ever requires prior written notice for withdrawals
- maintenance of records in a particular accounting format
- separate records kept for each beneficiary, property, or transaction
- records of funds received and paid out regularly reconciled with bank statements
- withdrawals only by the broker-trustee or other specifically authorized person

Commingling and conversion

Mixing of personal or company funds with client funds is grounds for the revocation or suspension of a real estate license. Depositing client funds in a personal or business account, or using them for any purpose other than the client's business, is also grounds for suspension or revocation of a license. It is important for the broker to remove commissions, fees or other income earned by the broker from a trust account within the period specified by law to avoid committing an act of commingling.

MODULE 6 SNAPSHOT REVIEW: RISK MANAGEMENT

I. Avoiding Misrepresentation and Reducing Risk

RISK MANAGEMENT STRATEGIES

- Avoidance — refraining from an activity that carries risk; complete avoidance in real estate is nearly impossible.
- Reduction — taking steps to lower the probability or severity of loss; often involves sharing responsibility for decisions with the client.
- Transference — passing risk to another party through contract or insurance; Errors & Omissions (E&O) insurance is the primary tool.
- Retention — accepting known risk and taking full responsibility; effectively self-insurance when no other strategy applies.
- The most practical strategies for real estate practice are reduction and transference, supported by education, disclosure, documentation, and insurance.

RISK MANAGEMENT PROCEDURES

Education

- Education is the first line of defense; familiarity with forms, contract elements, and license law reduces the likelihood of errors.
- Brokers have a legal obligation to train affiliated licensees; licensees must also seek outside education and meet continuing education requirements.

Disclosure

- Proper disclosure reduces the risk that clients will claim they were misled or acted on incomplete information.
- Required disclosures typically include agency relationships, property condition, personal interest in the transaction, and personal interest in referrals.

Documentation and Record Keeping

- Documentation provides evidence of compliance and proves what was said and done in a transaction.
- Key components include policy and procedures manuals, standard forms, communication records, transaction records, contracts, and accounting records.
- State laws require firms to retain written transaction records for typically three to five years after closing or termination.
- Trust fund accounting records must track depositor, deposit date, withdrawal date, payee, and other commission-required information for each transaction.

Insurance

- General liability insurance covers risks when the public or licensees enter an owned property but does not cover professional liability.
- Errors & Omissions (E&O) insurance covers negligent acts, errors, and omissions arising from professional services.
- E&O insurance does NOT cover violations of law, fraud, criminal acts, fair housing violations, mishandling of escrow funds, or environmental violations.

PRIMARY AREAS OF RISK

Agency

- Agency risks arise in two areas: the requirement to inform and disclose, and the requirement to carry out agency duties.
- Licensees must disclose their agency status verbally on initial contact, verbally before providing services, and in writing before signing agreements or presenting offers.
- Duties owed to all parties include honesty, fairness, reasonable care, and disclosure; duties owed to clients additionally include loyalty, obedience, confidentiality, and full accounting.
- The duty of confidentiality survives the termination of the listing agreement; confidential information may not be disclosed without the client's written permission.
- Conflicts of interest arise when a licensee's personal interests compete with a client's best interests; all self-interests must be disclosed.
- Penalties for breach of agency include rescission, loss of compensation, punitive damages, ethics discipline, and license discipline.

Property Disclosures

- Most states require sellers to provide written disclosure of known material defects before a purchase contract is accepted.
- Federal law requires lead-based paint disclosure for homes built before 1978; the licensee must ensure sellers complete the form and buyers receive it.
- Mold must be disclosed as a latent defect; flooding and water damage must also be disclosed because they can cause mold growth.

Listing and Selling Process

- Listing agreements must be in writing and must specify a selling price and compensation; net listings are generally forbidden.
- Licensees should use terms such as 'recommended listing price' rather than 'appraisal' or 'value,' which are reserved for licensed appraisers.
- Closing cost estimates should use the broker's approved form and be clearly identified as estimates, not statements of actual costs.
- Advertising must comply with fair housing law; discriminatory language and misrepresentations are prohibited and may result in license suspension or revocation.
- All actions requiring principal permission — such as placing signs, using the MLS, or appointing subagents — must be specifically authorized in the listing agreement.

Contracting Process

- All real estate contracts must be in writing to be enforceable under the Statute of Frauds.
- Common contracting risks include using an illegal form, failing to state inclusions and exclusions, missing contingency deadlines, and data entry errors.
- Licensees may complete blanks and make deletions on preprinted forms; additions should be drafted by an attorney; principals may make changes if all parties initial them.
- Giving legal advice or interpreting contract language constitutes unauthorized practice of law; licensees may express opinions but not make definitive legal interpretations.

Fair Housing

- The Fair Housing Act prohibits advertising that suggests a preference or limitation based on race, color, religion, national origin, sex, handicap, or familial status.

- When fielding questions that could lead to a steering charge, licensees should limit responses to property features and the buying or selling process.
- Before entering a listing, the licensee should obtain the client's written acknowledgment of the obligation to comply with fair housing law.
- Sellers may not refuse to sell based on a buyer's protected class status; agents must not participate in any such discriminatory act.

Antitrust

- The Sherman Antitrust Act prohibits agreements among competitors to fix prices, rig bids, or otherwise restrict trade.
- The Clayton Act prohibits mergers and acquisitions that lessen competition; private parties may sue for three times actual damages plus attorneys' fees.
- Even being present during a conversation about fixing commission rates can lead to antitrust charges.

License Law Compliance

- Licenses may be revoked or suspended for obtaining a license under false pretenses, mishandling escrow funds, failing to present written offers, or committing prohibited acts.
- Licensees may be disciplined for acting without a license, paying unlicensed individuals, demanding referral fees without cause, or entering into net listings.
- Licensees may be sued for fair housing and antitrust violations, breach of contract, agency duty violations, fraud, failures to disclose, and illegal practice of law.

Misrepresentation

- Unintentional misrepresentation occurs when a licensee unknowingly conveys inaccurate information, including information the licensee should have known was false.
- High-risk areas include reporting measurements, describing property, commenting on neighborhood growth, and making statements about hazardous materials.
- Intentional misrepresentation (fraud) involves knowingly conveying false information and is a criminal act subject to fines and incarceration.

Recommending Providers

- The safest risk management approach is to shift vendor selection responsibility to the consumer by offering a vetted list and letting the client decide.
- Any business relationship between the licensee and a recommended vendor must be disclosed.

Trust Fund Handling

- Brokers must hold escrow and earnest money deposits in a trust fund account at a federally-insured depository; records must be maintained in the format required by the commission.
- Commingling — mixing personal or company funds with client funds — is grounds for license revocation or suspension.
- Converting client funds for personal or business use is also grounds for revocation or suspension.
- Commissions and fees must be removed from the trust account within the time period specified by law to avoid a commingling violation.

MODULE 6 QUIZ – RISK MANAGEMENT

1. Four well-established risk management strategies include avoidance, reduction, transference, and ________.

   a. elimination.
   b. mitigation.
   c. sharing.
   d. retention.

2. Which insurance policy is a primary mechanism for transferring the professional liability risks of brokers and licensees?

   a. Errors & Omissions insurance
   b. General liability insurance
   c. Workers' compensation
   d. Consequential loss, use, and occupancy insurance

3. Which of the following duties requires the agent to act on the principal's wishes regarding the transaction?

   a. Confidentiality
   b. Disclosure
   c. Obedience
   d. Skill and diligence

4. An insurance policy is a common example of which risk management strategy?

   a. Retention
   b. Transference
   c. Reduction
   d. Avoidance

5. Which statute forbids brokers to band together to determine a set price on their listing services?

   a. Antitrust law
   b. Clayton Act
   c. Federal Trade Commission Act
   d. Statute of Frauds

6. Federal law requires sellers of houses built before _____ to make a lead-based paint disclosure to potential buyers.

   a. 1988
   b. 1964
   c. 1978
   d. 1950

7. What is the first line of defense against risk?

a. Education
b. Diligence
c. Liability elimination
d. Avoidance

8. Which type of insurance covers loss of rent due to a fire?

a. Fire and hazard insurance
b. Consequential loss, use, and occupancy insurance
c. Casualty insurance
d. Surety bond insurance

9. Which keyword should licensees avoid when preparing a CMA?

a. Market
b. Analysis
c. Comparables
d. Appraisal

10. Ella is buying an off-market home and asks her licensee friend to write a contract for her. The licensee agrees for a fee of $475. What can the licensee be accused of?

a. Fraud
b. Misadvertising
c. Unauthorized practice of law
d. Price gouging

11. How are federal antitrust laws enforced?

a. The FTC brings civil enforcement actions
b. With a $1,000-10,000 fine
c. With 30 days of incarceration
d. NAR brings criminal enforcement actions

12. Which of the following actions would be cause for license suspension?

a. Missing an education requirement
b. Handling earnest money improperly
c. Incorrectly renewing a license
d. Failing to complete continuing education

13. Which licensee duty applies to all funds involved in a real estate transaction?

a. Confidentiality
b. Disclosure
c. Accounting
d. Diligence

14. Which of the following would be covered by E&O insurance?

a. Claims that the licensee failed to carry out fiduciary duties
b. Violations of the law
c. Antitrust violations
d. Fair housing violations

15. Which statute requires that parties to certain purchase transactions be given accurate information reflecting their closing costs?

a. Clayton Act
b. RESPA
c. Sherman Antitrust Act
d. FTCA

MODULE 6 CASE STUDY

Risk Management

"WHAT IF" SITUATION EXAMPLE: Mitigating risks when dealing with buyers.

Abigail is a brand-new real estate agent and is hungry for her first deal. She is hosting an open house at a foreclosure property and an investor stops by. They chat briefly and, as he tours the home, he starts asking her for the cost to renovate the kitchen and what the future of the neighborhood looks like. Abigail has no experience pricing renovations but she is very eager to land her first client.

What would you say if you were Abigail?

Module 7: TYPES OF CONSTRUCTION

I. Construction Glossary

Module 7 Learning Objectives

1. **Identify common residential construction components and materials across the major systems of a home.**
2. **Recognize and distinguish residential house styles by their defining architectural features, such as roof type, exterior materials, ornamentation, and massing, and apply accurate terminology when describing properties to clients.**
3. **Explain the key systems found in a residential property, including electrical, plumbing, heating and cooling, insulation, windows, and doors, using correct technical terminology.**

I. Construction Glossary

HOUSE STYLES

bungalow Originally a one-story house with prominent roof and large overhangs.

Cape Cod A small one-story or one-and-a-half-story house with gable roof, clapboard or shingle siding, and no dormers (originally).

contemporary A modern house that emphasizes materials and structure rather than any traditional or derivative style.

Dutch colonial revival A house with a gambrel roof where the lower slope of the roof flares into the eave with a gentle curve.

Elizabethan A house using or simulating half-timber construction; cross gables; steeply pitched roof; large chimney stacks.

English colonial A saltbox, Cape Cod or other simple style with no ornamentations or classical details.

Federal An adaptation of classical and Georgian styles, featuring tall windows, curved stairs, elliptical rooms, bowed projections and octagonal bays, virtually flat roof, balustrade along the eave line, fanlight transoms, decorated sidelights, porticoes and columns.

Georgian A style characterized by symmetry, aligned windows, and conventional details; gambrel, gable or hip roof; windows capped with cornices or crown moldings; classical cornices on the eaves; pilasters often frame the doorway, but there is no covered porch at the front door; balustrade set high on the roof; building material varies regionally.

Gothic revival A variety of irregular, picturesque, rambling designs; steeply-pitched gable and cross-gable roof, vertical siding in earthy colors; carved ornamentation; verandas and balconies.

Greek revival A style based on the forms of the classical Greek temple; shallow-pitched gable roof, with gable end usually oriented toward the road; portico with columns; recessed front entrance with wide casings; white clapboard with dark green shutters.

Mansard A modern style featuring the mansard roof; often has arched dormer windows, double front doors, smooth stucco covering, and decorative corner features.

modern A house built with up-to-date materials. May be contemporary in style, or a reproduction or derivative style.

neoclassical revival A style featuring a two-story classical portico with columns, restrained decorative details, smooth exterior wall surfaces, often a hip roof.

Prairie Characterized by a low-pitched hip roof with wide overhangs; bands of casement windows; stucco covering; strong horizontal emphasis; low, heavy and solid appearance.

Queen Anne A multi-story, wood-framed and (usually) clapboarded style featuring turrets, towers, verandahs, wrap-around porches, gazebos, scrollwork, varied shingle patterns.

ranch Typically one-story; simple gable roof; built on a slab or shallow foundation; materials, coverings, ornamentation vary.

Romanesque A style featuring masonry construction, massive walls, round arches, masonry mullions, steep multi-gabled roof, turrets.

saltbox A two-story house with a gable roof, the back slope of which is elongated down to a one-story height; usually covered in clapboard siding.

Spanish mission Characterized by red tile roof, wide eaves with exposed rafter ends, open porches with rectangular piers, a dominant curved parapet, and stucco.

split-level A ranch-type house with a one-story section meeting a two story section midway.

Tudor A masonry or stucco building with parapeted gables, stone mullions, large leaded windows, and a Tudor arch.

Victorian Not a single style; often used to refer to Queen Anne or Gothic revival styles.

Williamsburg colonial A modern style featuring symmetrical facade, steeply-pitched gable roof with dormers; clapboard or brick covering.

DOOR TYPES AND PARTS

bifold A two-paneled folding door mounted in a track, usually used with closets.

bypass Doors set in a track so as to open by sliding past each other, usually used with closets.

Dutch A two-part door divided horizontally.

French A two-part door divided vertically.

hollow core A door constructed of exterior surfaces with air-space and filler between them.

jamb The sides and top member of a door frame.

raised panel A door constructed of shaped solid panels set into a solid frame.

sidelight Narrow window next to an entry door.

solid core A door constructed of exterior surfaces with solid wood blocks filling the space between them.

steel A door constructed of steel as a fire-proofing or security barrier.

threshold The bottom part of a doorway.

ELECTRICAL

240 volt service The type of electrical supply required by such household appliances as air conditioners, washers and dryers. Usually separate from the normal household supply of 120 volts.

amperage A measure of the overall capability of the household supply. 100 amp service is the modern minimum standard.

bus bar A solid metal bar in a service entrance panel or subpanel. A hot bus bar is connected to the main power source. A neutral bus bar provides a terminal for all neutral wires and is part of the grounding connection.

BX A flexible, metal-armored type of self-contained wiring that is installed without conduit. Also called AC (armored cable).

circuit breaker A resettable device that interrupts a circuit when there is an overload or fault on the line.

conduit Metal piping used to carry flexible wiring.

fuse A device that interrupts a circuit when there is an overload or fault. The fuse must be replaced after it has performed the interruption.

ground fault circuit interrupter A device that monitors the current entering and leaving a receptacle or circuit. When incoming and outgoing currents are unequal, the device instantly opens the circuit. Used particularly in bathroom, garage and outdoor receptacles.

junction box A box that contains wire splices or cable connections, but devices.

outlet box A box that protects wire connections and holds a device such as a switch or receptacle.

rheostat A dimmer switch that allows gradient control of current.

Romex A type of nonmetallic, sheathed, multi-conductor cable.

service entrance panel The main control box for a household electrical system, containing the connection to the power supply, the main disconnect, circuit breakers, and the grounding connection.

subpanel A panel containing hot and neutral bus bars to distribute power coming from the service entrance panel.

switch A device installed on a hot wire to break the connection between the hot bus bar and a device connected beyond the switch.

EXTERIOR COVERINGS

beveled siding Siding consisting of horizontally overlapped boards that are thinner on the upper edge than on the lower.

board and batten Siding that is applied in vertical panels or boards with the vertical joints covered by narrow strips.

brick Outside structural wall or veneer consisting of brick and mortar. In residences, generally regarded as
low-maintenance, fireproof and decorative.

clapboard A type of smooth beveled siding, generally narrow, that is common in older frame houses.

redwood siding Siding, usually beveled, made of cedar or redwood. Noted for resistance to weather, it may be installed with rough or smooth side out, and may be stained, painted, or only sealed.

shingle A type of thick, wooden shingle, also called a shake, which can be applied vertically as siding.

shiplap A type of wooden siding milled on both edges so that the edge of one board overlaps the edge of the next board.

siding Exterior finish or "skin" of a wall; typical types are vinyl, aluminum, beveled wood, shingle, and board and batten.

stucco A cement-based material applied in semi-liquid form over metal lath. A kind of false stucco is sometimes applied to plywood panels.

tongue and groove A type of wooden siding milled with a groove on one edge and a protruding "tongue" on the other so that the edge of one board fits into the edge of the next board.

FOUNDATION TYPES AND PARTS

brick A foundation of brick laid on a concrete footing, found in some older houses.

cement block A foundation of cast blocks laid on a concrete footing.

footing The base on which the foundation walls sit. Usually poured concrete, twice the thickness of the walls.

poured concrete A foundation in which the walls consist of concrete poured into forms.

slab A horizontal concrete section used as a foundation.

stone A foundation of field stone.

GENERAL STRUCTURE

balloon frame A house framing method in which studs extend from foundation to roof. Floor joists are hung on the studs. Generally replaced by platform framing after 1945.

basement An area below grade level, generally accessible from inside the house, with sufficient clearance that a person can stand up in it. A full basement covers the area of the entire first floor.

bay A portion of a building that projects beyond the face of the building.

beam A horizontal structural member. May be solid timber, laminated wood, or metal.

bearing wall A wall that supports part of the load above it.

blueboard A type of rough gypsum board used for sheathing interior walls.

bridging Diagonal bracing between floor joists to spread load.

building paper An asphalt-saturated paper used as a covering over wall sheathing, roof decking, or a subfloor.

casing Finish trim around a framed wall opening.

crawl space The area between first floor joists and ground in a house without a basement. Often filled with gravel. Clearance is not sufficient to allow a person to stand up.

deck A horizontal wooden surface attached to the exterior of a house.

dormer A windowed structure with its own roof that projects from the main roof of a building.

downspout An externally mounted vertical tube that carries rain water from gutter to ground or drain tile.

drain tile An underground tube that carries water away from the foundation footing or from the top of the foundation wall at the downspout.

drywall A type of smooth gypsum board used as an interior wall covering. Also called sheetrock and plasterboard.

eave The part of a roof that hangs beyond the external supporting wall.

facade The front face of a building.

fascia A board that covers the ends of the roof rafters.

flashing Metal sheets or strips installed as waterproofing at roof edges and around junctures of roof surfaces and other wall and roof locations where leakage must be prevented.

girder A horizontal beam that supports other beams.

greenboard A water-resistant type of gypsum board.

gutter A trough at the roof eave or other low point that collects rain water from the roof and carries it to a downspout.

gypsum board A wall paneling material composed of a core of gypsum between outer layers of heavy paper.

half-timber A type of timber framing in which the timbers and filled space between timbers are left exposed on the exterior surface.

joist One of the parallel, horizontal beams that supports a floor or ceiling.

knee wall A short wall from floor to rafter in a room with a sloped ceiling, such as an attic.

lath A wood or metal support for a semi-liquid wall covering material such as plaster or stucco.

lintel A horizontal supporting member across the top of a door or window opening.

masonry Construction using brick, stone, or concrete block..

partition A dividing wall, usually not a bearing wall.

plaster A mixture of gypsum, sand and lime applied by trowel over lath, plasterboard, or other plaster layer.

plate The top or bottom horizontal element of a stud wall.

platform frame A house framing method in which each floor is built up individually and serves as the foundation for stud walls. Also called western framing.

post A vertical structural member that supports a beam or girder.

rafter One of the parallel supporting members that holds the roof decking. Usually 2 x 6 or 2 x 8 solid timber (2 x 4 in some older houses).

rise The number of vertical inches per horizontal foot (run) of a sloped roof; the height of a flight of stairs; the height of one step.

riser The vertical board that covers the front of a stair.

run The horizontal dimension of a roof or stairway.

sheathing The rough covering of the shell of a structure, fastened to studs, rafters or joists as a support for a finish covering; typically composition board, plywood, or solid lumber (in older houses).

sheetrock Drywall.

shoe Sole plate; finish trim around edges of a finished floor.

sill Bottom horizontal member of a door or window frame; horizontal framing member bolted to a slab or foundation wall.

soffit The horizontal under-surface covering the area between the exterior wall and the end of rafters; the boxed-in area between the top of a row of cabinets and the ceiling

sole plate The bottom plate of a stud wall, attached to subfloor or slab.

span The distance between vertical supports.

stringer One of the side, supporting members of a staircase.

stud One of the vertical, parallel structural elements of a framed wall. Metal or wood.

subfloor Sheathing applied to floor joists as rough flooring.

suspended ceiling A ceiling supported by hangers attached to joists rather than being attached directly to the joists.

termite shield A metal or other barrier placed around foundation walls and wall penetrations to impede termites.

terrazzo A type of finished flooring composed of stones or stone chips imbedded in a hard medium.

top plate The upper plate of a stud wall, supporting joists or rafters.

tread The horizontal surface of a stair.

trim Woodwork, millwork, molding and other finishing material.

underlayment Plywood or other type of panel applied to a subfloor as a support for finished flooring.

wallboard Gypsum board or composition board used as an interior wall covering.

HEATING AND COOLING

central air An air conditioning unit, mounted outside a house, that cools the entire house by way of ducting.

duct work Sheet metal shafting and piping that carries hot and cold air in a house.

electric Heating by electric resistance cable or panels in floors, walls, or ceilings, or some other electrically powered radiation system.

forced air Heating by hot air blown by a furnace fan and carried in ducts.

gas Heating by means of a furnace powered by natural gas. May be forced air or hot water.

heat pump A device for recirculating heated air.

hot water Heating by means of hot water carried through pipes to heating coils, floor radiators, or baseboard radiators.

oil Heating by means of a furnace powered by fuel oil. May be forced air, hot water or steam.

register A grating in wall or floor to permit heated or cooled air to enter a room.

return A grating in wall or floor to remove cooled or warmed air from a room.

solar Heating by means of collection of solar radiation.

steam Heating by means of steam carried through pipes to radiators.

window unit A self-contained air conditioning unit installed in a window.

INSULATION

asbestos A fibrous mineral used for fireproofing, electrical insulation, around heating pipes and ducts, also applied as a spray covering on walls and ceilings; now regarded as a hazardous substance subject to environmental regulation.

batting Fibrous material, usually fiberglass, wadded together, backed with foil or paper, and formed into a roll; designed to fit between studs of a standard stud wall.

blown Loose insulating material blown into spaces between studs and wall surfaces.

fiberglass A cotton-like material consisting of glass and resin.

firestop A fire-resistant material used to impede the spread of flames.

foam Polystyrene or other expanding foam sprayed into gaps.

foam board Light-weight solid board composed of polystyrene foam and cut to fit between studs.

R-factor A measure of the efficiency of insulation against heat transfer.

vapor barrier A waterproof material that prevents warm, moisture-laden indoor air from meeting colder outdoor air and condensing.

PLUMBING

cleanout A removable opening in a drain pipe that allows cleaning out of clogging material.

cast iron Material traditionally used for soil stack and soil pipe, with joints poured of hot lead.

copper Material traditionally preferred for piping hot and cold water supply within a house, with soldered joints.

lead Material once commonly used to seal water supply pipes, now regarded as hazardous and subject to environmental regulation.

PVC Polyvinyl chloride, a thermoplastic resin used for piping, with glued joints.

soil stack Large-dimension vertical pipe that vents sewer gases through the roof

soil pipe Drain pipe that carries waste to sewer or septic system.

sump pump A pump installed in a basement to remove water from around and under the foundation and floor of the basement.

trap A U-shaped section of drain pipe that holds water as a barrier against sewer gases and odors.

vent pipe A pipe that allows sewer gases to vent above the roof line and prevents back pressure from building up; connects to a vent stack.

vent stack A soil stack.

well and septic A water supply and waste removal system that is self-contained on a parcel, usually in rural areas where city services are not available.

ROOF TYPES AND ELEMENTS

asphalt shingle Heavy felt impregnated with asphalt and coated with mineral granules; come in a range of colors; life span of approximately 15 years.

built-up A low-pitch or flat roof covered with layers of roofing felt laminated with tar, pitch or asphalt and topped with hot tar and gravel.

cross gable A gable roof that intersects another gable roof at right angles.

decking Boards or panels applied to the rafters as a support for the roof covering.

felt Asphalt-impregnated paper installed over decking as an underlayment for the roof covering.

flat A roof with little or no pitch; not suitable for shingles; requires a built-up or membrane type of covering.

gable A triangular end wall defined by the two slopes of a roof and a line joining the eaves; a pitched roof that creates a triangular end wall.

gambrel A roof that has two slopes on each side, the lower slopes being steeper than the upper slopes; typical of barns.

Gothic A ridged roof with sides that curve, often ending in a flair.

hip The outside corner formed by the perpendicular meeting of the outside edges of two roof slopes; a roof that ends in hips rather than gables or other end walls.

mansard A roof that has two slopes on all four sides; the upper slope is close to horizontal and the lower slope is close to vertical.

membrane A vulcanized sheet of rubber or other seamless material applied with adhesive directly to decking; used on flat and low-pitch roofs

pitched A roof that has a slope; pitch is usually stated as a ratio of rise (vertical distance) in inches per 12 inches of run (horizontal distance).

rafter One of the parallel beams that supports the decking of a sloped roof.

rake The slope of a gable.

ridge The horizontal line formed by the juncture of two roof slopes; the board to which the upper ends of the rafters of two slopes are nailed.

roll roofing Mineral-coated, asphalt-impregnated felt produced in long rolled-up sheets instead of as individual shingles; typically installed in overlapped pieces which are the length of the entire roof.

roofing paper Felt.

shake A wooden shingle, usually redwood or cedar, that can be installed as a roof covering or wall covering.

shed A pitched roof with a single slope.

slate A fine-grained rock that splits into thin, smooth layers that can be used as shingles; very heavy, but long-lasting.

tile Curved ceramic or concrete elements that fit together in such a way as to form a waterproof roof covering.

truss A framework of rafters and connecting beams installed as a unit to support part of a roof and tie together the opposite walls.

valley The inside corner created where two roof slopes meet; the opposite of a hip.

WINDOW TYPES AND PARTS

awning A window hinged along the top edge and designed to swing at the bottom.

bay A window or group of windows in a structural bay.

bow A curved window or a group of windows built as a unit to project beyond the surface of a wall.

casement A window hinged along one of the vertical edges.

casing Finish trim around a window opening.

double-hung A window with an upper and lower sash that slide vertically in separate slots.

eyebrow An arched window set in a rounded dormer that has no side walls.

fanlight A semi-circular transom window with muntins that fan from the center.

French A pair of casement windows hinged on the outer vertical edges so that they open inward or outward together.

hopper A window hinged along the bottom edge.

jalousie A window with adjustable, pivoting overlapped horizontal glass slats.

light A single pane of glass in a window; windows are described as two-light, four-light, six-light, etc.

louver A jalousie window, or one of the glass elements of the same.

mullion A vertical post or double jamb that divides two window sashes or large fixed panes.

muntin The horizontal and vertical cross-members that hold individual panes of glass within a single sash.

oriel A bay window on an upper floor.

rail One of the horizontal elements of a sash.

sash The frame which the panes of a window.

sill The base of a window jamb.

stile One of the vertical elements of a sash.

stool The ledge that sits on the sill of a window.

transom A small window above a door or a larger window; the horizontal divider is, technically, the transom.

MODULE 7 QUIZ – TYPES OF CONSTRUCTION

1. A buyer is viewing a two-story house with a gable roof whose back slope extends down to a one-story height, covered in clapboard siding. Which house style best describes this property?

a. Saltbox
b. Cape Cod
c. Dutch colonial revival
d. Georgian

2. During a listing appointment, a seller points to the roof and describes it as having two slopes on all four sides, with the upper slope nearly horizontal and the lower slope nearly vertical. Which roof type is the seller describing?

a. Mansard
b. Hip
c. Chalet
d. Shed

3. A home inspector notes that the house uses platform framing. Which of the following best describes this framing method?

a. Studs extend continuously from the foundation all the way to the roof line
b. The framing relies on half-timber construction with exposed beams on the exterior
c. Horizontal beams carry the full structural load without the use of vertical studs
d. Each floor is built up individually and serves as the working platform and foundation for the stud walls above

4. A buyer asks about the metal strips installed around the chimney and along the roof edges of a home she is considering. What is the correct term for this component and its purpose?

a. Fascia — a board that covers the ends of the roof rafters
b. Soffit — the horizontal under-surface covering between the exterior wall and end of rafters
c. Decking — boards applied to rafters as support for the roof covering
d. Flashing — metal sheets installed as waterproofing at roof edges and around junctures of roof surfaces

5. Which of the following electrical components is specifically designed to protect against shock hazards in bathrooms, garages, and outdoor receptacles by instantly opening the circuit when incoming and outgoing currents are unequal?

a. Circuit breaker
b. Subpanel
c. Ground fault circuit interrupter
d. Bus bar

6. A property inspection report states that the home has a crawl space rather than a basement. Which of the following statements correctly distinguishes between these two features?

a. A crawl space is below grade level with enough clearance for a person to stand upright
b. A basement has insufficient clearance for standing, while a crawl space extends the full area under the first floor
c. A crawl space has insufficient clearance for standing, while a full basement covers the area of the entire first floor with standing height
d. A crawl space and a basement are interchangeable terms for the same feature

7. A listing describes a home's exterior as covered in board and batten siding. Which of the following best describes this type of exterior covering?

a. Horizontally overlapped boards that are thinner on the upper edge than on the lower
b. Vertical panels or boards with the vertical joints covered by narrow strips
c. A cement-based material applied in semi-liquid form over metal lath
d. Wooden boards milled with a groove on one edge and a protruding tongue on the other

8. A plumbing inspection reveals that the home's drain pipes include a U-shaped section near each fixture. What is the purpose of this component?

a. It allows sewer gases to vent above the roof line and prevents back pressure
b. It holds water as a barrier against sewer gases and odors entering the living space
c. It provides a removable opening for cleaning out clogging material
d. It carries waste water from the fixture to the main soil pipe

9. Which of the following insulation materials is now classified as a hazardous substance subject to environmental regulation?

a. Fiberglass batting
b. Blown insulation
c. Asbestos
d. Foam board

10. A buyer notices that the upper-floor windows project outward from the wall of the home and asks the agent what they are called. Which window type correctly describes a bay window located on an upper floor?

a. Casement
b. Oriel
c. Transom
d. Awning

Answer Key for Quizzes

Answer Key for Module 1 Quiz: Missouri Agency Relationships & Agency Disclosure

1 a Transaction broker
2 b At the earliest practicable opportunity during or following the first substantial contact
3 b A definite beginning and expiration date
4 b River Bluff Realty and the listing client
5 a That the seller would accept less than the listed price
6 a Disclose all known adverse material facts to the client
7 c To allow two agents within the same firm to each fully represent their respective clients without dual agency conflicts
8 d Soliciting a brokerage agreement from a party already under an exclusive agreement with another broker
9 d The listing automatically expires at the end date unless both parties agree in writing to extend it
10 c Renunciation
11 d Confidentiality
12 c The agency relationships remain with the original broker, since clients belong to the broker

Answer Key for Module 2 Quiz: Missouri Seller Representation

1. a Any activity designed to generate listing prospects who have not yet committed to a broker
2. a Referral-based lead generation from friends, family, and past clients
3. a 7 to 8%
4. a Follow up with active buyers who may be in the market even if they do not purchase that particular listing
5. c An estimated net sheet, a detailed marketing plan, and all necessary listing paperwork
6. a Special or limited agency, restricting the broker's authority to specific transaction-related activities
7. d Any party, including the listing broker, a cooperating broker, or the seller themselves
8. b The seller finds the buyer independently without the broker's involvement
9. d Create an inherent conflict of interest by incentivizing the broker to encourage the seller to set the lowest possible price
10. b Call for a highest and best offer from all buyers to save time and ensure the strongest possible terms
11. c Submit the contract and earnest money to the managing broker without delay
12. d Offers of buyer agent compensation being published or advertised in the MLS
13. c Fully negotiable and not established or mandated by law
14. c Desire, utility, scarcity, and purchasing power
15. d An opinion of the price a willing buyer and willing seller would agree on in an arm's length transaction with full information and no abnormal pressure
16. b Pay no more for a property than the cost of an equally desirable and available substitute
17. c Deduct value from the comparable's sale price to equalize it with the subject
18. b A listing price is a strategic pre-contract market decision; the appraised value is an independent post-contract determination ordered by the buyer's lender

Answer Key for Module 3 Quiz: Missouri Buyer Representation

1. a A client receives the full set of fiduciary duties from the broker, while a customer receives only basic assistance without advocacy or negotiating representation
2. a Confidentiality

3. c Through any source during the agreement term, including the MLS, a For Sale By Owner, or any other channel
4. b Preserves the buyer's right to find a property independently without owing a commission
5. c The NAR settlement requires a written buyer representation agreement to be in place before a broker shows a buyer any property
6. d Special agency, authorizing the broker to locate properties, negotiate terms, and advise the buyer but not to bind the buyer to a contract without explicit consent
7. b The agreement must clearly state the compensation being sought and explain that the buyer may be responsible for paying the difference if the seller offers less than that amount
8. d It helps focus the property search, avoids wasted effort, and strengthens the buyer's position when making an offer
9. b Have a signed written buyer representation agreement in place before showing the property, with no exceptions
10. c A negotiated transaction term that may be included as a request in the buyer's purchase offer and which the seller may agree to, counter, or decline

Answer Key for Module 4 Quiz: Completing the Transaction

1. a Vendee
2. d The parties have yet to fulfill their respective obligations and promises
3. a Both spouses release homestead, dower, and curtesy rights to the buyer at closing
4. d A clause allowing either party to cancel for any reason at any time
5. a Specific performance, damages, or cancellation
6. d When the offeree communicates unconditional acceptance of all terms to the offeror
7. d When the buyer places the acceptance in the mail
8. a — The seller's change creates a counteroffer and voids the original offer
9. a — An agreement created when the offeree pays consideration to keep an offer open for a stated period
10. d Engaging in the unauthorized practice of law and exposing themselves to client lawsuits
11. c Unemployment benefits received after a layoff or termination
12. d Reflect the income's tax-free nature so it can be compared fairly to taxable income
13. a 27%
14. c Monthly grocery and utility bills
15. b Loan churning or loan flipping
16. b Written permission is obtained from the person providing the funds
17. c Making a good-faith determination of breach and giving all parties 15 days' written notice
18. b Ten banking days after receiving the next bank statement
19. b A fee paid to a title company for a referral when no actual title service is performed
20. c Three business days
21. c The brokerage commission owed at closing
22. b $984.00
23. c The VA usually requires no down payment, though the lender may require one
24. b A junior mortgage secured by the homeowner's equity in the property
25. b Receives a junior mortgage from the buyer and uses those payments to service the original first mortgage

Answer Key for Module 5 Quiz: Ethics and Standards of Conduct

1. a duties to REALTORS®.
2. a REALTORS® are not obligated to discover latent defects.
3. c Property.
4. a Commitment to Excellence
5. d REALTORS® must not disclose information ascertained from a hearing.

6. a To protect the public and promote homeownership
7. b procuring cause.
8. c mediation
9. b Article 15 of the Code of Ethics
10. d The Preamble
11. c The prohibition against undisclosed compensation
12. a Anyone
13. b $15,000
14. d Expulsion from membership for one to three years
15. c Ombudsman
16. b Declining to cooperate genuinely serves the client's best interest rather than the licensee's personal or financial preference
17. b Compensation and cooperation are separate matters; cooperation does not require sharing commissions or compensating another broker
18. c Publishing offers of buyer agent compensation in MLS listings
19. c The agency relationship remains between the seller and the brokerage firm, because the signed brokerage agreement establishes the relationship, not the source of compensation
20. d $4,500
21. d Sign crossing or broker interference, which is prohibited under Missouri license law

Answer Key for Module 6 Quiz: Risk Management

1. d retention.
2. d Errors & Omissions insurance
3. c Obedience
4. b Transference
5. a Antitrust law
6. c 1978
7. a Education
8. b Consequential loss, use, and occupancy insurance
9. d Appraisal
10. c Unauthorized practice of law
11. a The FTC brings civil enforcement actions
12. b Handling earnest money improperly
13. c Accounting
14. a Claims that the licensee failed to carry out fiduciary duties
15. b RESPA

Answer Key for Module 7 Quiz: Construction Glossary

1. a Saltbox
2. a Mansard
3. d Each floor is built up individually and serves as the working platform and foundation for the stud walls above
4. d Flashing — metal sheets installed as waterproofing at roof edges and around junctures of roof surfaces
5. c Ground fault circuit interrupter
6. c A crawl space has insufficient clearance for standing, while a full basement covers the area of the entire first floor with standing height
7. b Vertical panels or boards with the vertical joints covered by narrow strips
8. b It holds water as a barrier against sewer gases and odors entering the living space

9. c Asbestos
10. b Oriel

DEBRIEF GUIDE – POSSIBLE SOLUTIONS TO CASE STUDY EXERCISES

CASE DEBRIEF FOR MODULE 1:

Question 1. Because no written agency agreement was ever signed, Marcus was functioning as a transaction broker under Missouri law, which is the default status when no written agency agreement exists. Even so, Missouri licensees owe a duty to disclose their brokerage relationship status and to provide the Broker Disclosure Form at the earliest practicable opportunity during or following the first substantial contact. Marcus should have presented the Broker Disclosure Form at his very first meeting with Diane and established the nature of their relationship in writing before gathering any personal or financial information.

Question 2. Multiple disclosure violations occurred. As a transaction broker working with a seller, Marcus was required to disclose his status before the relationship was established and before receiving any personal or financial information. He was also required to disclose his existing relationship with Todd, a buyer, before showing Diane's property to him. The disclosure obligation to an unrepresented buyer or tenant is triggered no later than the first property showing.

Question 3. Marcus violated the confidentiality obligation that applies to all brokerage relationships in Missouri, including transaction brokerage. A transaction broker is specifically required to keep confidential the seller's motivation for selling and the minimum price the seller will accept. The absence of a written agreement does not eliminate this duty. Missouri licensees owe confidentiality obligations regardless of whether the relationship is formalized in writing, and sharing this information gave Todd a significant and improper bargaining advantage.

Question 4. If Marcus represents both Diane and Todd in the same transaction, this creates a dual agency situation. Under Missouri law, dual agency requires written disclosure to all parties and written informed consent from both the buyer and the seller before proceeding. Without that consent, Marcus cannot lawfully act as a dual agent. The firm's broker might also consider whether designated agency is a more appropriate option, assigning one agent to represent Diane and a separate agent to represent Todd.

Question 5. Every problem in this scenario traces back to three failures: not providing the Broker Disclosure Form at first contact, not executing a written brokerage agreement before gathering sensitive information or taking any action on the client's behalf, and not disclosing the existing buyer relationship before scheduling a showing. Module 1 makes clear that written agreements and timely disclosures are not optional formalities. They are the foundation of every lawful and ethical brokerage relationship in Missouri, and the practical protection they provide benefits the client, the licensee, and the brokerage.

CASE DEBRIEF FOR MODULE 2:

Question 1. Patricia had an obligation to complete a thorough comparative market analysis before recommending a listing price, and to clearly communicate to the sellers that her price range is not an appraisal and does not constitute a professional opinion of market value. By agreeing to $375,000 without supporting data, she failed her seller clients by potentially overpricing the property. An overpriced listing is unlikely to "appraise out", which is exactly what happened here. Missouri licensees who fail to provide competent, data-supported pricing guidance risk complaints to the Missouri Real Estate Commission, damaged client relationships, and transactions that fall apart during the pre-closing period.

Question 2. Missouri law requires that dual agency be disclosed to all parties and that written informed consent be obtained from both the buyer and the seller before a licensee can act as a dual agent. Patricia's casual mention of dual agency during the listing appointment, without explanation of its limitations or documentation, did not satisfy this requirement. Before showing the property to David, Patricia should have disclosed her existing relationship with him to Frank and Gloria, fully explained what dual agency means and what limitations it places on her ability to advocate for either party, and obtained written consent from both clients. The broker should also have been consulted to determine whether designated agency was a more appropriate option.

Question 3. By withholding the information that David was willing to pay more than his offer price, Patricia was protecting David's negotiating position at the expense of her seller clients. Under Missouri agency law, a licensee representing a seller owes duties of good faith, loyalty, and fidelity to the seller client. A dual agent, by contrast, is prohibited from sharing one party's willingness to pay more, or accept less, with the other party. However, before any written dual agency consent was in place, Patricia was still functioning as the listing agent and owed primary duties to the sellers. Withholding information that would benefit the seller while representing both parties without proper authorization is a serious breach of fiduciary duty.

Question 4. When an appraisal comes in below the purchase price, the lender will generally only finance up to the appraised value, leaving a $14,000 gap. The parties have several options: the buyer can make up the difference in cash at closing, the seller can reduce the price to $348,000, the two parties can split the difference and agree to a new purchase price somewhere in between, or the transaction can be canceled. Patricia's role is to facilitate communication between all parties, present the options clearly and without advocating for one party over the other in a dual agency situation, and help the parties reach a resolution in writing. An appraiser may also be asked to reconsider the value if there are factual errors in the report, or a second appraisal may be ordered depending on the financing type.

Question 5. The three most important things Patricia should have done differently are: first, complete a thorough CMA before the listing appointment and present a data-supported price range, including a clear explanation that it is not an appraisal; second, present the Broker Disclosure Form at the earliest practicable opportunity during the first substantial contact with the sellers, before gathering any personal or financial information; and third, have a full conversation about dual agency and designated agency before David toured the property, obtain written informed consent from both parties if dual agency was to proceed, and consult her managing broker for guidance. Every problem in this scenario traces back to the failure to establish the agency relationship correctly from the very beginning.

CASE DEBRIEF FOR MODULE 3:

Question 1. Jordan violated the written agreement requirement that took effect on August 17, 2024, as a result of the NAR settlement. A Missouri licensee may not show a buyer any property without a signed written buyer representation agreement already in place. There are no exceptions for a first showing, a casual appointment, or any other circumstance. Jordan should have scheduled a separate meeting with

Simone and Terrence before the first showing, explained the agreement in full, answered their questions, and obtained their signatures in a setting where they were not standing at a front door feeling pressured. Presenting the agreement at the property and characterizing it as a formality undermined the buyers' ability to make a knowing and voluntary decision, which is precisely what the signed agreement is meant to produce.

Question 2. Jordan failed to meet Missouri's requirement that licensees clearly communicate to buyers that broker compensation is fully negotiable and is not set by law. He also failed to explain the compensation section of the agreement in a transparent and accurate way. The agreement must clearly state the compensation being sought, how it will be paid, and what the buyer's potential financial obligation is if the seller declines to pay or offers less than the stated amount. Telling Simone not to worry and that sellers always cover it is both inaccurate and misleading. Jordan should have explained that the 3% compensation is what he is seeking, that it may be paid by the seller, by the buyers, or by a combination of both, and that if the seller does not agree to pay it, or pays less than 3%, Simone and Terrence could be responsible for covering the difference. That conversation must happen before the agreement is signed, not after problems arise.

Question 3. It was entirely Jordan's responsibility to ensure that Simone and Terrence understood the geographic scope and property coverage of the agreement before they signed it. A buyer representation agreement must clearly define the geographic territory and the type of property covered, and the licensee has a professional obligation to walk through those terms explicitly so that the buyers fully understand what they are committing to. Jordan should have explained that the agreement covered any residential property purchase within their county during the 90-day term, including For Sale By Owner properties, and should have confirmed that the buyers understood and agreed to that scope before they signed. If the couple later wanted to expand or adjust the coverage area, that change should have been made in writing and initialed by both parties. The dispute over the FSBO was entirely preventable and is a direct result of presenting the agreement as a formality rather than as a meaningful and binding document.

CASE DEBRIEF FOR MODULE 4:

Question 1 — Trust Fund Handling

Rosa's plan to wait until Monday is problematic. Missouri regulations require licensees to promptly deliver all trust funds to the broker. While the rule does not specify a precise number of hours, "promptly" means without unnecessary delay. The broker then has ten banking days from the date all parties have signed and initialed the contract to deposit the funds into the firm's escrow account. Students should understand that the ten-day clock runs from the contract execution date, not from when the funds are physically delivered to the broker. Waiting over a weekend without a compelling reason could expose Rosa to a regulatory complaint. The takeaway is that trust funds should move to the broker as quickly as practicable after receipt.

Question 2 — Undisclosed Debt and ATR/QM

When a credit report or underwriting review reveals a debt the borrower did not disclose, the loan originator is required to request a written explanation from the borrower and investigate whether the omission was deliberate. This is a core element of responsible lending under the Dodd-Frank ability-to-repay rules. As for the QM Safe Harbor, it generally applies when the borrower's DTI does not exceed

43%. Jerome's stated DTI of 38% would have qualified, but once the undisclosed co-signed loan is included, his actual DTI rises to 46%. At that level, the loan may still qualify as a QM but would fall under the Rebuttable Presumption rather than Safe Harbor, giving the borrower greater ability to challenge the lender's ATR compliance. More practically, many lenders will simply decline or restructure the loan once the true DTI is known. Students should recognize that omitting a co-signed liability — even unintentionally — can derail a transaction and potentially constitute loan fraud if done deliberately.

Question 3 — Asset Seasoning

The $12,000 deposit appearing only nine days before the application triggers the seasoning requirement. Lenders typically require that funds in a borrower's account have been there for at least 60 days to confirm they are legitimate savings and not undisclosed borrowed funds. A large, unexplained deposit that does not meet the seasoning threshold will require a paper trail and written explanation. If the funds were a gift, the borrower must provide a gift letter. If they were borrowed, they may create an additional liability that further affects the DTI calculation. Students should advise buyer clients to avoid moving large sums of money in the weeks leading up to a loan application.

Question 4 — Earnest Money Dispute and Broker Disbursement

The buyers properly invoked their financing contingency within the 21-day window, which means their failure to obtain financing does not constitute default — it entitles both parties to cancel the contract and the earnest money should be returned to the buyers. However, the sellers are refusing to sign a written release. Under Missouri regulations, the broker should retain the funds while seeking a written release from all parties or waiting for one party to file a civil action. Since 45 days have passed, the broker is approaching — but has not yet reached — the 60-day threshold that would permit unilateral disbursement. Once 60 days from the date of the dispute have elapsed, the broker may disburse to either party based on a good-faith determination that the opposing party is in breach of contract. Critically, before doing so, the broker must give all parties 15 days' written notice of the intended disbursement. Students should understand that the broker cannot simply return the money to avoid conflict — the regulatory process must be followed precisely to protect the firm from liability.

CASE DEBRIEFS FOR MODULE 5:

Case Debrief 5.1

1. Eric should have presented both offers. He then should have explained the pros and cons of each offer. The final decision is up to the sellers on whom they want to buy their house.

2. In this situation, the Professional Standards board determined that Eric violated Articles 1 and 3 of the NAR Code of Ethics.

3. The Standards of Practice violated are:
   SP 1.6 – Submit all offers and counteroffers objectively and as quickly as possible.
   SP 1.7 – The listing brokers must continue to submit offers they receive up to closing.
   SP 1.15 – When asked by the cooperating broker, the listing broker should disclose that he has other offers.
   SP 3.6 – The REALTOR® should reveal the existence of accepted offers.

Case Debrief 5.2:

1. Article 10 of the Code of Ethics was violated.
2. The agent violated Standard of Practice 10.5.
3. The agent may state their mind in the public forum; however, she may not use slurs or hate speech. She should have remained civil and not use derogatory comments against the County Commissioner. She would be guilty because she advocated violence against the Commissioner.

Case Debrief 5.3:

1. Article 16 of the Code of Ethics was violated.
2. The agent violated Standard of Practice 16.13.
3. At the hearing, Janet defended her actions because she had been invited to present the offer to the seller and begin the negotiations to sell the property. Janet had assumed that she had Dan's permission to talk with Joey about the property's sale. The ability of a REALTOR® to speak with another agent's customer must be expressed and not implied.

CASE DEBRIEF FOR MODULE 6:

Since Abigail is not a contractor she should not speak on the repair estimates for the home. Unintentional misrepresentation occurs when a licensee unknowingly conveys inaccurate information to a consumer concerning a property, financing or agency service. False or inaccurate information that the licensee, as a professional, should have known to be false or inaccurate may be included in the definition. Those found guilty generally have to pay fines and may be disciplined by state real estate regulators and professional organizations.

Instead of trying to win the client over with inaccurate estimates, Abigail should state that she is not a contractor but knows a few trusted contractors she could schedule to come out there for accurate estimates. This will show the potential client that she is resourceful and has his best interest at heart. It will also help protect her from any liability or misrepresentation issues.

If you liked Missouri Advanced Real Estate Practice (MAREP), check out the other titles of Performance Programs Company!

Cramming for your real estate exam? You need Missouri Real Estate License Exam Prep!

Where can you buy Missouri Real Estate License Exam Prep?
Missouri Real Estate License Exam Prep (MO-RELEP) is available as a printed book or e-book through nearly all online retailers.

Looking for a Missouri real estate principles textbook? Get what all the students love -- Principles of Real Estate Practice in Missouri 1st Edition!

Principles of Real Estate Practice in Missouri is invaluable reference material for real estate professionals. Its 560-pages contain the essentials of real estate law, principles, and practices taught in real estate schools and colleges across Missouri.

Where can you buy Principles of Real Estate Practice in Missouri?
Principles Real Estate Practice in Missouri is available as a printed book or e-book through nearly all online retailers.

Struggling with real estate math? The solution to that equation is Real Estate Math Express!

Real Estate Math Express is a concise, easy-to-study test preparation guide to help real estate students improve their real estate math scores to pass the state licensing test. The primary feature of Real Estate Math Express is that it contains all necessary formulas and practice questions in 100+ pages.

Where can you buy Real Estate Math Express?
Real Estate Math Express is available as a printed book or e-book through nearly all online retailers.

Publisher Contact
Ryan Mettling
Performance Programs Company
6810 190th Street East, Bradenton, FL 34211
ryan@performanceprogramscompany.com
www.performanceprogramscompany.com

www.ingramcontent.com/pod-product-compliance
Ingram Content Group UK Ltd.
Pitfield, Milton Keynes, MK11 3LW, UK
UKHW051508290926
15471UKWH00008B/1504